Archie Ferguson

Alaska's Clown Prince and "Craziest Pilot in the World"

Steve Levi

Master of the Impossible Crime

PUBLICATION
CONSULTANTS
WE BELIEVE IN THE POWER OF AUTHORS

PO Box 221974 Anchorage, Alaska 99522-1974
books@publicationconsultants.com, www.publicationconsultants.com

ISBN Number: 978-1-63747-046-6
eBook ISBN Number: 978-1-63747-047-3

Library of Congress Number: 2021945581

Manufactured in the United States of America

For my father, who was always
looking for a good laugh.

Contents

Forward

In photography, there is a term colloquially known as the "Magic Moment." This describes the heartbeat of time that occurs just after the sun has set. The blazing fireball disappears below the horizon and, momentarily, a golden glow of soft light washes the land. It gives just enough illumination for photographs but not so much light there are shadows. Photographers prize this "Magic Moment" – lasting no longer than a few minutes—and are careful to take full advantage of it.

Transferring this image to history, as this book was being completed, Alaska's frontier was passing through that "Magic Moment." The blaze of glory of the Wild, Wild North was fading fast and all that remained was in a momentary golden glow.

It was in this last, brief moment there was a chance to snapshot the story of Archie Ferguson, Alaska's Clown Prince and, as the *Saturday Evening Post* dubbed him, "The Craziest Pilot in the World." As Ferguson left few letters, his story was one of human memory that would pass with those witnesses to history. Even then, most of the people I interviewed only remembered Archie as a man who was their father's or grandfather's age. Very few of my interviews were with his contemporaries and now they are all gone.

The biography of Archie Ferguson was not an easy task. In every writer's life there is a book that never should have been. In my life, this is that book. It was an insurmountable task from the beginning, a project so complex that it should never have been completed. Yet, here it is, proof that just as bumblebees are not supposed to fly but do, a book about Archie Ferguson could not have been written but was.

This was by far the most difficult writing project I had ever undertaken. When I first decided to write a biography of Archie Ferguson, I assumed

I would have no trouble finding source material. After all, Archie was a significant part of the Arctic as well as a benchmark in Alaska's aviation history. It took me all of 15 minutes in the Anchorage library to realize just how wrong I was. Other than one chapter in each of Jean Potter's classic books, THE FLYING NORTH and FLYING FRONTIERSMEN, the only other references to Archie were a few paragraphs here and there in a handful of Alaskan books.

As far as Archie's personal papers were concerned, I was able to find a few letters along with an old radio logbook, but that was the extent of the written record. With the notable exception of Gene Joiner's *Mukluk Telegraph* that ran irregularly between June of 1950 and February of 1952, there was no newspaper in Kotzebue until long after Archie left the Arctic.

With scant written resources, I was forced to gather my information through interviews. This, as I quickly discovered, was the most frustrating of research methods. While I hear many historians beat the drum for the collection of oral histories, what these same people do **not** tell their audiences is that interviews are difficult to arrange, hard to interpret and riddled with inconsistencies.

Worse, no matter how truthful interviewees *think* they are being, all memories are flawed. It's not as though the subjects are *lying*; it's just that what they have always believed did happen, in fact, did not occur in just that way. Piecing together a composite profile of a man who had been dead almost 30 years before I even started the research was like searching for the truth with 40 witnesses to a crime that had been committed ten years previously.

Then there was the subject matter. Many of the interviewees for this book were worthy of biographies in their own right and some, I am sure, took great delight in "pulling fast ones" on me and continuing to present tall tales as history. Some of those stories I caught. Those of which I was unsure, I have noted in the text.

I clearly recognize that the major shortcoming of my book is the lack of reference to Archie's speech pattern. I only heard about 30 seconds of Archie on tape, and thus I cannot describe him in his linguistic glory. Jean Potter, on the other hand, quoted Archie verbatim, as he was speaking. Her book thus has a dimension mine could never have.

With regard to the contents of the book, as much as possible, I avoided using material from Potter's books. Potter met and interviewed Archie and her material on Archie is from Archie. Mine is a biography based on interviews with people who knew him.

There are quite a few people to thank for making this book possible. Edith Bullock and Cliff Cernick top the list. Also on the honor roll are Thomas E. Wiltsey, R. Bruce Parham, Diana Kodiak and Sally Dunn at the National Archives in Anchorage – now defunct –who became numb from my bizarre questions. Others whose help was indispensable include Pam Vizenor, Chris Capps, Marilyn Richards, Tommy Richards, Sr., Hadley Hess, Dorothy Richards, Georganne Phillips, Ed Yost, Bill Boucher, Jim Ruotsala, Tony Schultz, Mary Oldham, Jean Oldham, Sam Shafsky, Bob Erwin, Don Ferguson, Fred Goodwin and more than eighty other people who talked with me about Archie.

Edith Bullock deserves special credit for the hours she spent answering my questions on Kotzebue and Archie. She was a fountainhead of information and without her assistance Archie Ferguson would still be a character known only in bits and pieces to me. All Alaskan historians miss her.

If there is any one person to whom I owe an incredible debt and without whose help I would not have started this project, that person is Victoria Eubank. Before I began this work, Victoria was doing a statewide, weekly radio program called "Neighbors" which highlighted living Alaskans across the state and their contributions to modern Alaska. Then, as now, I was – and am – a starving freelance writer. She hired me on a story-by-story basis and taught me how to use the tape recorder. I had never thought of using the tape recorder as a tool of historical research. Even if I had, I did not have the money at that time to buy a top-notch recorder. So I used Victoria's recorder until I made enough money to buy my own equipment. Only then did I realize that I could go after the Archie Ferguson story on my own. Without that push, this book would never have been completed. My 70 odd interviews with those who remembered Archie Ferguson are available at the Anchorage Museum of History and Art.

A note to readers in the Lower 48. The term Eskimo has no real meaning in Alaska. That is because – generally speaking – there are two "kinds" of Native peoples in Alaska that fall under that term: Inupiat and Yupik. The Inupiat live in the Arctic regions of Alaska and Siberia while the Yupik live in Southwest Alaska. For the purposes of this book, the term Eskimo is not used because Ferguson lived and worked in Kotzebue where almost all of the Native people were Inupiat. Where the term "Eskimo" was used in a quote or the title of an article, it has been left intact.

. . . Steve Levi

ARCHIE JUST BEING ARCHIE

"Now, Theodore, you don't have to worry about anything. Everybody who flies with me is insured for $10,000."

... Archie Ferguson

Nobody could tell Archie Ferguson how to fly. He did exactly as he pleased. That was "just Archie being Archie." Any one of his mistakes would have killed far better pilots than he ever was. But Archie didn't get killed. He kept beating the odds. He seemed to live a charmed life with disaster being a way to liven up his life rather than threaten his existence.

One wintry day in the early 1940s, Archie flew over to Kiana to pick up two passengers on his way to Fairbanks. There was actually another of his planes stopping in Kiana that day but since his mistress, Beulah "Bobby" Levy, lived there, Archie used the passengers as a convenient reason to be away from his wife in Kotzebue.

The two pilots spent the night in Kiana and the next morning, Archie's pilot got up early and went through the ritual of getting his plane ready to fly. Archie, who usually rose at 4 a.m., slept in, so to speak. When it got light enough to fly, the other pilot left. Winter in the Arctic did not offer many daylight flying hours and pilots have to take advantage of every minute they have.

When Archie finally did roll out of bed and discovered that his employee had left for Fairbanks, he began rushing around madly to take off. He started the engine up and perfunctorily knocked what frost he could off his plane's wings. Then he loaded both passengers, Laurenz Schuerch, a storekeeper in Kiana, and Theodore Kingeak, an Inupiat from Kiana. When Schuerch suggested Archie spend more time on his pre-flight than simply sweeping the frost off the wings, Archie just replied quickly. "She'll fly! She'll fly! I don't want that son-of-a-bitch to beat us to Fairbanks."

Archie was able to make it off the frozen river but he didn't make it very far. The cold engine labored to keep the frosted aircraft aloft but lost the battle with gravity. The plane came down hard and bounced to a stop in a deep snowdrift.

Angrily, Archie spun the plane around for another try. But before he took off, he wanted some of the frost off his wings.

"Theodore," Archie snapped. "Get out there and shake the end of the wings. She'll fly! She'll fly!"

Archie was right. This time the plane did fly. Then, once aloft, Archie began talking incessantly as he usually did and pulling antics for which he was famous. He slyly shorted some wires to make sparks fly in the cabin which made Scheurch and Kingeak uncomfortable. Then, when Archie switched from one gas tank to the other, he purposely let the engine momentarily stop.

Halfway to Fairbanks, Schuerch looked out his window and was horrified to see there was only half a ski of the landing gear on his side of the plane. Worse yet, that half was perpendicular to the ground.

"You got a ski on your side?" Schuerch asked Archie.

"Yeah," said Archie.

"Well, you've got half a ski more than I do on this side," Schuerch replied.

"Nooooooo," replied Archie. "Don't go kiddin' me."

"Well, why don't you lean over and see for yourself?"

This time Archie believed him.

All three men knew what missing a ski meant. Now it was just a matter of choosing where to crash. The best possible outcome was all three men would walk away. The worst-case scenario was chilling.

Archie thought about it for a while and then decided against crashing in Fairbanks. After all, that's where the hated CAA was based, the forerunner of the FAA, and those were the last people Archie wanted to crack up in front of. So he turned the plane around and headed back to Kiana.

Babbling into the radio, Archie told Beulah to get every Inupiat in Kiana out on the frozen river.

"I'm gonna bring the plane in," he told her, "if she turns over and rolls, drag us out quick before the plane burns."

Beulah did her job well. By the time Archie reached Kiana, the sides of the frozen Kobuk River were lined with Inupiat. Archie started on his final approach when Kingeak, who had been silent up to this point, suddenly began to express a great deal of nervousness. Archie looked over his shoulder and issued a classic line:

"Now, Theodore, you don't have to worry about anything. Everybody who flies with me is insured for $10,000."

THE FERGUSON FAMILY COMES NORTH

"Rustguard"

. . . Ed Yost

He was the King of Kotzebue, Alaska's Clown Prince.

Some called him the "World's Craziest Pilot," others, "a buccaneer" and the slipperiest of Arctic businessmen. But everyone who ran into him considered him one of the most colorful characters in Alaskan history. Specifically, he was Archie Ferguson of Kotzebue, a remarkable man whose fame and notoriety were so widespread that even decades after his death, people who had never met him burst into laughter when his name is mentioned.

But Archie was more than a colorful character of the Last Frontier. He symbolized the transitional period of the Arctic. Arriving above the Arctic Circle before the airplane changed the face of Alaska, he died at the end of the heyday of the wild and reckless days on the Northern frontier. He was the consummate frontier businessman, con and character combined. As such, Archie Ferguson shaped an incredible chunk of American history that will never be again.

Physically, he was sight to behold. In his younger days he could have been described as thin and wiry. By the time he reached his prime in his 50s – and weighed around 190 pounds – he was "short and built like a potato."[1] He stood all of five-foot-four and in his middle age that was probably the dimension around his girth as well. Other descriptions applied to him include "gnarly," "dumpy," "roly-poly," "dwarfish," and "impish." He looked like one of Santa's middle-aged elves who had somehow escaped from the drudgery of North Pole toy-making to opt for the good life in Kotzebue.

If his physical features did not put him in a class by himself, his voice surely did. Archie didn't talk; he cackled, "like Donald Duck."[2] He usually wore a belt that was too large for his waist size and left the end of it dangling in the wind. He never walked anywhere; he ran. He was always singing the same few, distracting bars of a song no one knew, the lyrics of which Archie only knew one word: "today." He couldn't "carry a tune in a bucket," Baptist minister Richard Miller, remembered, and was always "rocketing about from one thing to another."[3] Comically, Archie ran around so much that all of his shoes had their toes turned up. When he came into his restaurant from the snow he would put his wet shoes under the oil stove. As the shoes dried, the toes would curl up on their own.

He was always laughing, telling stories, most of them about himself, epitomizing the fine Alaskan art of absurding – treating absurd notions about Alaska as if they were the unvarnished truth. His high-pitched, whiney voice was always going "the one speed he had," former Alaska Governor Jay Hammond remembered: "full throttle." He would converse at great length on any subject, whether he knew anything about it or not, and just as often answered his own questions before anyone else had the chance to break into the conversation.

Archie spoke a strange English. He "Archie-fied" words, slaughtering the English language unmercifully. "Siberia" invariably came out "Serbia," "Cabaret girls" became "carrot girls." "Cessna" changed in his lingo to "Cessn." "Meteorology" was always "metricology." "Navigation" was "nadigation" and "Manchuria" emerged as "Mankura." There was absolutely no word Archie could not mis-pronounce.[4] Adding to his unique verbal style, his pithy speech pattern was punctuated with vulgarities, a great number of them broadcast over the radio, a personal failing of which the FCC (Federal Communications Commission) was constantly reminding him and concerning which they maintained a growing pile of complaints.

Archie's date and location of birth, like much of his life, remains a matter of conjecture. According to his death certificate, he came into the world in "Fallmont, Ohio." However, no such city exists on any map of Ohio and the Ohio Historical Society has yet to discover its whereabouts.[5] Other sources, including Archie, list his birthplace as Fremont, Ohio—also where a birth certificate for Archie does not exist – and the date of birth as January 24, 1895. Had he been born there, Fremont was exactly the kind of a place to attract an entrepreneur like Archie's father, Frank R. Ferguson, known throughout his life as simply "F.R." There had been a gas boom in the area between 1886 and 1891, followed by an oil boom. But with the oil boom came lots of people and F.R. probably felt the urge to move along to a less confining community.[6]

By 1900, Archie's family had moved west to Beaverton, Oregon. Here the family of three children, Archie, his older brother Warren and a sister by the name of Juianta (spelled in a non-traditional manner) settled for the next 15 years while the parents ran a small store. It can be presumed that the children were educated in the local school but Beaverton Schools could "find no information" on any of the Fergusons.[7]

Though some people interviewed stated the older Fergusons were missionaries, there are no documents to substantiate this claim. More likely, F.R. and his wife, Clara, were restless entrepreneurs. F.R. held a number of jobs, including working for the railroad, from which he saved a nest egg that was used in opening the Beaverton store. Then, in 1915, the family went north to the Territory of Alaska, first to Douglas, then Nome and finally above the Arctic Circle to the village of Shungnak.

For most Americans, the Arctic is the least understood region of the world. In fact, it would probably be a good bet to say that most Americans know more about the deepest, darkest jungles of Africa than that acreage of their own nation stretching from the Arctic Circle to the Arctic Ocean and the Chukchi Sea.

The prevailing attitude is that this region is nothing more than a vast, featureless, wind-swept, landscape covered with deep snowdrifts during the six months of winter and virtually impassable with chest-high tundra during the summer. Wolves, of course, travel in packs of several hundred and attack caribou herds mercilessly leaving half-consumed corpses scattered like hillocks on a plain with no other features but horizon in all directions. Then there are the solitary polar bears stalking unwary Eskimo who, in turn, hunt the herds of penguins whose only escape is to dive into the open water leads in the ice pack known as *polynyas*. Further, common perception continues, with the exception of the Eskimos, the only human life north of the Circle are the truckloads of oil company employees who care more for getting oil out of the ground than any environmental damage their companies may cause. None of these views of the Arctic is accurate though each has a grain of truth – with the exception of the penguins. Penguins live in the Antarctic, not the Arctic.

To burst a few more bubbles of perception, in terms of precipitation, the Arctic is a desert. Fewer than a handful of inches of rain or snow actually fall each year. While the Arctic does have blasting storms, the snow in the drifts has been blown in from somewhere else.

During the summer, the Arctic is low-lying swampland impossible for humans to traverse on foot. There are some trees, but these are not very tall or rotund. This is primarily because their roots cannot break the permafrost, a layer of perpetually frozen earth two or three feet below the soil's surface. When the spring snow melts, the Arctic soil turns into a sponge. As the temperature rises, pools of water unfreeze and grow in size. Billions of insects appear from their winter hibernation filling the ponds with their larvae. As the larvae mature, they cover the short grasses of the tundra until the plants are black with insects. In turn, this fecundity of insects brings hundreds of thousands of birds from around the world who feed on this bountiful harvest. Tundra, the generic term for plant growth in the Arctic, rarely reaches chest-high. There are patches of plants in some parts of the Arctic that can get to mid-shin but for the most part the grasses are only ankle-high and the greenery grows in what would be called a swamp anywhere else in the United States.

With regard to the animals, wolves do live in the Arctic and will sometimes travel in packs. But these groupings average six to eight animals, not several hundred. Caribou are a primary food source for the wolves when they migrate through the wolves' hunting ranges, but, for the bulk of the  year, wolves survive on lemming, ptarmigan, Arctic hare and whatever else they can catch. Wolves eat what they kill; they don't leave scores of carcasses littering the landscape. Polar bears do prowl through the most northern fringes of Alaska, but rarely do they get as far south as the Arctic Circle. Polar bear attacks, and wolf attacks for that matter, are extremely rare.

Another myth of the northland is that Eskimos live in ice-and-snow igloos. Alaska's Eskimo do not and probably never have lived in these structures. Throughout antiquity they have built their homes of whalebone, driftwood and sod and are called *barabaras*.

But the greatest mistake many people make is in assuming that Alaska *is* the Arctic. While the Arctic is part of Alaska, it is by no means all of the state. Technically, the Arctic is that area which lies north of the Arctic Circle, the latitude on which the sun does not set on the summer solstice (June 21) and does not rise on the winter solstice (December 21). Geographically, it is 66 degrees, 33 minutes North though this varies slightly from year to year.

In terms of miles, consider the distance from Los Angeles to Seattle is roughly 1,000 miles, about the same as from Boston to Atlanta or Houston to Denver. From Seattle to Anchorage, the most populous city in Alaska, the distance is another 1,500 miles. Then, from Anchorage to Kotzebue, 35 miles north of the Arctic Circle, there are another 550 miles. Though there are sections of the Arctic Circle that are closer to Anchorage, the area most people associate with the far, far north is still substantially distant from the heavily-populated areas of the state. Finally, the geographic North Pole, which many people seem to believe is "just on the other side of the Arctic Circle," is actually 1,500 miles north of Kotzebue.

Why the Fergusons headed north is a matter of some dispute. A few sources state they were trying to avoid the impending World War I draft. By moving north, their children would be out of harm's way. This version, however, may have sprung more from Archie's tall tales than any truth. Legendary bush pilot John Cross of Kotzebue noted that while it may have been true that the Fergusons came north to avoid the draft, neither of the Ferguson boys would have been taken as they were both were "small for their age, just over the line" and may very well would have flunked the draft physical.[8] Further, even if the Ferguson boys had been in the Territory of Alaska, they would still have been eligible for service.

This may be all part of the legend of Archie. For the record, both Archie and Warren did register for the World War I draft. But both listed deformities: Archie claimed rheumatism and Warren stated he had a "rupture." But they did register in August of 1917, well ahead of many other patriotic Alaskans.[9] Fred Goodwin, who came to Alaska in 1939 and worked for the Episcopal Missions in Nenana driving dog teams and hauling wood before flying, remembered that Archie had indeed been ordered to report for induction. As he recalled, Archie and Warren were sent a telegram ordering them to report to Nome. The two brothers were 300 miles west of Nome at the time and started walking. "By the time we got to Nome," Archie told Goodwin, "the War was over. 'Course we didn't walk very fast."[10]

While the elder Fergusons scrounged a living in Nome, Archie, in his twenties, worked at a sawmill and operated the water nozzle at a gold operation. Looking further east, F.R. saw an opportunity he could not pass up. Tom Berryman, who ran a string of trading posts across the Arctic, was looking for a responsible manager for his post in Shungnak, a community of no more than 100 people on the Kobuk River. F.R. took the job and became Berryman's employee at the Shungnak branch of the Kotzebue Fur Trading Company. After F.R. acquired another nest egg, he bought out Johnny Cleveland's store at Kobuk. The Ferguson's oldest son, Warren, ran the second family store at Koutchak Creek, halfway between Shungnak and Kobuk.

F. R. and Minnie Ferguson

The next Ferguson store, which Archie ran, was in Selawik. Translated from Inupiat, *selawik*, meaning "place where the female shee fish spawns," was an ideal spot for a store. It was a hub community attracting patrons from far up the Selawik River. Three rivers fed into nearby Selawik Lake, making it an excellent place to fish, as the community's name clearly implied. Selawik was also known as the "Venice of the Arctic" because of the streams that flowed through the community.[11]

By this time, the family had splintered. Warren was in Kotzebue running the new Ferguson store while Archie remained at the Ferguson store in Selawik. Both brothers had married Inupiat women in the Friends Church in Selawik. In January of 1919, Archie had married Hadley Vayluk (Wood), the granddaughter of the Chief of the Kobuk Inupiat. (Warren later married Minnie Gallahorn in 1931.)

Even while he was running a store, Archie did a wide variety of other jobs. He found time to work at the family gold operation, hauled freight for the Ferguson stores and even did a stint as a floating peddler. In those days, a peddler was someone who possessed a Peddler's License. This gave the peddler the right to buy from and sell to Native people on a reservation but only from the deck of a boat in reservation waters. This was the way the federal government got around the problem of not having any whites with stores on reservations but still allowing the Natives access to store-bought products. While Alaska did not have "reservations" in the Arctic as the word applied in the Lower 48, at least two Arctic communities were considered as such: Noorvik and Noatak.[12]

Though Archie didn't know it then, the ten years he spent in the Arctic as a miner, dog team freight hauler and river peddler were to become invaluable to him as a pilot. While other airmen came north and had to learn the country, Archie already knew it from the ground up. He knew the dog trails, river bends and sand bars. Even more important, he knew the Natives individually and collectively and he spoke the three area dialects as fluently as he spoke English. However, considering how Archie spoke English, this was not saying much.

While Archie was far from the safest, most cautious pilot in the Arctic, he was without a doubt the most knowledgeable when it came to getting around. The United States Marshal for the Kotzebue area, Burt Neily, often commented that he preferred to fly with Archie rather than any other pilot, because, his noted antics aside, Archie "never got lost."[13]

At that time, Kotzebue was truly on the most far-flung edge of civilization. Residence there meant living on a treeless stretch of gravel where there were 36 days of 24-hours-a-day sunshine during the summer. Temperatures could rise as high as 80 degrees Fahrenheit and mosquitoes would come out of the wetlands in clouds. Then there were the other biting insects: the white socks, flies, gnats and no-see-ums. On the flip-side of the seasons, 50 degree below zero days were not uncommon during the winter and the 36 days of perpetual darkness was a phenomenon that still staggers the imagination of Americans in the Lower 49.

Kotzebue homes were hardly palatial. When Edith Bullock, Kotzebue entrepreneur and barge line owner, arrived in Kotzebue in 1948, the housing conditions were "horrible. Little huts lined the beach, some of them with sod roofs." Some of the shacks had been built with plywood and plasterboard without adequate insulation. Heating was primarily with fuel oil or coal, both of which had to be shipped in.[14] There were trees up the Kobuk River and those who could not afford coal or oil had to move cords of wood to the homes before freeze-up.

KOTZEBUE IN WINTER

Sanitary conditions were appalling. When the first missionaries settled in the Kotzebue area in the early decades of the twentieth century, health concerns were high on their agenda. Toilets were introduced, even though they were just open containers – euphemistically known as "honey buckets." During the summer, human sewage was segregated out of town. When winter came, it was transported in buckets out onto the ice of Kotzebue Sound where it was dumped into piles. It froze quickly and remained a black spot on the ice until spring breakup transported the frozen feces far out to sea on ice cakes that disappeared into the maw of the Bering Sea. (Later it was put in barrels that sank into Kotzebue Sound.)

But even with the new accent on health, the cleanliness of America was a difficult standard to emulate. As late as the 1950s, bathing was reasonable during the warm months but close to impossible during the winter. Drinking water was relatively plentiful when the shallow lakes surrounding the community were aqueous but once the lakes froze, water came from ice that had been sawed in slabs.

KOTZEBUE WATER WORKS

These slabs would be taken to town by dog sled where they were stored outside the homes – high enough so that dogs would not urinate on them. The slabs would be shattered during the winter and the shards brought inside and placed in buckets. Gradually the room temperature would turn the ice to drinking water. This system was used until the establishment of the water filtration system in the mid-1960s.

Transportation was a problem as well. Until the Second World War it was possible to count the number of motor vehicles on one hand in most Arctic villages.[15] While some readers might believe the lack of vehicles would have resulted in periods of blessed silence, this was not the case. As dog teams were the primary source of transportation during the winter there were hundreds of dogs in Kotzebue. This lead to another form of noise pollution. When a howl started for some unknown reason at one end of town, it would carry across Kotzebue, each dog adding its own voice to the melee until the wave of dog howls moved like the wind from one end of the community to the other and then back again. Many Kotzebue residents believed – and some undoubtedly still do – that when the dogs howl, "sing," someone died. A more likely cause of the dogs' nightly yowls, Dr. Neilson remembered, was the 11 pm curfew siren for the kids during the summer. As far as numbers are concerned, as late as 1960, Dr. Charles Neilson remembered that in Kotzebue "there were 1,200 people and about 2,500 dogs."

It was into this era that the airplane was introduced. Archie first trip in an airplane was with another legendary bush pilot, Noel Wien, one of the founders of the company that was to buy Archie out: Wien Alaska Airways. Noel came to Kotzebue in 1927, barnstorming his way across the Arctic. Interested in this new form of transportation, Archie screwed up his courage and paid his money for that memorable first flight asking Noel to "pour it on and give me my money's worth."[16]

Noel did exactly that. Once aloft Wien proceeded to scare the living daylights out of Archie by performing a series of barrel rolls and loops watching in amusement as a terror-stricken Archie gripped the sidewalls of the plane so hard his "fingers left dents."[17] For years, Archie relished telling of that first flight. "Wien looped me 'n I purty near fell out," he would recall with self-deprecating laughter. "Gosh, I was so scared I couldn't get my hands loose from the sides of the airplane!"[18]

But far from convincing Archie he should stay on solid ground, the flight only sharpened his desire to fly. Perhaps a more persuasive reason Archie wanted to learn to fly was Hans Mirow, the Nome pilot who was doing most of the air cargo and passenger hauling in those days. Mirow was not proving dependable. Archie had a let's-do-it-right-now personality. When Mirow or his pilots couldn't keep to Archie's rigid schedule, Archie decided to take matters into his own hands and became a pilot.[19]

But learning to fly was not that easy. First, Archie had to locate a plane in the Lower 48, have it disassembled and transported to Kotzebue where Archie was spending most of his time. Next, somebody had to teach him how to fly the contraption. Then, of course, were the associated problems of a consistent supply of fuel and spare parts. And mechanics would be needed to maintain and repair the aircraft. These minor considerations aside, the aviation venture had to make money. Bush flying was not a profitable business and profit margins were thin at best. To show a profit, Archie would have to compete head-to-head with seasoned veterans of the sky like Frank Whaley, John Cross, Frank Pollack, Hans Mirow, and Jack Jefford, just to name a few.

None of this deterred Archie in the slightest. He was going to fly. He made the final decision in Selawik in 1930, Jim Hutchison remembered. Hutchison, who was working as a reindeer herder then, remembered Archie had fallen into conversation with Jim Robbins of Pacific Alaska Airways – a subsidiary of Pan American — who had taught flying in San Diego before coming to Alaska.

After the two talked about aviation all night long, Archie made up his mind to fly, not that he needed much of a push. Robbins suggested Archie learn in a Great Lakes Trainer, an open cockpit bi-plane that Archie considered ideal for his purposes. The next year, 1931, Archie scraped together $4,000 and bought a Great Lakes Trainer. He spent another thousand to have it taken apart and shipped to Kotzebue.

When it got to Kotzebue, he and Jim Hutchison had to replace the fabric because that which was not rotten was badly ripped. Now that he had a serviceable plane, Archie needed a sky-teacher. Leafing through a flying magazine, Archie came upon an advertisement for a "flight trainer," Chet Brown of Colorado. He hired Brown by telegram and Brown came north to what he probably thought was the edge of the earth.

For all his enthusiasm, Archie was hardly a star pupil, even in a class of one. It could not be said that he was an average student of aviation either. In fact, in all honesty, it could only be said that Archie was one of the worst students imaginable. For all his drive and energy, he had a terrible time mastering even the most elementary aviation skills. After 60 hours of training, seven times longer than an ordinary student would require, Brown was still unwilling to let Archie fly solo. Archie thought differently. He was *ready* to fly solo. He *wanted* to fly solo and he *was going* to fly solo!

Finally, after much whining and arm-twisting – not to mention a lot of practical jokes along the way – Brown relented and released Archie into the sky to fly solo. But, taking a page from Archie's book of practical jokes, Brown slipped an alarm clock under the pilot's seat. It was set to go off ten minutes after Archie left the ground.

"Go right up over town," advised Brown suppressing a smile. "Climb to a thousand and circle around. And be sure to take your time."

All went well as Archie flew steadily for nine minutes and 59 seconds. Then, when the alarm went off, the plane began wallowing about in the sky, as if a wild man was in the cockpit – which one was. A shaken Archie brought the plane down quickly, managing to land safely on a gravel bar in Kotzebue Lagoon rather than on the landing strip.

"Gosh I was scairt," Ferguson said for years. "I thought [the alarm] was some kind of a signal!"

Brown quit the same day. Since Archie still needed more training, he hired another pilot by telegram, Maurice King, out of Davenport, Iowa. Maurice, pronounced "Morris," also came north at Archie's expense. But even under the tutelage of this second expert instructor, Archie was still unable to master even the most basic of commercial aviation skills.

Then along came Burleigh Putnam who was working for the CAA (Civil Aeronautics Authority), the aviation watchdog. Burleigh gave Archie a few pointers to enable him to pass his commercial license and "make him as legal as possible." Burleigh remembered going aloft in Archie's Fairchild 24 to teach him spins, and Archie "pretty near went through the roof of the airplane when it stalled," Putnam recalled. "He'd never had anything like that happen to him before."

Little wonder that it took Archie *five years* to get his license. Even then it was widely rumored and quite possibly true that Archie bribed a CAA inspector to pass him.[20] (That inspector, incidentally, was *not* Burleigh Putnam. Putnam steadfastly maintained a reputation for being squeaky clean.)

With his hands, at long last, on his pilot's license, Archie quickly earned a reputation as one of the worst pilots – if not *the worst* – in the Arctic. He quickly became known and acclaimed as the most erratic flyer in Alaska, if not the United States. Every landing he made, it was said of Archie, was merely a "controlled crash."[21] He didn't so much *land* as *arrive*. Other more earthy descriptions of his lack of flying skills were accurate as well. "More bull shitter than pilot," said Ray Petersen, founder of Northern Consolidated and later part owner of Wien Alaska Airlines. "Maybe he's a pilot," a lot of other bush pilots used to say of him, "but he shouldn't be."

Even Sam Shafsky, who worked for Archie for a number of years, remembered Archie's flying as a phenomenon that was beyond belief. "He wasn't orthodox," Shafsky said shaking his head sadly. "He'd panic. He'd get in a tight jam and panic every time. [He'd make] wild turns right down on the deck and we'd be loaded to the gills." After about four trips together, during one of which Shafsky had to wrestle control of the aircraft away from Archie, both men agreed to remain friends – but never to fly together again.

Tommy Richards, Sr. –Kotzebue's first mayor and Wien's first jet pilot – also remembered Archie's flying with trepidation. "He didn't fly like he was supposed to," Richards, recalled. "He never flew more than 50 feet off the ground. Once [I and some passengers were with him when Archie] saw this fox crossing the Selawik River. Archie had to show us this fox and he just banked. He used his rudder [in a] completely uncoordinated turn and I thought the ball in the ball bank was going to shoot right out of the tube."

Why was Archie flying so low? Early in his career, he experienced a fire in his plane at 5,000 feet and barely made it to the Nome Airport before the plane was engulfed in flames. After that episode, his attitude was that if "the airplane burned up, he wanted to be close to the ground."[22]

F.R. and Clara, more aware than most of their son's inability to fly safely, looked up in trepidation every time Archie came visiting. They had good reason to be concerned. On his first trip as a pilot for hire, he was transporting Jimmy Donovan, a carpenter, to Shungnak in his Great Lakes Trainer. Archie hit the landing strip too hard and the plane bounced. When it landed it came down on its nose. Then it flipped over, leaving Donovan hanging from the open, back seat cockpit with his tools falling all around him like a metal rain.

For years, Archie told a story about flying into Shungnak and not knowing from which direction to land because there was no windsock at the field. Calling his mother on the radio, Archie told her to toss something into the store's wood stove so he could tell from the smoke which way the wind was blowing. His mother, legend has it, grabbed the nearest thing and tossed it into the stove. As it turned out, she had tossed in F.R.'s trousers. This story, like so many other legends of the north, fits Archie's personality like a pair of trousers.

The 1930s were a grand time for the Ferguson clan and they enjoyed a significant list of "firsts." They imported the first truck, an International, and the first cow north of the Arctic Circle. Warren and Archie flew the cow to Selawik. On mild days they would give the cow some exercise by letting it loose in their fox pens. "At first the foxes ran for shelter when the strange animal was put in with them," Warren told the *Nome Nugget,* but after the animals got used to each other they would "play around in the pen together."[23] Later the Fergusons also imported a bull, but there are two stories as to the size of that animal. Potter stated that the "bull" was actually a ten-month old calf, much to Archie's dismay, because, as he stated, "we didn't git a damn bit o' milk after he arrived." This obviously stalled Archie's plans for a herd of dairy cows.[24]

Some residents of Kotzebue remembered it as a full-grown beast. When the bull came off the barge, according to Segundo Llorente, the Catholic priest in Kotzebue at the time, everyone stood back to give the animal room while the dogs "howled in fury." It was suggested that Llorente, "a Spaniard, should treat the town to a bull fight." Llorente did. He entered the enclosure that housed the bull, walked right up to the beast and, with his cane, "hit him gently on the head." The bull looked up from his meal of tundra in surprise. Llorente then grabbed the bull by the horns at which time the animal backed up, dragging the priest with him. Only after the priest had fallen to the ground did the bull stop. Then, Llorente wrote in his memoirs,

> *I let him have it with a couple of blows in the horns with my cane. He did not like it and ran in total defeat with his tail up in the air, while I stood there with my cane raised to the sky — a symbol of victory.*[25]

The Fergusons also imported the first motorcycle. Archie set an Arctic motorcycle speed record roaring from Selawik across the ice to Kotzebue in three hours. The record stood for quite a few years, primarily because there were no other motorcycles in the Arctic. Archie also claimed he used that motorcycle to do the first flying in the Arctic when he used the cycle to hurtle Evel Kneivel style, across an ice lead.

In 1932, Archie and Warren used the spark coils out of an old Model T Ford to rig a transmitter to an antenna. As soon as they and their wives learned Morse Code, they went on the air. It wasn't long before quite a few other residents joined in and everything was going well until the FCC clamped down. Their homemade sets were transmitting all over Alaska and causing annoying communications problems. When one of the Fergusons got on the air, everyone else was wiped off.[26]

When voice communications came to the Arctic, Archie was one of the first people on the air. He delighted and riveted the collective ham operators within range with on-the-air ongoing spats with his wife, Hadley. Hadley, no slouch when it came to using the radio, competed word-for-word with Archie though she did not use language as pithy as that of her husband. Archie took the abuse as long as he was in range of Hadley and then he would talk to anyone he could reach. Moving out of one ham's range and into another's, he would talk his way from one end of the Arctic to other.

Always talking, always laughing, pilots remarked that Archie would "fly 300 hundred miles, ask 300 hundred questions, answer them all himself and then fly 300 hundred miles back." Jim Hutchison, long-time airplane mechanic, remembered one time when Archie landed in a village, rounded up a guy he was looking for and "talked to him for 20 minutes and never g[a]ve the fella an opportunity to say anything, [and then Archie got] in his airplane and flew home."

Flying passengers in those days was financially risky for everyone involved. If a pilot had to fly a carpenter out to a construction site, often the carpenter had to fly first and wait for his tools to catch up to him. This was terribly expensive for the construction company because the carpenter could not work while he did not have his tools yet he would still have to be paid since he was on site. Certainly the carpenter could borrow tools, but a worker without his own tools is only half-efficient.

If that carpenter was a specialist, he might have no choice but to sit around on payroll until his gear caught up with him. The bad news for the employer could get worse if the weather closed in. Then the carpenter would be sitting for days, on payroll, waiting for his tools. This set of circumstances did not endear that flying service to the construction company.

Some of the passengers were wage earners of another kind. If the miners could not come to town for a "good time," then the "good times" came to the miners. Thus the prostitutes of the era made their circuit by bush plane. They would rent a cabin for a few weeks, curtain off the back and ply their trade until they had extracted all the money, nuggets and dust that they could from the area. Then they would move on.[27] They, like the ministers, magistrates, game wardens, marshals and territorial engineers, established peripatetic routes that served their purpose best.

Sometimes passengers could be problems. Don Emmons, flying for Archie, was taking his common-law wife to Fairbanks when she decided to commit suicide. Halfway to Fairbanks she opened the fuselage door and stepped out into thin air. Another passenger, Dr. Anthony, grabbed the woman by the foot and held on tightly. Since the woman was hanging lower than the wheels, Emmons had no choice but to order her dropped before he landed on the airstrip. The woman, legend has it, fell into a deep snow bank unhurt and was rescued within a few minutes.[28] This story spawned quite a few similar tales. Shafsky, who knew both participants well, filled in the gaps of the story. Don Emmons and the woman had just parted company and she had drawn a .38 and appeared to be intent on killing Emmons when she suddenly decided to commit suicide instead by stepping out of the plane. Dr. Anthony held on to her as long as he could but finally had to drop the woman. But she did not escape unscathed. She broke a great number of bones and remained in a full body cast in Kotzebue for almost a year.[29]

Over the years, the plane proved to be a versatile tool for the Arctic. Bill Munz, flying out of Nome, even showed how an airplane could do double duty and help a dog team. In December of 1945, he was north of Teller flying a pregnant woman into Nome when he spotted a herd of reindeer being chased by a runaway dog sled. He followed the coastline until he came across Frank Ahnangatoguk four miles away. Munz picked up Ahnangatoguk and then flew back toward the runaway dog team. There he "execute[ed] a treacherous landing between the dog team and the reindeer herd thus stopping the team." Ahnangatoguk got out and Bill Munz landed in Nome shortly thereafter. But he had an extra passenger on board; the pregnant woman had given birth before he made it into Nome.[30]

Passenger service in the Arctic between 1930 and 1950 was a far cry from what it is today. "Rustic" would be the best word to describe the service. Whether someone liked to fly or not, they flew. They did not have a choice. If someone had a fear of flying, they drank heavily, bit their lip and left their fingerprints on the underside of the arm of the seat. But it was fly or walk and it was a long way between places on foot.

One aspect of passenger service has not changed that much in the bush. Today, as then, passengers fly on a "call and wait" basis. Passengers would call for their favorite pilot and wait until he or she showed up. There was a great deal of loyalty among passengers to pilots – until something went wrong. Then the loyalty would switch to another carrier. In the Arctic, Pilgrim Springs had a Catholic orphanage and they wouldn't fly with anyone but Hans Mirow. But that was only until one of Mirow's pilots, Jack Jefford, crashed while taking off. After that the orphanage wouldn't fly with anyone but Wien.

As long as no one crashed, passengers stuck to their favorite pilots and would continue to call for a specific person. But the turnover rate was high. Often a pilot who had been in Nome in the spring might not be there in the fall. He might be in another part of the Territory, in a hospital or even dead. A new pilot would show up and begin building passenger loyalty of his own – a practice that continues to the present day.

Sometimes when a new pilot arrived instead of the pilot requested, chicanery was involved. Archie was famous for stealing passengers and he was very good at his trade. He would be in the air and hear on the radio that someone in Selawik was calling for Jack Jefford. Archie would beat Jefford to Selawik and tell the passenger that Jefford had "cracked up in Deering." It would only be later that the passenger would realize that he or she had been snookered. But Archie already had their money.

Archie was also an expert at stealing passengers in the large communities as well. While his certificated route was between Kotzebue and Fairbanks, sometimes he would take a charter into Nome. On these trips, he would often swing through Candle and Deering looking for other passengers to take west. Once he arrived in Nome, he would start looking for passengers who needed to go east. Starting on one side of Front Street he would hit every tavern and store from one end of Nome to the other and then start back on the other side of the street.

Since he knew by sight the people who usually flew, as soon as he spotted someone he knew who was from out of town, he would cut a deal. Usually the deal was best for Archie but it would be, nevertheless, a deal the passenger could not afford to bypass. This infuriated the other pilots of course, particularly those who had the certificated route. "He was an expert at swiping our passengers," remembered Robert Jacobs who was flying for Alaska Airlines, "which he did a good bit of the time."

But loyalty to a pilot was not given easily. When a pilot left an area, it was not always easy for his replacement to win the loyalty of the old customers. Fred Chambers learned that to be a fact when he cracked up in Buckland. He was doing fine until he hit a rut on the runway and knocked off one side of the landing gear. When he got back to Nome, his boss, Hans Mirow, told him, "You've still got your job but I don't know if people will ride with you." Mirow was right. Mirow Flying Service would get a call to pick someone up at a mining camp and Chambers would fly out to pick them up. But, recalled Chambers, "they'd see me taxiing and they'd turn around and walk back to camp."

Finding pilots was hard; finding good ones was close to impossible. Because of the distance to the Lower 48, particularly from the Arctic, pilots were hired by wire through Western Union. In those days "when you hired a new pilot [you knew] it was going to cost you a new airplane," Chambers noted. That was part of the price of doing business in the Arctic. You put a new pilot on payroll and pretty soon he was going to "wash out an airplane. You couldn't afford to fire him then because he had learned [a valuable lesson] at your expense."

When it came to the business of flying, Archie was as cold-blooded as a corpse on the polar ice pack. While he was always more than willing to steal any other pilot's passengers, he was not going to allow anyone – and particularly Hans Mirow – to steal his. To keep a firm grip on his clientele, Archie and Hadley developed a system of codes that would let Archie know that a passenger was waiting in Shungnak or Deering even though Hadley might *say* on the radio the passenger was in Kiana. This baffled the competition. If Hans Mirow or another pilot were trying to snatch one of Archie's passengers, he would show up at the village where Hadley *said* there was a passenger only to find that he had wasted time and aviation gas going to the wrong village.

When it came to operating the radio, Hadley Ferguson was a professional. In the days of Morse Code, she learned to handle the key better than many white operators who had been speaking English their entire lives. Hadley was also an incredibly intelligent woman and an excellent businessperson. While Archie was essentially a schemer and conniver, Hadley was a knowledgeable, hard-core, nuts-and-bolts person. She knew how to handle money and did well with it. Archie, on the other hand, didn't have a clue as to how to *keep* money once it found its way into his hands.

Hadley in 1950

The only thing Archie spent money on willingly was his pilots. "Ferguson College of Technical Knowledge," he called his business laughingly. But he paid his pilots well remembered two of his pilots Ed Yost and Sam Shafsky. "We were the highest-paid pilots in Alaska," Shafsky recalled.

When it came to having a good time, Archie's fun-loving side was infectious. Pilots loved to sit by the hour and listen to his wealth of stories – most of them barefaced lies. Then there were his practical jokes. Archie loved practical jokes! One time at Selawik, he was told that Hans Mirow would be flying over on his way to Nome. Archie hired some Inupiat to hurriedly dig a depression at the end of the runway. Then he taxied his Cessna Airmaster over and tipped its nose into the hole. Archie's plane was clearly identifiable from the air since the name FERGUSON was printed out in huge block letters across the top of the wing.[31] Mirow, flying very high as was his style, circled Selawik to get a better look at the aircraft that had apparently nosed into the landing strip. Then, as soon as Mirow turned back and headed for Nome, Archie righted his Airmaster and flew like the blazes, picking up some miners at Cleary Creek, and beat Mirow into Nome. "Boy, was he surprised to see Archie in Nome!" Sam Shafsky laughingly said of Mirow.

By the end of the 1930s, the Fergusons were among the wealthiest people in the Arctic, if not Alaska. They owned trading posts in five Arctic communities. They had a sawmill, mink farm, and a greenhouse and owned the only movie theater north of the Arctic Circle. Additionally, they also owned and operated a hotel and restaurant and had interests in several gold operations as well as some jade claims.[32]

But they were not the only entrepreneurs in the Arctic. In Kotzebue alone in the 1930s there were a handful of stores. In addition to Ferguson's there was Magid's, run by the Magid brothers, Boris and Sam; Eckhardt's, owned by the husband-wife team of Hugo and Gretchen; and N. G. Hanson's, an enterprise that Archie eventually won on an $85 bet in 1948.[33] Later, Bess Cross, wife of bush pilot John Cross, opened a store and restaurant. There was also a collection of other traders and fox and mink farmers in the area.

Then there was Archie's business nemesis and archenemy, Louis Rotman. Rotman, known as "Louie," was one of the sprinkling of Jewish merchants who had come north to take advantage of the opportunities the Arctic had to offer. He started as a fur merchant in the 1920s and later expanded into the general store business. Oddly, he had worked for Tom Berryman early in his career, just as F.R. had.

But it was not just Louie Rotman and the Fergusons who were business and personal adversaries. It was everyone against everyone. After all, the entrepreneurs were all operating in a small town with only so much money to go around. If the Fergusons were not fighting with Bess Cross, then they were crossing swords with the Magid brothers or Tom Berryman. Sometimes it was a combination of the above and at others it was with the universally hated federal government. But while he was alive, it was Louie Rotman that the Fergusons fought with the most.

Rotman was about the same size and age as Archie. Both men were equivalent when it came to their enthusiasm for "indoor sports." Louie eventually married Clara Levy, one of three daughters of a Jewish store-keeper in Kiana and an Inupiat woman — but not before having a steamy affair with her sister, Beulah.[34]

This particular liaison is significant because Beulah was to become Archie's long-term mistress from the mid-1940s to the end of her life in 1956. Beulah's son from Louie, Billy Levy, died at the age of 20 in a plane crash 10 miles from Shishmaref in April of 1953. But while Billy was alive, Archie treated him as though Billy were his own son, which came as a surprise to many of the Kotzebue pilots since Louie and Archie hated each other with such a sizzling passion.[35]

One of the many aspects of Inupiat culture that did not change with the arrival of the white man in Kotzebue was the sexual proclivity of the Natives. Sexual intercourse was viewed as a natural function and performing it did not carry any of the social or religious stigma of shame that the Christian religion tried to inject. Sexual relations were open, frequent and unrestrained, a fact of life terribly distorted by Hollywood movies which insinuated that Inupiat men would "share their wives" with travelers. This was a grotesque over-simplification of what was actually occurring.

Archie and Beulah

Sexual intercourse was widespread with some taboos but little regard to race or age spread between the participators. As a result, when family trees were drawn, their trunks and outstretched branches were so intertwined with so many other trees that the expression "one big happy family" had a real meaning north of the Arctic Circle.

While the Inupiat were doing publicly what many whites were doing privately, this did not mitigate the social stigma in the eyes of the whites. Inupiat were grossly discriminated against in the same way as the blacks of the Deep South during the same era. They were often required to sit apart from whites in public gatherings and inter-racial marriages were looked upon as miscegenation.

For the white males in the Arctic, however, the free sex attitude of the Inupiat was a satyriasis's dream come true. Here were women of every body type and facial configuration free for the taking. And take them the men did, to the point that the genetic family tree of the Arctic contains as many Non-Natives as Native genes. Regardless of the efforts of the missionaries, singularly or combined, the "indoor sportsmen" of the Arctic made the concept of the alleged superiority of European morals laughable.

In Kotzebue specifically, a good example of the pride with which some white men expressed their sexual prowess was Paul Davidovics. A legend in the Arctic in the 1930s, Davidovics used to carry the mail by dogsled from Nome to Barrow. So famous was he that Will Rogers was going to interview him after he and Wiley Post had gone to Barrow to visit Charlie Brower. The visit never occurred for Post and Rogers died in August of 1935 in a lagoon south of Barrow.

A storyteller *par excellence*, "the world [did] not have paper enough to copy all the stories that Paul told," reported Father Llorente. One of the few that has been recorded, and is probably true, was of a night when Davidovics was lost in a driving storm. More dead than alive he stumbled upon an abandoned shack where he immediately sought shelter. He fed his dogs in the dark and then crawled inside his sleeping bag using a log on the floor of the cabin for a pillow. When he awoke the next morning, he discovered that the "log was not a log at all; it was a frozen, dead man."[36]

In 1939, Davidovics was invited to the Golden Gate International Exposition, dubbed the "San Francisco World's Fair." Before his introduction, he had been quite boisterous in his claim of having "99 children," an allegation that was quite possibly true. But, as the Exposition was in San Francisco, and the Lower 48 was in the grip of a serious case of sexual repression, the Master of Ceremonies attempted to down play Davidovics' record as an indoor sportsman and introduced him as a man with "25 children." But Davidovics was not to be denied any of his paternity. When he made it to the podium, he was incensed. "Dammit!" he said to the crowd. "I said 99!"[37]

Depending on the source, Archie's archrival in Kotzebue, Louie Rotman, was either an amiable, bland businessman who rarely smiled or he was one of the most disliked entrepreneurs in the Arctic. "Only the people who knew him didn't like him," said Jack Lee of Lee's Flying Service. "He was only interested in making money." Gene Joiner, the Kotzebue eccentric, referred to Rotman as the "virtuoso of the cash register."[38] On the other hand, Sam Shafsky, who had worked for him, found him "a shrewd individual with a heart of gold if you were a friend."

While it could be certainly said of both Archie and Warren that they, like Louie, were "only interested in making money," the difference was that the two brothers were blessed with personalities that made it hard to dislike them. Louie was regarded as cold and unfeeling thus giving others the impression that all he cared about was making a profit.

It didn't take much to start a spat between the Fergusons and Louie. If it wasn't something one of them said, it was prices at their respective store or what was happening in the villages where their stores were in competition as well. In a lot of ways the three men were similar. They were all about the same physical size, had the same temperament, were in the Arctic for the same reason, had Inupiat wives, had stores in many of the same villages, were sexually interested in the same women and probably could not have lived anywhere else on earth and been so happy.

But in other ways they were very different. Louie was a drinker; Archie and Warren were not – though Warren sold liquor.[39] Louie was frugal with his money; Warren was but Archie was not. Louie was a passive man and while Archie was a "lover not a fighter" and Warren was a boxer. Warren was such an aggressive fighter that once Logan Varnell, miner and seasonal worker, had to break up a fight between Louie and Warren over a woman. For good reason, Varnell believed, Warren might damage Louie with more than a bloodied nose.[40]

The older of the two Ferguson boys, Warren, was particularly well liked in Kotzebue. A boxing enthusiast, he used to hold July 4th matches on the Ferguson barges, events that were very popular with the Inupiat. There was also a touch of the grandiose in Warren. In April of 1936, as an example, he hitched "100 dogs" to move a mining elevator 1,600 feet to a new location. Undoubtedly with a mischievous smile on his face, Warren asked the reporter from the *Nome Nugget*, "Some 'horsepower,' what do you think?"[41]

But the Ferguson success story was not without its dark clouds. Tragedy struck in the latter half of the 1930s. One of Archie's children, Stanley, died early in the decade when he fell down a flight of stairs and broke his back.

Archie and Hadley's second and last child, Glenn, died of pneumonia in Nome in June of 1935. F.R. passed away in October of 1937, and his wife followed him the next year.

While the death of a parent is to be expected, the loss of a brother is another matter altogether. On October 22, 1939, Warren and Logan Varnell were driving on the ice of Kotzebue Lagoon. They had run rope to the Ferguson tug, the **Helen Lee**, and were trying to pull it ashore. Suddenly the truck went through the ice.

The truck sank 15 feet and both men came out of the submerged cab, clawing for the surface against the tide. Fortunately for Varnell, there were some Inupiat nearby at the time. One of them, Duffy Henry, could clearly see Varnell's shadowy, struggling figure through a section of clear ice and pounded an escape hole open with a two-by-four. Varnell came out of the water and dove back through the hole made by the truck looking for Warren. But Warren was gone, swept under the rougher ice where his struggles could not be seen. Warren could not have lasted long under the ice. It was so cold that within minutes of coming out of the water, Varnell's clothing became so frozen that it had to be sawed off his body.[42]

Though Archie was able to retrieve the truck, Warren's body could not be found before the hole in the ice hole froze closed. Knowing that if the corpse could not be retrieved before spring it would drift out to sea with the shore-fast ice, Archie put out a reward of $100 for retrieval of the body. The next June, Harold Brown recovered the corpse by stretching some nets across the mouth of the lagoon slightly below the level of the ice. When Warren's body drifted by, Brown was able to snag it.[43]

The residents of Kotzebue sorely missed Warren. Unlike Archie, he was trusted in Kotzebue. He was a sharp businessman but lacked Archie's infamous conniving streak. Even so, recalled Shafsky, Warren was "just as neurotic and just as crazy as Archie." The Inupiat particularly liked Warren and gave him the affectionate name "*ongooporuk*," which fit him perfectly because of his size, body shape and warmth of personality. The Inupiat term meant "bossy little man" or "little boss man."[44]

Warren's death may have also created both a financial windfall and a curse for Archie. Warren was an astute money-handler and at the time of his death, the Fergusons had accumulated an empire estimated at an amazing $7 million.[45] But Warren's death created a major problem for Archie.

Warren had three children – Don, Ray and Frank – and an undependable wife. Archie immediately moved to Kotzebue from Selawik permanently and established the three boys in his house where he and Hadley raised them as his sons, later adopting them.[46]

Warren's wife, Minnie, in the words of Kotzebue pilot John Cross, then went to Fairbanks where she "made a fool of herself."[47] She worked at the Wonder Bar Cafe in Fairbanks for years before returning to Kotzebue where, in 1991, she was living in the Senior Citizens Cultural Center. Minnie's lack of a grip on reality was apparently a lifelong affliction. In 1990, she told this author that Warren had "committed suicide" and that she and Warren had "five children: three boys and a girl." One of Warren's grandchildren, Hadley Hess, responded to Minnie's comments by saying that she was "crazy" and that fact had been well-known for quite a while by the rest of the family.

For Archie, the awful string of deaths must have been devastating. In a period of four years he had lost two children, a brother, both parents and acquired responsibility for three boys, the oldest one, Don, being only four years old. But even in Warren's death, Archie managed to find a silver cloud. For years afterwards, any time one of his pilots asked for a raise, Archie would unreel a long, tearful story of how Warren had died with "thousands of dollars" in his pocket, money that was never recovered and how he, Archie, was still struggling to recover from that terrible loss. Archie was still using this excuse as late as the 1950s, almost 20 years after Warren's death.[48]

But then again, it was Archie's nature to do anything to create confusion. He never told anyone his birth year and was equally as reluctant to tell anyone his middle name. For years, one of his mechanics, Ed Yost, tried to find out what the "R" in Archie's middle name stood for. Whenever he asked Archie, Archie would give him a strange look as if the middle name was something exotic or embarrassing, a name like Rupert or Ringermorton. All Archie would ever say was that the "R" of his middle name was the same as that of his father, F.R.

While Archie may have been able to insinuate that he had a name of which to be ashamed, his pilot's certificate revealed nothing exotic at all. The "R" stood for "Robert." But for years, Yost called Archie by a middle name he concocted to fit the letter R: Rustguard. (Archie's father's middle name, it should be added, was not Robert, even though Archie claimed it was. The "R" is F.R. stood for "Ralston.")[49]

ARCHIE FERGUSON, ALASKA'S CLOWN PRINCE

"Ya hear that noise? That ain't static; that's a bear! Yeah, I got-ta bear in the plane with me, and he's broke loose! He's climbin' right up here beside me, growlin' an' showin' his teeth – big sharp teeth! Oh Jeezus, he's tryin' ta eat up the fuselage! There's two of us up here now, but it looks like purty soon there's only gonna be one 'n' it ain' gonna be me! Stand by, I'll call ya every other minute!"

. . . Archie Ferguson giving his blow-by-blow description of the baby polar bear which became loose in his plane while he was aloft.

* * *

"The best landing that Archie Ferguson ever made."

. . . anonymous bush pilot when he was told that a baby polar bear had been at the controls when Archie's plane landed.[50]

Once he got his license, it didn't take long for Archibald "Rustguard" Ferguson to become Alaska's Clown Prince. From the time that he bought the Great Lakes Trainer until he died in 1967, Archie deliberately wove a tapestry of zany achievements that would have been worthy of the Marx Brothers.

Perhaps the truest assessment of Archie's career as a pilot was that it was a hodgepodge of incidents rather than an ongoing drama. Archie did not appear to learn from his mistakes; he just repeated them. First he would crash a plane, tell a great story about how the plane had gone up on its nose and, shortly thereafter, crash again. But he survived every crash. He was like a flying cat with a never-ending sequence of lives, each with a tale of its own.

By the early-1940s, his notoriety was so widespread that Jean Potter, who was then writing her classic THE FLYING NORTH, was told by Jack Jefford that no book on Alaska aviation would be complete without Archie. **BUT**, he warned her, "do not fly with him." Other pilots gave her the same advice. Potter reported that the only reason she went up with Archie was because she got trapped into it. "Oh Jeezus," Archie told her, "here yer writin' a book on aviation 'n' ya don't even have no faith in it!" So she went up with him.[51]

Potter's chapter on Archie made him a national celebrity overnight. Later she admitted that the chapter on Archie was the easiest section of her book to write. "I didn't really write it," she said in 1989. "Archie did. Mostly I just wrote what he said." The section so impressed her agent that it was sent to the *Saturday Evening Post* where it was accepted at once and printed in December of 1945 under the title "World's Craziest Pilot." "I didn't even know [the article had been published] until I got the check," Potter recalled.[52]

But Jack Jefford was right. Archie was a *terrible* pilot. He was so bad that even today, seasoned pilots wonder how he was able to survive. "The most amazing thing that Archie did in aviation was live through it," Neil Bergt, owner of the now-defunct MarkAir, said with a laugh. "He survived in a country where navigational aids were virtually absent and anyone who had done it for as long as he had obviously knew something about what he was doing." Former Governor Hammond, another seasoned bush pilot, felt the same way. "He never got killed. He must have been good."

With the advent of airplane, Alaska changed faster than ever before. "God may have created Alaska," Alaskan humorist Warren Sitka once noted, "but it was the airplane that truly carved the face of the Last Frontier." Even this could be an understatement. Alaska had a unique role in the history of aviation. Its rugged landscape and unbelievably miserable weather should have been two factors that limited air travel. To a certain extent they did. But not for long. By the Second World War, there was no village that could not be reached by the airplane. The transportation of goods and passengers throughout Alaska was thus the proof positive that planes could consistently supply goods, mail and other necessities of life every month of the year – even over an area more than twice the size of Texas with some of the worst weather in the world over the ruggedest terrain in North America.

Even today, an era when men have walked on the moon, one-third of the population of Alaska still lives in communities that are not connected by a road. In these areas, known collectively as the "bush," the airplane is the only consistent link with civilization. In these remote areas, the airplane became more than a means of transportation: it was the lifeline.

Archie's CAA Pilot's Certificate File is a good indication of his attitude toward flying. He misplaced his license and had to request another. Other times his license was suspended. In 1941, he failed navigation, meteorology *and* the flight test – after flying for *ten years* – and had to try again. On more than one occasion, he allowed his license to expire.[53] But Archie didn't care. He was "anti-establishment of the first order. Anything that had any authority to it, well, he was against it."[54] and high on his list of authority figures to which he was irreverent with was the CAA, which he viewed as the serpent in his Garden of Eden.

Then again, the CAA was evil incarnate to most Alaskan pilots and just plain evil to the rest. Pilots did not look on the CAA as a safety-oriented agency. They viewed it as a bureaucracy full of incompetents intent on putting every pilot out of business. Pilots had good reason to be concerned about CAA motives. The pilots had their collective hands full just struggling to survive in Alaska. Having the CAA looking over your shoulder was like butchering a moose with one's back to a grizzly just out of hibernation.

Supposedly the CAA was in Alaska to make sure that the pilots flew safely. But, from the way the agency enforced regulations, there was no way anyone could stay in business and still follow regulations. At least that was how the pilots saw it. On the other hand, CAA inspectors were amazed at the condition of many Alaskan planes and wondered how the crates could get off the ground, much less fly cargo and passengers.

So the pilots played an on-going cat-and-mouse game with the CAA, dodging the Feds while the inspectors tried to catch them unaware. If it had not been so serious, it would have been comical. Whenever CAA inspectors went to Kotzebue on business, by the time they arrived in town every pilot who could fly had flown the coop. Wherever a plane crashed on takeoff, it was a race to see who got to it first: the CAA or every other pilot at the airstrip. The CAA would come with scales to see if the plane had been overloaded. The pilot's buddies would be busy helping the unlucky airman unload his plane so the CAA inspector would not find that the aircraft had been grossly overloaded when the pilot tried to take off. Once Don Emmons went off the runway at Weeks Field in Fairbanks and by the time the CAA inspector got there the only cargo left aboard was "about two cases of beans."[55] Understandably, the CAA had a rough time enforcing the hated regulations, but CAA activities did have a noticeable impact on flying in the Arctic. Just as the State Trooper who sits visibly along the interstate slows traffic simply by being there, the CAA changed aviation in Alaska just by showing a presence.

The CAA also served another purpose. As a federal agency, the CAA could coordinate federal activities that individuals and companies could not. Upon occasion, the CAA asked the military to bomb ice bridges. In June of 1948, the CAA requested and received the services of the P-51s of the 64th Fighter Squadron to bomb an ice jam. The military complied and the ice jam "weakened after several 500-pound bombs were dropped." When the ice dam broke, the Kobuk River dropped two feet in 15 minutes.[56] The CAA could also coordinate transport of supplies to Federal hospitals and installations as well as streamline permission through the bureaucracy.

The CAA had a right to be concerned about the state of aviation in the Territory of Alaska. Aviation in that era was a grim business and crashes were everyone's problem. Good pilots got no headlines. They did their job. Bad pilots became notorious when they went nose-down on a runway and spilled their passengers.

But, in the final analysis, the bottom line governed. To stay in business, a pilot had to fly. He had no choice. If rules had to be violated along the way, that was the cost of doing business. "If you want to make a living [in the Arctic] you have to fly," veteran pilot Bill Munz told Vincent Doran who was considering buying Munz Airways. "[And when you] fly in good weather and bad long enough, your digestive system goes to pot." Above all else, Munz said, "You've got to stay away from the CAA. All they want to do is ground you."

Munz, like many pilots, had a seething hatred for the United States government for no other reason than it was a government. Occasionally it flared and Munz, who had a political point of view that was "to the right of Genghis Khan," went far out of his way to show his contempt for anything related to the government. "For a while he wouldn't land at the Nome airport because he had to talk to the government people there," Dick Gelleher stated when Munz died in 1992. "He didn't want anything to do with the government."[57]

Because flying in the Arctic was tough, pilots had to take whatever advantage was offered. Munz, as Doran learned, took this lesson to heart. "[Munz had] the most unique flying service in the world." At any one time during the summer "he had at least six planes ready to fly but he was the only one who flew." Doran learned that Munz would buy planes from people who went bankrupt, tune them up and let them sit in his hanger. All winter he would work on the planes, then, during the summer, when a plane started giving him problems, he just grounded it and used another. "I never bought a plane I couldn't completely pay off in 100 hours of flying," Munz told Doran.

Munz is also remembered as a practical joker. "Don't slam that door it might fall off," he might tell a *cheechako* (tenderfoot) when he or she scrambled aboard looking for a bit of adventure with a *real* Alaskan bush pilot. For sourdoughs who didn't know him, he'd take off and fly straight toward a power line while talking to the passengers, apparently oblivious to the impending danger. Then, at the last second, he'd pull the stick back and b-a-r-e-l-y make it over the wire.

Practical joking aside, death was a pilot's constant companion. "You don't have to go up," the old saying went, "but you do have to come down," and every pilot knew that whenever he went up, he might not have a choice of where, when and how he was going to come down. When Fred Chambers was missing on the Nulato River in December of 1939, Hans Mirow and a score of other pilots went out looking for him. On the first day, Mirow got caught in a whiteout while following the wide swath cut in the forest for General William "Billy" Mitchell's telegraph wire. Mirow nicked some trees about eight miles from Kaltag and came down hard. It took rescuers several days to find his body. That was the price flying in the North sometimes exacted. (After a very cold week, Chambers was rescued.)

While the best pilots refused to take unnecessary risks, some took no risks at all. At the head of this pack was Mr. Caution himself, Sig Wien. Sig would fly only under the best of conditions. Like most other pilots, he flew only in daylight. When it started to get dark, he landed. If the weather closed in, he stayed until it cleared. But Sig took his caution to the extreme. In the late 1950s while flying an Arctic route, Wien personnel sometimes wouldn't know where Sig was for days. If the weather got bad, he'd land.

Sig Wien's cautious behavior was attuned to the Arctic's often-rotten flying conditions. Arctic weather closed in suddenly and remained unflyable for days. Sometimes flying weather would deteriorate so quickly pilots would be forced to land wherever they were and wait on the ground until clouds lifted. In December of 1946, Archie was flying his neighbor, Representative Bess Cross, back to Kotzebue. Following Archie was a second plane carrying Cross' $2,500 fur coat along with a case of Scotch whiskey, several pounds of pork chops and a load of vegetables for her store, the Kotzebue Trading Post. As the two planes headed out along the Bering Sea coast, the second pilot lost Archie in the fog. As the weather front moved in, the pilot landed on a sand bar to wait for the clouds to pass. When Archie found him seven days later, the pilot was sitting bundled up in Cross' fur coat and guzzling her whiskey. He had already devoured every one of her pork chops and all the produce.[58]

In comparison with the Lower 48, the tempo of flying in Alaska was staggering. On a per capita basis, by the end of the Second World War Alaska had 116 times as many planes engaged in commercial activity which flew 70 times farther carrying 23 times as many passengers along with 1,034 times as much cargo and 48 times as much mail when compared to the Lower 48. At the same time, Alaska's population was equivalent to barely .05 percent of the nation's 1940 total.[59]

This was a different era, an Alaska that is no more. Things happened that could never happen again. Crime was low because the cities were isolated. There was no road out of the Territory until the Second World War. Thieves could neither leave the territory with their booty nor sell it in the small communities from which it had been stolen. No one locked doors. Hotels didn't have room keys. It was not until into the 1960s that the Anchorage Westward Hotel, today the Anchorage Westward Hilton, even had door keys. As late as the 1970s, Alaskans routinely left keys in the ignitions of their cars.

Bizarre aviation incidents happened regularly. Sam Shafsky, long-time bush pilot who flew for Archie, remembered a flight from Ruby, up the Yukon, around Tanana and then into Fairbanks. The weather had been pretty good when he started but between Tanana and Manly Hot Springs clouds moved in, forcing him to fly lower and lower until he was skimming along inside a canyon a few hundred feet off the river bank with mountains on each side.

"I could see something dark comin' up so I pulled over a little bit kept looking and saying to myself, 'What is that?'" With each passing instant, the object became darker. Then, in the last instant before it snapped into focus, he realized it was another airplane, flying down the same canyon coming directly at him! Neither pilot had time to change course. "I looked out the window and it was Jimmy Stewart in a Pilgrim on the mail run from Fairbanks to Nulato! I looked at him and he looked at me [as if to say] what are you doing here?!" Both men shot by each other and talked about the incident for years.

Not everyone considered flying as the way of the future. Sam Shafsky said of Ed Stroecker, president of the First National Bank of Fairbanks: "He had a bad heart. If you wanted to give him a relapse you'd go in and ask for a loan. 'What's it for, Sam? Is it for one of those airplanes?' Then he'd just turn his back on you, walk out of the office and slam the door."

There was good reason for Stroecker to consider airplanes a bad risk as there was also good reason for the CAA to keep an unblinking eye on pilots like Archie Ferguson. Few aviators disputed that Archie was an "accident looking for a place to happen and frequently did." Claiming to have had more crack-ups than any other pilot in Alaska, Archie's company, Ferguson Airways, had as its motto "Anywhere, Anytime." Archie meant it too. He'd fly anywhere for profit. He had a small fleet of airplanes including a Waco, Cessnas and Stinsons and did as much flying as his pilots did. But Archie remained the flying clown, a reputation he built upon monthly.

His takeoffs and landings were events. As a young man, Doug Millard was working for Wien in Nome during the summer of 1946 when Archie came to town. As Millard was about ready to drive back to Nome from the Airport, his boss, Dick Webb, Manager for Wien in Nome, saw Archie about to take off. Webb stopped Millard from going back into town. "Let's stay and watch Archie take off," Webb told the young Millard. "We hope nothing happens but if it does, you sure wouldn't want to miss it."[60]

There was good reason to watch. Robert Bruce Clifton, author of MURDER BY MAIL, reported one of Archie's many encounters with movable objects. After Archie took off from Kotzebue, the operator at the field stated

No one else is flying, but Archie just took for the Kobuk. With this wind, he could be in Kiana in a few minutes. His departure was routine; he knocked over several oil drums at the end of the field as he left.[61]

John Paden, Principal of the Alaska Native Service School at White Mountain, 75 miles from Nome, vividly remembered another of Archie's more memorable takeoffs. Archie had asked Paden to call Nome and tell them he was on his way. Paden did a few minutes of paperwork and then, in his words, "I pulled the phone over toward me, and first thing I know the danged thing flew off the desk away from me and bounded across the floor and hit the wall." When he went outside, the mystery of the flying phone was cleared up. Archie had taken off right into the telephone line strung around the school, snagging a good portion of it around his propeller. Unperturbed, off Archie flew to Nome with yards of telephone wire flapping wildly in the Arctic sky.[62] (Some pilots felt that it was more likely that Archie had snagged the wire on his landing gear. Though hooking an unexpected rope is rare, it does happen. One of the first licensed polar bear guides, Mary Oldham, remembered seeing Eddie Clark of Naknek "flying down the beach at Egegik in his Super cub with 2-foot floats hanging from his tail.")

Archie also gave his passengers more than a few moments of terror. One winter his plane broke through the ice at Shungnak shearing off several inches of one end of the wooden propeller. Hefting an axe, Archie hacked off a few inches of the undamaged side to balance the prop.

"I'll fix this baby," Ferguson declared jovially, "We're r-e-a-l-l-y going to fly today!"

It took the plane more than three miles of skipping along the ice "rattling like a sawmill" before it finally took off.[63] "She turned up like hell," Archie later told Fred Goodwin, "but she didn't go very fast." Archie proudly displayed that propeller in his restaurant for years. Archie also kept another propeller in his restaurant. This one was "missing most of one blade" and had become damaged, Archie swore, when he "attempted to taxi between two trees."[64]

When it came to the mechanics of keeping a plane in the air, Archie knew very little and never cared to learn. This, itself, made him a dangerous pilot. One passenger, Al Doyle, was flying with Archie when the engine started to smoke. Archie landed, opened the engine cowling, snatched some wires and ripped out a handful.

"That," he said to Doyle, "takes care of that. Let's go." And they did.[65]

Archie's landings, more precisely his "controlled crashes," were often unbelievable. Once, while coming in for a landing to pick up some stranded sheep hunters, Archie found them on a sand bar that was "crooked like a dog's hind leg." Just before he landed, Archie saw one of the hunters running in front of the airplane. Archie suspected that the hunter was showing him the best part of the crooked landing strip to use so he followed the hunter so close, he later commented, that he "almost took off a couple of his back pockets."[66]

Again and again, Archie's landings were the stuff from which Laurel and Hardy could have made movies. But there was a kind of pride in Archie's voice when he spoke of his accidents. "I've piled up five airplanes and only broke one leg," he told Ray Heinrichs. "You just gotta know how to do it."

If there was any one thing Archie knew how to do superbly, it was crash. Most of the time, crashes were not planned. In 1943, Archie hit the ground and did seven cartwheels and wore the plane "right down to the seats."[67] Another time Archie landed in a snowstorm with one of his employees, "Smiling Jack" Herman, bush pilot Gene Jack's wife and her little boy. Just before the plane landed, a cross wind or down draft flipped it over and it hit the ice upside down. The plane skidded for "three miles" on glare ice before finally coming to a stop.

The next day an Inupiat, John Nelson, found Archie and the passengers by following the deep scratch marks the plane had left on the ice. He thought the scrape marks had been made by someone dragging willows near where he was ice fishing. When he came to the end of the ruts, there was Archie sitting on a five-gallon can waiting for someone to come and find them. No one was hurt except Archie. In the excitement he had bitten his own tongue.[68]

Smiling Jack Herman

For a while Archie averaged a crash of some kind each year. Though no crash is funny, Archie's escapades in the re-telling warmed many hearts and produced endless chuckles that took the bitterness out of howling winds and bone-chilling cold. When Archie crashed, everyone was expecting a great story. They usually got one and whenever Archie described what had happened, the stories brought something precious to life in the northland. Once Archie was racing some other pilots to pick up some passengers when disaster occurred. As was his daily routine, he got up at 4 a.m. and headed out, flying in drizzle beneath a low ceiling. Ten miles out of Kobuk he dropped lower to find the lake covered with a dense fog. This deprived him of a horizons on which he could lock his eyes. Visually trapped, he flew right into Kobuk Lake.[69] Later, when he returned to Kotzebue, he told "Smiling Jack" Herman's wife of another problem he had when the plane struck the water. "My teeth bit me!" he snapped. Archie possessed only three teeth by the time he reached middle age and carried his choppers in his back pocket – when he bothered to take them with him at all.[70]

Mrs. Don Emmons remembered Archie and his teeth well. "He'd always check to see who was coming in on the plane and then decide if he'd put in his teeth or not. When he didn't, he had this big, wide grin with no teeth at all!"[71]

Archie's flying wasn't much better than his landings and takeoffs. He always flew incredibly low, so low that it would make "your toes curl," Edith Bullock remembered. In 1949, Bud Miller flew to Candle with Archie to ferry a plane back to Kotzebue. The whole distance Archie flew no higher than 100 feet "except when [he] chose to dive on any walrus that happened to be basking on the ice." (It is more likely these were seals. There are very few walrus in this area.) The plane would buzz the walrus and they would disappear into the water. "A couple of times I thought we were going in after them," Miller remembered.[72]

One of Archie's favorite passengers was his good friend Jim Robbins, the pilot who talked him into buying the Great Lakes Trainer in Selawik. When Robbins quit flying commercially, he owned and managed a mine in Candle. The men would trade off flights and pull practical jokes on each other while aloft – one very good reason the CAA took a dim view of the antics of the bush pilots in the Arctic. Jim Hutchison, the mechanic who had to put Robbins' plane back in flying condition every time it crashed, remembered the pair of clowns well. "First they would fly in Robbins' airplane and then in Archie's airplane. And they would pull stunts on each other like shut the motor off or pull out the mixture control and they'd be flying along and all of a sudden the engine would quit. Neither one of them would do anything. One time neither of them did anything and they had to land because there [really] was something wrong. The engine'd quit."[73]

JIM ROBBINS

Archie loved nothing better than to pull a practical joke. Life, he believed, should be accompanied with laughter. Often he just stirred the pot and see what happened. Sometimes it would be as piddling as telling someone that another person had said something rude about them. Other times he would take advantage of the situation as it arose. As an example, there wasn't a landing strip in Point Lay so the Inupiat set out flags on the smoothest part of the Arctic Ocean ice to identify the landing area. This gave the two pilots who flew there regularly – Archie and Sig Wien – a landing strip. But Archie liked to move the flags and after Sig Wien had his first bumpy landing, he learned to fly over the marked strip and give it a c-a-r-e-f-u-l look before he came in for a landing.[74]

Once Sam Shafsky, who was working for Archie at the time, radioed Archie that he was out of gas and had landed on the ice. There happened to be a CAA inspector in Kotzebue at the time so Archie figured he would pull a practical joke on Shafsky. Archie went over to the CAA office and talked the CAA inspector into flying out to Shafsky with him. The inspector was new in town and didn't know Archie that well, so he said fine. The two men flew out to where Shafsky was stranded on the ice and Archie helped Shafsky fill up his tank while the CAA inspector nosed around, much to Shafsky distress because he didn't know if he was overloaded or not. No pilot wanted the CAA looking at his plane too closely. *Every* plane had something wrong and sometimes it just took a close inspection to find it. When it was time to take off, Shafsky fired up the engine and had a carburetor fire. This wasn't unusual in those days. But it was never a good idea to have such a dangerous situation occur in front of a CAA inspector. The minute the fire started, the CAA inspector popped open Shafsky's door and grabbed the fire extinguisher. While the CAA inspector was moving toward the fire, Archie was hurriedly pulling the mail out of Shafsky's plane. (Archie concentrated on the First Class mail out of the plane because that's where the checks were and he didn't want them burned. Rather, that's where *Archie's* checks were.)

When the CAA inspector turned the fire extinguisher on, nothing came out of the canister. It was empty. Using snow and some cloth, the inspector was able to extinguish the fire – while Archie kept snatching the First Class Mail out of the airplane – at which time the irate CAA employee confronted Shafsky with the empty fire extinguisher.

"Didn't you know your fire extinguisher was empty?!" he snapped.

"Should be," replied Sam. "This is the third fire I've had this trip."[75]

Fred Goodwin remembered being in Kotzebue with another CAA inspector and trying to maintain as professional an image as possible when Archie pulled yet another shenanigan. While Goodwin and the inspector were sitting in Archie's restaurant, the Kotzebue Grille, Goodwin decided to call the weather station to find out what conditions were between Kotzebue and Nome. By the time he got back to his reindeer steak, Archie had figured out that Goodwin's passenger was a CAA inspector.

As Goodwin sat down, he told the Inspector that there was freezing rain between there and Nome so they had best spend the night in Kotzebue.

Archie chose that moment to innocently saunter over, as if he had just heard Goodwin say he was not going to fly because of bad weather.

Archie whined. "I never heard you go over and ask for the weather in all of my life that I've known you. You just *always* flew. You never *asked* for the weather. What's goin' on here? You must have a CAA inspector with you."

Goodwin was not above pulling a practical joke himself, particularly when it came to Archie. One time, Goodwin had a CAA inspector aboard as he was flying into Kotzebue. He had been listening to Archie yack away on the radio for a while and by his own count he figured that Archie had at least six and possibly seven passengers in his four-seater Cessna Airmaster. This was clearly a case of overloading.

"Boy, I'm going to get ol' Archie this time," Goodwin snickered to himself. So he timed his arrival to be just ahead of Archie's.

"Say," said Goodwin innocently to the CAA inspector. "Have you ever met Archie Ferguson?"

"No," replied the inspector, thrilled at the prospect of meeting a living legend of the Arctic. "But I'd sure like to meet him."

"Well, he's going to land in about five minutes and I'll go over and introduce you."

The inspector was all smiles and Goodwin figured he was going to let the CAA catch Archie with a at least six people aboard – clearly a violation of aviation regulation as well as good sense.

Five minutes passed. Then ten minutes went by. Finally, 15 minutes later, Archie landed on the ice with skis. But when he opened the door to his Airmaster, only three passengers got out. Goodwin introduced the CAA inspector to Archie. After the small talk, Goodwin pulled Archie aside.

"Where are the rest of your passengers?"

"You son-of-a-bitch," snapped Archie. "I knew you had that inspector aboard and I figured you'd want to pull something like this. I landed over there on a lake. I left four of them boys over on the lake. I gotta go over there and pick 'em up and bring them over here."

One of the problems with talking the way Archie did, as he painfully discovered, was that sometimes his mouth moved faster than his brain. It had been raining heavily in the area and Archie was flying his Travelaire 6000 searching for a place to land. Passing over a likely landing strip, he was pleased to see that a plane was already down. What he didn't know was that the field was very muddy and the plane on the ground, Frank Whaley's, was there because Whaley had not been able to take off.

Left to right, Fred Goodwin, Tom Richards and Harry Hough, courtesy of The *Senior Voice*, Anita Nelson.

The minute Archie hit the ground, he knew he was going to have trouble getting off again. He was right. With the mud gripping his wheels he slowed suddenly and stopped. It was very clear that he would not be able to break the Travelaire's wheels free of the mud in time to get aloft.

Talking to some of the villagers, Archie learned that Sig Wien had been stuck in the same situation recently but had managed to take off. Archie asked the Inupiat how Sig had been able to take off from such a muddy field. It was not that difficult, the Inupiat said. Sig had taken everything he could out of his airplane, drained most of the gas out of the tank and, with some Inupiat pushing him down the field, he had gotten just enough speed to take off and skip over to a sand bar which the villager pointed out to Archie.

"That's what I'll do," roared Archie and he proceeded to strip his Travelaire of all non-essential weight and drained the gas until he only had a gallon in the tank. Once he got over onto the sand bar, he figured he could reload everything and take off again. Then, with four or five Inupiat pushing and the throttle open wide, Archie got just enough speed to lift off the field and leap frog onto the sand bar. The minute he hit the sandbar, he knew he was in trouble again. The bar was so soft that he went on his nose.

Archie was furious! "I thought you told me that Sig landed here?"

The Inupiat looked at him stoically and said "Yes. Sig Wien land here an' he go up on his nose too."[76]

Other times, Archie's libido got in the way of his good sense. Being the indoor sportsman he was, whenever opportunity knocked, Archie answered. Archie was coming back from a village on the Noatak, Neil Bergt recalled Archie telling him, and Archie "picked up a girl from one of the villages who was crazy about him. [She] fell to love with him on the way back to [Kotzebue] and he couldn't wait until he got back to town so he landed on a sandbar, cracked up the airplane and spent 22 days floating down the river before he got home."

Archie wasn't just a terrible pilot; he was a terrible passenger as well. Though Shafsky was working for him, he was living in Candle. Archie was flying an Airmaster when he hit some turbulence and his door popped open. Because of the way the wind was blasting, it snapped the door off its hinges. One second the door was closed and the next, Archie was looking straight down at the tundra.

A shaken Archie landed in Candle and asked Shafsky to fly him back to Kotzebue. Cutting across Kotzebue Sound at 4,000 feet, Shafsky was caught by a freak wind.

"Land this son-of-a-bitch," shrieked Archie pointing toward Jefford Field. ("Jefford Field" was a big, wide stretch of black sand near Kotzebue where "you could land a B-25, no problem," noted Shafsky.)

"We're over water!" snapped Shafsky.

"Over there! Over there!" shouted a frantic Archie, pointing toward Jefford Field.

"Where do you think I'm trying to go?" retorted Shafsky.

The two men were screaming at each other and finally Shafsky cut power and put the plane into a dive. But the wind was so strong it began blowing the plane backwards!

Archie yelled in terror, mispronouncing his words as he was prone to do, "we're gonna go to Serbia!"

Fighting the wind for a half hour, Shafsky decided to tack and cut his way toward the shore. Archie, in the meantime, was hysterical with fear and was promising Shafsky, his employee, all kinds of incentives including a "new airplane" and a "raise in pay" just to get the aircraft they were in on the ground.

With a frenetic, animated Archie wiggling in the co-pilot seat, Shafsky was finally able to make shore. Just as they started up the beach looking for a place to land, Shafsky saw a pack of wolves on a ridge, "their heads down and [the wind] blowing their fur."

Archie, who a moment earlier had been firmly convinced he was going to die and his body sink to the bottom of Kotzebue Sound, spotted the wolves and his entire attitude changed. "Look at the wolves. We can get $75 apiece for them! Get on the ground. We'll come back down and get those wolves!"

When it came to the technology of flying, Archie would have none of it. He was a truly fly-by-the-seat-of-your-pants pilot. Worse, he just flew. When Archie wanted to fly, he just went out, got in his airplane and flew. He didn't check the gasoline or the oil or the weather report. He just got in the plane and left. For Archie, a pre-flight consisted of starting the engine. If the engine turned over, the plane was ready to fly. If the weather was bad and Archie wanted to fly, he went up just to see if the weather was as bad as people were saying it was.

Archie didn't have much use for instruments either. While most pilots flew VFR (Visual Flight Rules) or IFR (Instrument Flight Rules), Archie and quite a few of the old timers flew by line of sight. Such instruments as the newer planes had installed were viewed as new-fangled and many seasoned pilots shied away from using them. It was a standing joke that if a *cheechako* asked a bush pilot if he flew VFR or IFR, the pilots would sometimes jokingly say: "IFR," an acronym to the veteran pilots for "I Fly the River" or "I Follow the Railroad."

When the artificial horizon was first introduced to Alaska, many bush pilots were thrilled with the new technology. Archie, however, was unimpressed but he stunned other bush pilots by saying he was going to buy four of them.

"Four?" asked another bush pilot. "You only need one. Why four?"

"Because," chortled Archie, "I can put one on each side of the cockpit. Then everywhere I look I'll see a horizon."[77]

But Archie lacked more than just the inability to fly by instruments. He lacked the patience to learn. However, Art Fields wasn't too sure Archie couldn't fly by instruments. Fields and Frank Davidovics were hunting on the Squirrel River one winter when a storm moved in. After the storm passed, there were snowdrifts all over the river ice. When Archie came in to pick the two men up, he landed on a snow drift and hit so hard that his windshield shattered. With the two men and their caribou aboard, Archie flew back to Kotzebue with his head ducked down as the wind blasted through the gaping hole where the windshield used to be. But even then, "whether Archie actually flew instruments, I wouldn't swear to," said Fields.

What makes this story unusual is that the Cessna Airmaster was not supposed to be able to fly without its windshield. When Archie landed and the plane was examined, Archie learned that the fabric in the back was just beginning to strip. Had he stayed in the air just a few more minutes, the Airmaster might have fallen out of the sky, its skin in shreds. (As a side note, when Archie had been aloft he had called Kotzebue to get the wind speed. He was told that the wind in Kotzebue was about *15 miles an hour.* "It's more than that in the cockpit, Archie replied")

Archie loved his Airmaster and if Cessna had continued making them that was all Archie would have ever bought. "I just love them Cessners,"[78] Archie used to say but Cessna ceased production on the model at the beginning of the Second World War. Unfortunately for Archie, he had decided to buy another one just as the last one was rolling off the assembly line. When Cessna told him they had no Airmaster to sell, Archie sent a wire to the company asking for the names of everyone who had ever bought an Airmaster. Cessna offered to send it by mail but Archie demanded it be wired. It was and Archie proceeded to send a telegraph to everyone on the list to see if they wanted to sell their Airmaster. He finally found an airplane in Wilmington, Delaware, owned by the DuPonts. He bought the aircraft and when he made it back to Kotzebue he amused the other bush pilots with his statement, "ain't nothing too good for them millionaires and me."[79]

An extremely rare photograph of Archie with a tool!! Photo courtesy of Burleigh Putnam

Actually, there was one instrument on which Archie was an expert: the radio. He loved to talk on the radio. But when it came to maintenance of parts of the radio other than the microphone and dials, Archie had no interest. His disdain of any kind of basic maintenance of the only instrument he cherished often led to comedy.

At that time there were two types of high frequency radio antennas. One was a wire on a reel that fed through a lead in the roof of the cockpit. The wire ran free through a loop on top of the tail where it was attached to a little parachute or a plastic ball, the latter being similar to the black ball one could find in the back of a modern toilet. (Some pilots used plastic funnels.) When the pilot wanted to use the radio, he would unwind the antenna wire to a prescribed length and send his message on a specific frequency.

However, if the pilot forgot to pull in the antenna when landing, it could snag on the ground and break the antenna wire. The rubber ball was considered the superior alternative, obviously, because if the pilot forgot to reel in the antenna wire, the ball would just bounce along the ground and the wire would usually not snap. But this didn't always happen. At the landing field in Nome, for instance, there was a power line that stretched across the south end of the airport. For years there were a myriad of rubber balls and snapped antenna wires hanging from it, mute testimony to the number of pilots who forgot to reel in their antennas.

Archie was famous for not pulling in his antenna. More than one person remembered watching Archie taking his loose antenna wire and wrapping it around his rudder for a rudder lock. Later Archie changed to a belly antenna. This antenna reeled off a wheel through a fairlead in the floor of the cockpit and was attached to a lead weight. The lead weight kept the antenna wire taut. But the pilot had to be very careful because if he landed without reeling in this antenna, the lead would hit the ground and the antenna wire snap. Under the right conditions, the weight could even bounce up and damage the aircraft.[80]

Flying with the belly antenna down could be a problem as Archie discovered. In October of 1946, Robert Jacobs was flying with Archie in a search pattern for a mail pilot who had gone down in the Kotzebue Sound area. The two men were hopping from one Inupiat summer camp to another dropping notes to the reindeer herders. As they approached the mouth of the Kobuk River they spotted a reindeer camp and Archie took his plane low so Jacobs could drop the next note. What Jacobs distinctly remembered about that camp was a ten-foot pole in the center of the compound with dogs tied to it. Archie came in *very* low, forgetting that he was dragging an antenna. The antenna wire caught the pole and snapped the antenna lead from the plane. But the metal ball was still traveling as fast as the airplane and, at 50 miles per hour, it wrapped itself around the pole like a tether ball in an elementary school playground.

Jacobs, incidentally, was the inventor of the Alaskan air cowl flap system. Flying in the Territory, and particularly during the winter, forced pilots to develop a new way of thinking about flying. Winter always brought treacherous conditions. Along with snow and ice came the extremely low temperatures, particularly in the Arctic and the Interior. Even the most experienced pilots considered the cold an enemy of the aircraft. It affected the plane, its flying ability and, most notably in Fairbanks, landing conditions. Since Fairbanks sits in a geologic bowl surrounded by mountains, on many winter days, temperature inversions make it far colder at ground level than at 1,000 feet.

This often lead to disaster. A pilot at 2,000 feet might be flying in minus ten temperature but when descending, the plane would drop into the cold belt of air lying on the ground. There the blanket of air over the landing strip could be 50 below zero. While the pilot in a relatively warm cockpit might not feel the change in temperature, the plane's engine most certainly would. "On the air-cooled engines," remembered Jacobs, "the engine would sometimes freeze. Here you were coming in for a landing and the engine quits at 100 feet. If you weren't lined up for a landing, you were dead."

These conditions called for new technology and sometimes that technology just required a bit of brain-power. Jacobs solved this problem in a unique manner. He invented a cowling system that forced air to circulate *around* a hot engine *before* it was used to cool the engine. Only in Alaska, he said laughing, would you have to *heat* the air before you used it for cooling.

When it came to modern technology, there was instrument that Archie made certain was in his plane: a radio. There were no radios in the other planes he owned, but in his personal plane there was always a radio. Since there was a CAA rule that all planes had to have a radio onboard, Archie just took the outer casings of a radio and stuck it where the instrument should have been. Then he hung headphones nearby so that a superficial look in the cockpit would make it appear that the aircraft had communication equipment.[81] This was not an unusual attitude toward the radio. Other pilots had bad attitudes toward radio as well, even when they were required in control zones around airports with a manned control tower. Bob Reeve for instance, **_hated_** the radio and put one in his airplane only after the CAA threatened to ground him if he didn't have it. Then, once it was installed, he didn't use it. "What do I want with a radio," he asked, "I have enough troubles of my own without fooling with a gadget like that."[82]

While Archie may not have been particularly interested in learning how to fly on instruments, he was specifically interested in making money. He was in the business to make money and he was the busiest flier in the Arctic. He was also good at taking advantage of any situation. Goodwin remembers a time when the Canadian authorities asked him, Goodwin, to check on an old timer on the American side of the border near Fort Yukon who hadn't been seen in a while. Goodwin flew over the sourdough's cabin but did not see any sign of life. He reported the absence of any activity to the United States Marshal who could not investigate until he had received permission from the local Commissioner, who happened to be his wife. The couple wrangled over whether they should go or not, and whether to pay for the pilot until Goodwin finally said he was going back that way anyway so he'd take the Marshal along *gratis*. When the two men arrived at the remote cabin, sure enough the sourdough in question was dead.

The incident was written up in the Fairbanks paper, (either *Jessen's Weekly* or the *Fairbanks News Miner*), and the next time Goodwin was in Kotzebue, Archie pulled him aside and said sharply, "Fred, never go up there and find one of them old timers dead in a cabin of natural causes. Always come back and tell 'em you found this guy dead up there and it looks suspicious to yuh and that they should have a coroner's jury go up and there and determine how this old man died. They're gonna have to charter you and that's good for $900 to a $1,000."

Another advantage Archie used was *not* paying his own bills. If he could figure a way of not paying, he would. When he had to pay, he did it piece-meal, shelling out just enough to infuriate the party to whom he owed the money. Usually it was so difficult collecting from Archie most people just quit dealing with him. That was fine with Archie. He came from the P.T.

Barnum School of Skullduggery that preached there was a "fool born every minute." On the other hand, when it came to making money with the airplane, Archie was a professional. No scheme passed through his mind unconsidered seriously. One summer month he logged 185 hours.[83] Had the CAA known, they would have been very distressed since the maximum pilots were legally allowed was well below that.

It was not just businesses that took a financial hit from Archie. So did the federal government. Just as the Second World War started, Archie was able to wrangle a contract with the United States Army to fly inductees to Fairbanks. He made 30 trips in one month and was flying so frequently that he didn't want to take the time to open his gas tank so he just chopped a hole in the side of his fuselage and stuck the gas hose right inside. (This is a fine tale and vintage Archie but it has some fatal flaws. First, the tanks on an Airmaster are in wings so chopping a hole in the side of the plane would not have helped Archie fuel his tanks. Second, Mary Oldham said she once forgot to put the cap on her gas cap and once aloft the "suction emptied my tank.")

But that was only half the story. Archie, a draft dodger from the First World War who was on the Selective Service Board for the Second World War, hauled a planeload of men to Nome to be considered for the draft. But Archie, ever attuned to making a profit, flew only those men with obvious physical defects. In this way he could charge the government for trips both ways. Ironically, at the end of the war he received a medal from the United States Selective Service for hauling men to Nome to be considered for the draft![84]

Ferguson's record with both cargo and passengers was replete with unique incidents and humorous anecdotes. In the summer of 1949, Harold Little incredulously watched as Archie jammed a boiler into his Fairchild 24. The boiler was in Point Lay and "Archie wanted that boiler in his plane in the worse way." When the boiler wouldn't fit, Archie "chopped a hole in the roof of the Fairchild and flew it with the stovepipe sticking through the top of the airplane."

Cargo in those days was a mix of products, some living and others so bulky they had to be taken apart to be fit inside. If the plane was too full, the cargo was sometimes lashed to the outside. Sig Wien remembers flying a bed spring outside his plane. Some of the photos of early aircraft show them so bulky with cargo strapped to the outside of the plane that it was a wonder the plane lifted off. Once in the air, it is surprising that the pilot could see over the sacks tied to the front of his aircraft. Many pilots lived the adage that "If it'll fit; it'll fly."

Russ Merrill, overloaded and about to take off from what is now the Anchorage Park Strip. Photograph courtesy of the Anchorage Museum.

Then there was the live cargo. Transporting walrus to zoos in the Lower 48 was not unusual. "They'd cry real tears when they'd be aboard because they were stressed and it just hurt your feelings," remembered "K" Doyle, the first stewardess for Wien. In the larger planes, horses and dogs were not uncommon, and once Wien flew an elephant to Nome – but in a larger cargo plane.

When an airline could get cargo, it could usually haul it in whatever quantity it felt safe, regardless of what the CAA may have felt was a safe load. But then, the chance of being caught overloaded was slim. There were too few regulators for the vast area to be covered and pilots routinely ignored the load limits of the CAA and its other rules anyway.

Sometimes there were good reasons for ignoring CAA regulations. In many cases, the CAA's rules were ludicrous. For instance, while the limits for legal loads were quite strict, when pilots were carrying full tanks of fuel there wasn't much room for cargo. Even Burleigh Putnam, who headed the CAA in Alaska during the 1940s, admitted that "payload didn't mean a thing. Our own CAA airplane, when it was full of gasoline, could only carry 20 pounds legally and I flew it one time with a 1,050 [pound] overload."

To non-pilots it is important to note that planes get lighter the farther they fly. While this may seem to be impossible, keep in mind that fuel is weight. As a plane flies, it burns fuel which lightens the weight of the aircraft. Seasoned pilots with nerves of steel often overloaded their planes knowing that by the time they encountered a mountain range they had to leap over, the plane would be substantially lighter than when it took off and the extra lift would get them over the peaks.

Everyone was fudging on the cargo loads. Even after the CAA moved maximums to more reasonable levels, pilots continued to overload. But there was a good reason for the fudging: profit. The bigger the load, the greater the profit. It was not a case of greed; it was a matter of staying solvent.

Veteran bush pilot Ray Petersen, in a conversation with Beth Day, author of GLACIER PILOT, made the truest statement regarding overloading in the 30s and 40s:

> *Our loads were determined by the length of the field and whether we could make it off the ground. We'd fill up all the seats, throw in all the freight our passengers' laps would hold, fill up the gas tanks, and take off. On a long trip we could take an extra load, because as the gas burned out we got the additional lift we needed to make it over [a] pass. When [the CAA Inspector] was around, we'd wait [until] he went to lunch, then everybody would overload their planes and take off fast."*

But there was great danger in overloading. Many pilots thought they knew what the safe limit was and would throw in an extra box. After all, it was only a box. So the box went on board. The next time it was two boxes or a heavy bag. This attitude could lead to tragedy. It was, as Ray Petersen noted, "that last ten bucks worth of freight" that killed the pilot. Maybe he needed more feet of runway than he had and went off the landing strip into the trees. Or he increased his stall speed so he, quite literally, fell out of the sky on final approach.

Just as likely, the plane became less maneuverable in the sky. Archie, heavily loaded, clipped a tree on the Hog River. "That was certainly close," one of his passengers muttered.

"Sure was," replied Archie peering through the windshield. "But those two trees up there are the ones that are going to stop us."

Archie pointed ahead to a pair of trees coming up fast. Too overloaded with cargo on the inside and icing up on the outside, the aircraft could not rise above the pair of trees and, as Archie predicted, the plane hit the trees and crashed to the ground.[85]

(The men spent five days on the ground, and were only saved after Archie told searchers to "Tell Maurice King I'm right where we had all that trouble with the parrot." King knew exactly where he was. Two years earlier, Maurice and Archie had been flying a parrot back to Kotzebue from Fairbanks. They hit some bad weather and the parrot became quite animated and began swearing at the two men with "every cussword in the English language." King rescued Archie and, as Archie liked to say for years, he was none too soon. Archie was eyeballing his passengers suspiciously because all the food was gone and, in Archie's words, "I thought maybe they was gonna eat me up. I kep' the snowshoes on and laid awake all night so if they started fer me I could get away."[86])

Archie was also infamous for monopolizing the airwaves – even during the war years when radio silence was the established rule. When a radio was used for commercial purposes, like getting a weather report, the call had to be made with a code. This was to make sure that no Japanese pilot who happened to be flying in the area – 2,000 miles from the nearest battlefront – could get a report. This requirement made it particularly difficult for pilots who were flying in soupy weather. The pilot would end up fighting the wind while he dug around the cockpit for his codebook and then the page that had the code of the day. Only in an emergency was a pilot allowed to bypass the code. Once a radio operator in Nome who was not familiar with Archie and his antics tried to get him to stay off the air.

Ferguson began the conversation in his own inimitable style: "Nome Radio, Nome Radio. This is Cessna Two Zero Seven Six Six. Gosh it's startin' to rain up here! Looks like some awful dirty stuff ahead! Gimme yer weather in the clear!"

Mindful that the only authorized wartime chatter on the radio was for an emergency, the operator asked innocently: "Cessna Two Zero Seven Six Six, do you declare this an emergency?"

"Yer darn right," snapped Archie into his microphone, "Any time I'm in the air it's an emergency!"[87]

Another version of this same story had Archie requesting to land because he "only had one engine." After he landed, the control tower in Nome realized that he was flying a Cessna 180 – which only had one engine.[88]

One of the cherished wartime legends of the North was when Archie reported seeing a Japanese submarine. While some writers use this as yet another example of Archie's craziness, facts shed a different light on this incident. Did Archie really see a Japanese submarine? "Absolutely," confirmed Ed Yost. There was a Japanese submarine making repairs in Kotzebue Sound. "We could watch them 24 hours a day." Archie sent a telegram to

Fairbanks and reported the submarine. Fairbanks wired him back that he had "Civil Air patrol money to keep track of the submarine."

"I'll take care of 'em," Archie wired back. "Send me some guns! Send me some guns!"

Perhaps the best-known story of Archie and his flying was the time he was bringing a baby polar bear to Kotzebue from Point Hope. The two had been aloft about ten minutes when Archie became aware that the cub had gnawed through its bonds of *babish*,[89] tanned caribou rawhide rope, and was roaming around the back of his plane. Not familiar with aircraft fragility, the cub would take an occasional bite out of the pilot's seat or claw at the fuselage. Finally the bear settled down. As long as the flying was smooth there was no problem, but whenever there was turbulence, the bear became rambunctious.

This is one of a number of bear stories and Archie, all of them humorous. But the most reliable one came from Sam Shafsky. That was because Shafsky was there when it happened. Shafsky remembered Archie buying two bears in Point Hope. Unfortunately he tied them inside his Cessna with *luftack*,[90] dried seal sinew. What Archie didn't realize was that the bear could eat the *luftack*. The first time Archie knew the bears were loose was when on them struck him in the head with its paw. Archie turned around, saw that one of the cubs were loose and knew he was in trouble. Things got worse when a cub crawled into the co-pilot's seat. When it reached for the controls, Archie gave it a shove. The cub, thinking this was a game, shoved Archie back. Archie shoved the cub away from the controls again and the cub continued the game.

Then Archie got on the radio and started the way he always did with his pet expression, "Oh, Jeezus, lovely oh Jeezus." At this particular point in his career everyone knew that Archie was in deep trouble because the FCC had clearly warned him that one more profanity on the air and they would jerk his operator's license.

Rattling on about the bear, every other phrase an obscenity, Archie began talking wildly about the loose bear – in the singular – in the plane. It didn't take long for that to change.

"Now the *other* one is loose!" shrieked Archie into the microphone.

By this time everyone in the Arctic who had a radio was tuned in to Archie's latest sky escapade. In the Kotzebue Grille, which kept the pilot's frequency on all day, everyone went wild with laughter. Every time Archie came back on the air the restaurant roof would shake. For 15 minutes, Archie kept the Arctic on its toes and roaring, with every explicit, mule skinner expression or the specific four-letter word on which the FCC routinely frowned.

When Archie's plane appeared over Kotzebue, it was "all over the sky." His Cessna was stick-controlled so every time he moved his legs, the plane lurched in response. Archie landed fast and brought the plane to a screeching halt not far from his restaurant. In an instant he was out the door of the Cessna even as the prop was winding down.

Out he came, just ahead of the two bears, which tumbled out the door after him. There was Archie, running down the street with two polar bear cubs at his heels. He ran all the way to his restaurant and exploded through the door knocking the Inupiat cook aside. Up the stairs he went, into his apartment and locked the door. Close behind him were the two bears. But when they could not get through the door, they began scratching on the door.

"Who is it?" shrieked Archie hysterically.

"It's the bears, Archie" said the cook. Archie let out another shriek and went out his apartment window screaming "Jeezus, the sons-of-bitches are gonna eat me!"

One of the bears, which Archie named "Pola," appeared on the front cover of *Alaska Sportsman* in April of 1944. It was eventually sold to Keith Hedreen and George Madsen who owned a bar in Nome named, appropriately enough, the "Polar Bar." A year later the two men regretted their decision because the bear was, quite literally, eating them out of house and home – at the rate of "two dozen eggs a day."[91] The other bear cub was shipped to a Baltimore zoo.[92]

Archie also brought another bear into Kotzebue where it remained for years. During the winter, it would stay under the Wien Hotel – polar bears do not hibernate –but throughout the tourist season it would lounge around in the sun attracting the attention of Outsiders. This bear was also adept at frightening tourists. Sometimes it would lie on its belly hiding the chain with its body. Whenever a tourist the bear didn't like approached, it would explode off the ground and charge to the very end of its chain. The shocked tourist would usually stumble backward, often ending up seated in a muddy pool of water.[93]

In 1949, while the polar bear was just a cub, Graham Mower remembered seeing Archie being chased around town by the cub. "It was a pretty good-sized cub," Mower remembered. "The bear hated Archie and every time he'd see Archie he'd take out after him. Archie was running half the time around town because the bear was just loose and if Archie went somewhere and the bear happened to come by, why he'd take right out after Archie. I don't think he ever caught him. And Archie was funny with those turned-up shoes and little short legs."[94]

As time went on, Archie's schemes got bigger and bigger. At one time the Archie even tried to start a turkey ranch. "Goin' to raise my own Thanksgiving," he told everyone. He had the birds barged to Nome where he picked them up and flew them to Kotzebue. However, as there is no further reference to them, it would be safe to say that this particular entrepreneurial venture was not successful.

But it did give Archie a good story.

Because the crates in which the turkeys were confined were too large to fit into his plane, he took the turkeys out and put them in the cabin individually. But, allegedly, as he started to take off he realized that the load of turkeys was too heavy for the plane. He was saved, or so he claimed, because at the last moment he hit a bump on the runway that frightened some of the turkeys into flying around in the cabin. This, he asserted, lightened the load enough for him to take off. Then, as long as he kept waving his arms occasionally, the turkey continued to fly around in the cabin so that Archie could make the trip to Kotzebue safely.[95] This was a great story, but the fact of the matter is that turkeys can't fly.

But then again, neither could Archie.[96]

Turkeys weren't the only animals that gave Archie problems. So did wolves. Warren, unlike Archie, had been an excellent wolf hunter. In April of 1937, Warren received permission from the "Bureau of Air Commerce" to use a commercial plane to fly low enough to get a shot at the wily predators. Warren also indicated that he was requesting that the Bureau of Air Commerce allow him to use a machine gun against the wolves. With a typical Ferguson flair, Warren swore that the predation in the "Selawik, Shungnak and Noatak ranges during the past year [had] resulted in about half of the reindeer herds being exterminated by marauding wolves which have been multiplying rapidly in these sections around Kotzebue."[97]

Archie, on the other hand, became so excited while hunting wolves that he actually shot off his own propeller. In reality, this is not as bizarre as it sounds. A wolf will make erratic turns when being hunted from the air. Often a hunter will be aiming at a wolf and it will make a sudden turn. The hunter will follow the wolf with the shotgun not thinking about where the propeller is in relation to the shotgun. All a hunter has to do is have one pellet of OO buckshot hit the turning blade and it will unbalance the prop's equilibrium.

Even with this excuse, Archie was still a terrible wolf hunter. When Jean Potter asked him if he hunted wolves, Archie proudly said yes, he had killed 16 wolves from the air, "n' cracked up every time."[98]

But of all his escapades, Ferguson is best known for what is called the "Arctic Bump." For Archie, there was no such thing as a trip without excitement; even if he had to create that excitement. Flying between Kotzebue and Nome he had to cross the Arctic Circle and often he would cut the gas as he approached the hypothetical line on the ground.

"We're comin' ta the Arctic Circle!" he would shout to his nervous passengers as he secretly reached for the gas line switch. "Ya can't see it but ya'll sure know when we hit it. The engine'll quit! There's no air in that darn circle for eight hundred feet!"

Then, when the engine sputtered to a stop, the plane would go into a steep nose dive. Passengers would shriek and cry in terror as the plane dropped hundreds of feet until Archie surreptitiously re-opened the gas line and restarted the prop. (Goodwin swore that the teacher who suffered from Archie's first Arctic Bump signed on for a second year rather than take *another* ride with Archie across the Circle.)

Historically, the man who truly popularized the Arctic Bump was Fred Goodwin. While he never turned his engine off to frighten his passengers, while flying for Wien he would "push it over and give the tourist the same sensation as when they went over the top of a roller coaster." But he flashed the seat belt sign first to make sure everyone was strapped in.

Even with this warning "women would scream and cameras would take photos of the ceiling." After a while word about the Arctic Bump got around and "it got to be where we had to do one on each flight! I got it from Archie but I never cut off the engines." To this day, many commercial airlines still "bump" as they cross the Arctic Circle.

Even when he wasn't flying, Archie was a master of the practical joke. One time when Fred Gentry of the CAA came to Kotzebue, Archie pulled one of his best practical jokes on his friend and employee Shafsky.

Whenever Fred Gentry of the CAA came to town, everyone was on their toes. Archie got a load of fresh produce for the Kotzebue Grille for inducement – Archie was always bribing someone – and he called Shafsky to come up from Candle.

Shafsky flew in, tied his plane down, and went in for dinner and conversation. Sitting around the table were Ed Yost, Don Emmons, Fred Gentry, Gene Jack, Archie and a few more pilots. It was an amiable meal and then the cook, Flo-Flo, brought out some tomato pie. Shafsky was about to start his second piece when Gene Jack got up and said he had to go up to the hospital to get a shot. A few minutes later, Archie said he had to go find someone, so he left as well.

What Shafsky *didn't* know was that Gene Jack and Archie had rounded up a crew of Inupiat and had moved Shafsky's plane around behind the Magid brother's store so it could not be seen from the ice at the front of town. Then they went to the hangar and got an old Fairchild wing that had been in Kotzebue for years, and dragged it back onto the ice where Shafsky's plane had been tied down. As soon as the wing was in place, Archie took two barrels of gasoline and drenched the area. The Inupiat dragged the barrels away and Archie torched the wing.

BOOM! As soon as the gasoline lit, Archie came charging through the door into the restaurant yelling wildly, "FIRE! FIRE! My Fairchild's on fire!"

Everyone jumped up and rushed out onto the ice and there, lighting up the Arctic sky was a blaze with the flames leaping 20 or 30 feet into the sky. It only took Shafsky a minute to realize that the fire was where his plane was supposed to be, not Archie's.

"There goes my airplane," thought Shafsky wildly, and "there goes the $1,200 I still owe on it!"

As everyone else stood back, Shafsky started walking around the fire and looking at the wing and peering into the fire. But the longer he walked and the more he looked, the less he could see of his airplane. Nor could he see any debris, much less anything that looked like the skeleton of an aircraft.

As he turned to ask Archie what was going on, he saw Archie and the entire contingent of bush pilots from the restaurant rolling on the ice in gales of hysterical laughter.

"This isn't my plane!"

"Where's your plane?" asked Archie as he stopped laughing for a second. "Probably over in Serbia!" And with that Archie and the rest of the pranksters continued to roll about on the ice in laughter.

Sometimes humor just came Archie's way. To repair a leaky gas tank on his Great Lakes Trainer, Archie had his plane flipped over. As the tank was being fixed, Archie noticed a strange plane circling the field. Concerned that this could be the CAA making a surprise visit, Archie had his plane turned right-side-up quickly. When the strange plane did land and disgorge a team of CAA inspectors, they were amazed to find that there was no plane upside down as they had seen from the air.[99]

But Archie did not get along with everyone. In addition to Louie Rotman, anyone working for the government and, particularly, anyone working with the CAA, there was also Elizabeth M. "Bess" Cross. Bess, then bush pilot John Cross's first wife, was, in the words of Fred Goodwin, "a double-barrel bitch." [100] (This is not Bessie Cross, John Cross' second wife.)

That was one of the nicer things people called her. "She didn't have to look for trouble," Sam Shafsky remembered, "She *was* trouble." Others referred to her as "Queen Bess" and "Vamp of the Arctic[101]" and commented on how she was a social climber and political groupie. It was one of the great riddles of the North, Shafsky noted, as to why John Cross remained married to Bess considering that even they did not get along that well.

Archie and Bess Cross despised each other and were always fighting. Bess would complain to the CAA about Archie and the CAA would send an agent to investigate. The agent would look into Archie's operation and, as Archie kept no records, there was nothing the CAA could do. Then Archie would tell the CAA about Bess Cross's transgressions and the CAA would investigate her. Unfortunately for Bess Cross, Edith Bullock recalled, "Bess kept records." Once Bess complained to the Office of Price Administration that Archie was selling cigarettes without charging a tax. After an investigation, which led nowhere since Archie had no records, the investigators were tipped off by Archie that Bess was doing the same thing. Bess kept records so they caught her not charging the same tax she had complained about. Another time, the authorities were tipped that Bess was a bootlegger. She was caught red-handed and sentenced to a six-month jail term.[102]

The animosity between Bess and everyone else went on and on and John Cross sometimes found himself caught in a squeeze between the antics of his wife and the welfare of his friends. In l940, Bess ran for one of the four Territorial House seats representing Nome and Kotzebue. The candidate she had to beat was from Nome, Frank Whaley. (Whaley, like Cross, was a Wien pilot. Later Whaley became Vice President of Wien.) Bess, intent on winning at any costs, had a pamphlet printed in Fairbanks that contained scurrilous information on Whaley. Bundling the campaign pamphlets, she demanded that her husband fly over the villages in the election district and toss the pamphlets out so they would flutter to the ground like descending leaves.

Sam Shafsky coutesy of Ed Yost

But John Cross, for whatever reason, didn't like the idea. So he did the absolute minimum. He flew over the remote villages and tossed out the pamphlets. But he did not untie them as his wife requested. As a result, they fell as a bundle, hit the snow and buried themselves. Most of them weren't found until the next spring, months after the election.

However, at Kivalina, one of the bundles was recovered. When Archie Ferguson flew into Kivalina a few days later, he was approached by an old Inupiat who was puzzled by the bundle of election pamphlets. The Inupiat knew John Cross had delivered the bundle because everyone knew the pilots by their planes. But, since the Inupiat could not read, he did not know what the bundle was.

Ferguson knew instantly what had happened. Well, he told the Inupiat, this was toilet paper. Why didn't he go use it on his trap line this winter? So the Inupiat did, pleased that John Cross had thought so kindly of him and delivered that bundle personally.[103]

Whaley beat Bess Cross that year by more than a hundred votes and became one of four representatives from the Second Division in the Alaska Territorial House.[104]

As an interesting legislative sidelight, Bess Cross ran for the Territorial house again four years later. Whaley was running for the Senate at that time but even then Bess still did not have an easy go of the campaign. Even after blitzing Nome with shee fish which she passed out to buy votes, she tied with B. G. Baker. To break the tie

Almer Rydeen, clerk of the court [in Nome], placed two cards in a container and prevailed up[on] a high school girl, Loretta Snyder, who was selling tuberculosis stamps in the post office lobby, to come into his office to draw one of the cards.[105]

Thus was Bess Cross elected to the Alaska Territorial Legislature in 1945.

Whatever Archie did, he managed to do it unforgettably. Even his letters were classics. When his communiqués arrived at CAA headquarters in Anchorage, they were so hilarious that 40 years later staff members still recalled reading them and passing them around. One time he wrote Burleigh Putnam and stated that he had crashed and added the postscript "Ha. Ha. Ha."[106]

Another time he complained about a "very dangerous obstruction" in the Fairbanks area which were, specifically, "a bunch of radio towers." These were, he wrote angrily, "one helluva hazard" to flying and "if the CAA keeps improving the airway with their damn towers and wires, the only way we can fly in Alaska is underground."[107]

Archie wrote like he talked. He had a beaten typewriter in his store where he would type out his angry letters using one finger and "go a mile a minute" and couldn't spell worth a darn. Then he would send the paper down to the Alaska Communication System (ACS) building – the Alaska equivalent of Western Union – where someone would try to decipher what it was Archie was trying to say before it was sent.

While Archie may have hated the CAA, he was exactly the kind of a pilot the CAA was trying to put out of business. As far as Archie was concerned, the CAA wanted to put all pilots OUT of business and, to a certain extent he was partially right. Pilots like Archie were a danger to everyone in the air – and on the ground. So, certainly, the CAA would have been happy if Archie had not had a license to fly.

So enjoyed the cat-and-mouse game he played with the agency as he skirted their agents and regulations. If he thought he could get away with something, he'd try. The CAA was not innocent of any wrongdoing either. One of the biggest problems was that Alaska was looked upon as a place to dump men and women of less than average talent. While not all were cretins, a good number were.

Another problem the CAA had in Alaska was enforcing rules that made sense in Kansas and Florida but not in Alaska. One requirement, for instance, was no pilot could depart before he had left behind a passenger manifest. This, in itself, was stupid because many of the passengers were picked up on frozen lakes, beaches or sand bars where there was no one to whom a passenger manifest could be given. Archie once gave a manifest to a ditch digger because he happened to be there – and received the wrath of the CAA because he gave the paperwork to the wrong person.

Another idiotic CAA move was to state any pilot who carried mail three times a week into a community could have an air service monopoly in that community. Wien cleverly sent two letters a week to every postmaster along its route: one to the postmaster and the other asking the postmaster to mail it back. In this way they secured their mail contract and routes.

As a footnote, Archie soon discovered a way to take advantage of Wien's mail route monopoly. Tom Packer, who later worked for Wedbush Morgan Securities in Anchorage, ran the Post Office in Kotzebue in the early 1960s and remembered Archie trying to get milk out to his Selawik store on a day when his plane was being repaired. "Wien wouldn't take the milk as cargo because they didn't want to go to Selawik so Archie dragged all the milk into the Post Office and mailed it to Selawik. We're talking about 100 cases of milk. Then Wien had to go to Selawik because mail was a priority item."

For many of the carriers, the difference between success and failure were the United States mail contracts. Here was a cargo client who could be depended upon to pay – late, perhaps, but the pay was consistent and many an air carrier today is in business because of mail contracts at a critical time in its history. To fully understand the impact of the United States Postal Service in the Bush, consider that in 1991, Kotzebue – with a population of 3,000 – received 15,216,000 pounds of mail. By comparison, all the mail from New York to Washington D.C. for an entire year is only about 45,450,000 pounds. This is primarily because Alaska has what is called "bypass mail." Since cargo to the bush is critical to those living there, the United States Post Office will allow just about anything to be mailed. While in the Lower 49, there are restrictions, in Alaska there are few as the poundage indicates.[108]

On smaller planes, mail and cargo meant revenue so it went aboard first. Passengers sat where there was room – and, by regulation, with seat belts. Sometimes this meant passengers sat on mailbags stacked between seat belts that were bolted to the floor. If there was no room, passengers sat would on top of the cargo, which was strictly illegal but not unusual. Many of the pilots preferred cargo to passengers because, as Bob Reeve put it succinctly, "Cargo don't talk back."

The CAA caused even more problems when it assigned routes. In 1939, the Agency ruled that everyone flying on a certain date would have that particular route as their regular run. This was fine for someone like Archie who picked up the Fairbanks to Kotzebue run, but not for Bob Reeve who had suffered a wreck shortly before the critical time period. He didn't get a route. Neither did other pilots who came later, particularly Gene Joiner, who made harassment of the CAA a holy quest unto itself.

To say that many of the CAA inspectors were hated would be like saying Baptists dislike the Devil. While there were a handful of well-liked inspectors, many of them were lucky they were able to survive a tour in the Arctic. If one of these inspectors had a plane that needed repair, every private mechanic was suddenly "out to lunch." If a CAA plane went down, not a lot of pilots spent much effort looking for them. On one occasion, several very hated CAA inspectors had gone down and were missing for a number of days. When the CAA finally pulled them out of the Interior, it was revealed that several days before they had been rescued a pilot had spotted the wrecked plane, flown over and "dropped a snow shoe." "Snow shoe" in this case was in the singular. Fred Goodwin was accused of being the pilot in question but he denied it. "Wasn't me," he said in 1989. "I wouldn't have wasted one snowshoe on them."

Whenever CAA inspectors came to Kotzebue most of the pilots knew they were on their way. Everybody used the transmitter in Archie's Kotzebue Grille and there were no secrets. Self-service atmosphere was how people survived. Pilots would walk in off the street and use the radio or, if aloft, use the plane's radio to order their steaks so they would be ready when they landed. There was no waiting at the Kotzebue Grille.

It was not hard for the pilots to figure out that a CAA inspector was aboard an incoming plane. The pilot bearing the bad news would tip the pilots in the Grille and by the time the inspector landed "anyone who wanted to leave would." Sometimes there would be 10 or 15 pilots in the Grille when the call came in. By the time the inspector was on the ground, there would only be one or two airplanes left. The rest of the pilots had flown the coop because the CAA, in the words of Goodwin, "couldn't get them in the air."

Some of the CAA personnel, like Burleigh Putnam, were competent. Burleigh's attitude was "that if [a pilot] didn't do something stupid and they knew what they were doing, I didn't worry too much about the regulations." But others were from a different planet. One night when Goodwin was flying into Kotzebue for Wien he radioed ahead to have the flare pots lit. This meant two flaming pots at either end of the landing strip and one pot midway on the left side of the strip as the plane approached. Goodwin had a CAA inspector aboard, right out of the United States Air Force, and as soon as Goodwin started his final approach, the inspector became quite animated and refused to let Goodwin land. The inspector was standing in the cockpit and arguing violently with Goodwin and his co-pilot that "the book doesn't say you can land on ice" and, furthermore, "it was illegal to land on a field with open flames." Goodwin landed despite the outrage of the CAA inspector. With personnel like this, it is no wonder that many pilots gave CAA inspectors so little respect.

After the war, the Arctic changed dramatically. The hostilities brought thousands of people north and the United States military began laying plans for air bases, radar installations, early warning radar systems and other defense structures. There were even some paved landing fields and more durable hangars. Suddenly there was more money to be made flying on a contract than flying passengers. Archie smelled the profit in cargo handling and swiftly sold his certificated route to Wien in 1946. "Everyone is buying an airplane," he said and as history was to show, he was correct.[109]

Archie was far from being through as a pilot or, for that matter, as an entrepreneur. He was 51 years old and as active as ever. Now, with his certificated route gone, he could concentrate on doing what he did best: skinning people alive as a businessman. Some of his antics were purely penny ante. Since Archie had the only fuel service in Kotzebue, everyone had to buy aviation gas from him. Unfortunately, the only way he would sell fuel, no matter how much a pilot needed, was in a 50-gallon drum. The pilot had to pay for the drum and add another $5 so Archie's son, Don, could roll the barrel under the plane's wing.

After the pilot had filled his tank to capacity, he would tell Archie, to "put my name on the barrel and when I come back through I'll have some gas." Archie would agree but just as soon as the plane took off, Archie would have Don roll the barrel back down to the end of the field and top it off. Then he would sell it to the next pilot coming in. When the first pilot returned for his left-over gas, Archie would claim he had lost track of the original barrel.[110]

Another scam was Archie's handling of the mail. Ida Evern remembered when Archie had a contract to deliver mail to Kiana "once a month." Often he would show up on the last day of the month and deliver some mail. He would fly out and be back the next day, the first day of the next month, and deliver another load of mail and thus fulfill his contract.[111]

Sometimes this was more method than madness. Since Archie hated to pay bills, he went to extraordinary lengths to delay payment as long as possible. Federal Judge von der Heydt remembered Archie from his early legal days in Nome when von der Heydt had been retained by Union Oil to file suit against him. "Archie had a bad habit of not paying bills," von der Heydt remembered. "He would write a check, fly to Point Hope and mail his letter there." That would really slow it down. The letter might sit there for 10 or 15 days before it was picked up and taken to Fairbanks. From there the mail went down the railroad to Seward and to Seattle by ferry. By the time the letter actually reached its destination, six weeks or two months would have passed. "Then the check hadn't been signed, and it had to be sent back," von der Heydt recalled laughing. "Then the check would come back and Archie would sign it and the process would start over again."[112]

Von der Heydt also remembered the paper chase Archie led him on when Union Oil tried to collect for oil they had sent north. What they discovered was Archie would start a company, burn through its assets and then walk away from it. By the time the legal eagles went after him, there was nothing left but a corporate shell. "He had a lot of problems with Union Oil mainly because he seldom paid for the oil,"[113] von der Heydt recalled. "I had two or three suits against Archie and [Union Oil] never got a nickel out of him. The creditors would throw him into involuntary bankruptcy and Archie would never bother to show up."

Union Oil finally gave up trying to collect from Archie. They were running up legal expenses and getting nothing for their paperwork. It was also very clear that they were not going to get anything for their effort: Archie had no identifiable assets to attach.

For Archie no chicanery was off limits. He could lose entire loads of coal or anything that happened to be on a barge. Or he would take a Caterpillar apart, slip it off the barge in some remote location and then claim it had been swept overboard. Even when he wasn't the barge owner, things would disappear.

"Archie's claims were always bigger than his freight bills," Ray Heinrichs remembered sardonically. "When he was building The Eskimo Building, the B&R barge, [the Bullock & Rotman barge], unloaded and Archie swore he never got his nails. That was 40 to 60 kegs of nails.

'I never got the nails,' Archie told me.

"We didn't believe him so Archie said, 'Come search my warehouse.' So we did and we looked everywhere. Finally I saw this Inupiat kid in a truck and I went up and asked him if he had unloaded some nails. The kid said 'Yes' so we knew Archie had the nails. We looked and looked and we finally found them, those 40 to 60 kegs of nails, in an old warehouse under the floorboards behind some stacks of wood. I was mad, but Archie just laughed. "'Well, I pretty near got away with it.'"[114]

Archie also had no problem using other people to do tasks that he considered too dangerous to do himself. Bud Miller should have been suspicious when Archie offered to pay him $25 to fly a plane back to Kotzebue. When Miller got in the plane he discovered that it had no brakes. He flew it Kotzebue anyway. Later he learned that Archie thought the plane was jinxed and had been approaching "every strange pilot who flew into Kotzebue" with the $25 proposition.[115]

Archie's attitude was that if it wasn't bolted down, it was his. In July of 1941, the United States government had to take Archie to court for putting up a fence on its property and moving "parts of an abandoned airship and a small building" onto the property. Further, he was using a strip 30-feet wide along the southern boundary of the federal property "as a roadway and airplane landing field." When asked to remove the property, Archie just ignored the government. He was summoned to show up, which he failed to do, was found in default and ordered to show cause, which he did not, and was then ordered off the property.

Going through Territorial and state court records in Fairbanks, Nome and Anchorage, Archie had suits against him of every sort. He refused to pay bills, did not honor contracts, did not set prices as per the Emergency Price Control Act of 1942, failed to pay wages along with other transgressions of ethics and law.

While any term of disrepute would have fit Archie like a glove on a wide variety of occasions, the bottom line remained: Archie was Archie. He was an anomaly. The only person on earth who could do what he did and get away with it. Everyone tore their collective hair out by the roots when confronted with the way he did business.

But for Archie, business was a not cold-blooded venture. It was a game. Certainly he made money, a lot of money, but he looked upon taking other people's money as a challenge rather than an act of plunder. When it came to statutes, laws and regulations, it wasn't so much that he chose to break them 'because they were there.' Rather, he did what he wanted to do without even bothering to check to see if what he wanted to do was legal. "He never broke the rules," Harmon Helmricks said, "He just didn't bother to find out if they were there."[116]

George Grant said it best. "No one considered Arch[ie] to be crooked or anything. That's just the way it was in the bush in those days. You did everything it took to make a living. Cheating is not a good word to use. All of the old traders up there did things that way. It was their form of entertainment."[117]

But there was more when it came to Archie. The big difference between Archie and other people doing the same thing, Edith Bullock said, was that "no one could stay mad at Archie. He'd cheat you, then sue you, and four weeks later you'd be getting along with him so well that you'd take his handshake on a contract – and then the process would start all over again."

GENE JOINER, THE ARCTIC ECCENTRIC

14 BABIES MURDERED

Civil Aeronautics Board Prevents Bush Pilot Flying Serum to Stricken Area. All babies in Wainwright Die in Whooping Cough Epidemic.[118]

... headline from Gene Joiner's

Mukluk Telegraph, August 31, 1950.

Archie was the King of Kotzebue. He owned a piece of every industry in the community, and sometimes the whole industry. He had a store, a restaurant, a hotel, the movie theater, a flying service, a fur farm, and a sawmill. He owned mining operations, fresh water and fuel services. His empire also included quite a bit of land and more than a few buildings. He was the richest man in the Arctic, lived openly with his mistress and did exactly as he pleased whether it was legal, ethical or moral. Almost everyone living in the community had to deal with him because they had no choice. One and all, he skinned them with a smile. But, he was such a loveable, disarming character that it was hard to dislike him.

However, there was one person in Kotzebue of whom Archie could not take advantage. This man took no grief from Archie – or any other individual for that matter. He lived like a hermit in the center of town and though his personal contact with Archie was minimal – as per the choice of both men – this individual had his own way of making Archie squirm.

He was a thorn that tortured Archie's side for a decade and a half. He was a plague in Archie's kingdom of Kotzebue. That man was Gene Joiner, the Kotzebue eccentric.

Gene Joiner was a character too unbelievable for fiction. He was the kind of a person for whom the phrase "truth is stranger than fiction" fits like a glove. If such a character appeared in a novel, any self-respecting editor would have red-lined him out as being too unrealistic. Hollywood could not have made a more outrageous character. No dramatist could have created a character like Joiner because he was, in a word, "unbelievable."

But this is a chronicle of Kotzebue. It is not fiction. In Arctic Alaska in the twilight of the frontier such an individual as Gene Joiner existed.

In the truest sense of the word, Joiner was an anomaly. He was in a class by himself. There probably has never been anyone quite like Joiner in Alaskan history – or any country's history. Life may certainly be richer having met a man like Joiner, but the meeting would leave one wondering where such a person fit into the evolutionary process.

Joiner was a slight man, about 5' 9" tall, five inches taller than Archie, but slender as opposed to Archie's rotund frame. But that was all that was "normal" about Gene Joiner.

Basically, he was slovenly but not in the sense that his clothes were pervaded by the stench of body odor or that he wore a good percentage of the last three meals he had eaten. Rather, Joiner was a sophisticated slob.

But a slob nevertheless.

First, were his clothes. Actually, as he wore the same shirt and pants all year long, any description of his clothing should be considered in the singular. Joiner did not care what he looked like and did not care if anyone else cared. As a consequence, he would buy a new shirt and pair of pants only when his old ones, quite literally, fell apart on him. Then he would wear the new clothes until they too disintegrated. While it was certainly true that *everyone* was wearing dirty clothes in Kotzebue in those days, Joiner's clothing were in class by themselves.

Then there was his smell. He didn't have the mephitis of a locker room or reek of body odor, but he did smell of his last meal. If you happened to talk to him when he came in from his jade claim, you could not help but notice that he smelled quite strongly of garlic. That's what he used for mosquito repellent. It must have been effective because Joiner never complained about mosquitoes.[119] Humans were not the only ones who found Joiner's personal hygiene offensive. Animals did as well. Rose Marie Lauser, a nurse in Kotzebue in the 1960s, remembered seeing a dog urinate on Joiner's leg.

Then there was his home, a two-room house he built for himself in the late 1940s. Outside during the winter it looked like any other home in Kotzebue. But during the summer, Joiner had a little lawn of weeds that he would cut with a push mower.[120] In July of 1952, when *National Geographic* came to Kotzebue for an article on the **North Star**, Joiner, identified only as the editor of the *Mukluk Telegraph*, proudly showed the reporter the "most northerly lawn in Alaska" which he was trimming with a pair of scissors.[121]

Later, Joiner grew turnips in the lawn. In the mid-1960s, Joiner had a brilliant idea. He approached Ray Heinrichs, who also had a lawn by this time, and told Heinrichs to "mow my lawn for a dollar." Heinrichs didn't know why but did so. When he was finished, Joiner handed him a dollar as said, "Congratulations. You're now the first commercial landscaper in the Arctic." Heinrichs was amused at this thought. But Joiner was not through. "Now," he said, "buy my turnips for a dollar." Heinrichs complied and, with a satisfied smile, Joiner handed Heinrichs the turnips and said, "Now I'm the first commercial farmer in the Arctic."

But it was the interior of Joiner's home that most people remembered. Inside, winter or summer, Joiner rarely threw anything out. He just threw it on the floor. Whether it was an old newspaper, a recent letter, a half-eaten sandwich, an airplane engine part, a cash receipt or a tire patch, he just tossed the item. Where it fell, it lay. Those who have been in his house remembered discarded paper being "a good two inches thick" on the floor like a paper rug and so deep "you needed snow shoes pretty near to walk through there."[122]

When Neva Whaley, Frank's wife, went to Joiner's house, she remembered he had "trails" through the two-room house because he had books and magazine in piles all over the floor. She suggested that he put up some book shelves and Gene agreed that was a good idea. Shortly thereafter he rounded up some old, stained gasoline cases and stacked them on top of each other for bookcases. (These were wooden cases that contained two, square five-gallon cans of gasoline, Blazo or kerosene.) Ray Heinrichs remembered Joiner's room as "filthy" and laughed when he recalled how Joiner had used narwhale horns as "curtain rods" on all of his windows.[123]

Then there was his furniture. What pieces he did have were broken. They were also strategically located so Joiner had the maximum use of his main room. Whenever he had to repair an airplane engine he dragged the greasy machine into his living room. There, on the debris-covered floor, he would completely dismantle the engine. The addition of the airplane engine and the associated oil and gas which spilled freely on the papers that made up his floor, turned Joiner's living quarters into a bonfire waiting to occur. As he heated his house with a large, upright oil furnace that sat in the very center of the room, Joiner spent years one spark away from a disastrous conflagration.

Then he added yet another fire hazard!

He was a heavy smoker. When he could get them, he smoked OPs; or, as polar bear guide Harold Little recalled, "Other People's" cigarettes. When he had the choice, Joiner preferred unfiltered Camels. If he couldn't get them, he would buy filtered camels, tear the filters off and toss them into the growing mounds of debris on his floor. Then he would walk around his house smoking until he was through with the cigarette in his mouth at which time he would spit it out onto the floor. Sometimes he would crush out the glowing embers underfoot. Other times, his foot would miss and he would let the cigarette burn out of its own accord.

Joiner only cleaned out his room when "it got so deep he couldn't walk around," Jack Lee remembered. Ozrow Martin, a jade dealer from Anchorage was one of the few people living, or dead, to have ever seen Gene Joiner's floorboards. He remembered them as being tongue-in-groove but "there wasn't a spot that didn't have a cigarette burn."[124]

Actually, Joiner did clear his home occasionally. All winter long he would use the papers to absorb the grease and oil from the engine work he did indoors. As the papers were soaked, he burned them. Then, every spring he would remove all the papers that had not been burned during the winter.

Then there was Joiner's personal hygiene. He never washed anything; not his clothes, not his dishes, not his cooking utensils. When guests came over for a glass of wine, Joiner just wiped out the dirty glasses with the shirt he had been wearing for months and filled the glasses with wine. Dishes were treated in the same manner.

Joiner's hygiene was appalling as well. After a night of heavy drinking with Martin – who was repelled by Joiner's living conditions – Joiner asked

Martin how he wanted his eggs. A badly hung-over Martin said that he "didn't want any eggs t'all."

"Well," said Joiner. "I'll scramble 'em" and Martin vividly remembered Gene Joiner standing in front of the wood stove in his filthy long johns and "that son-of-a-bitch was scramblin' eggs with one hand and a pissin' in a five gallon bucket with the other."[125]

Joiner was also unbelievably cheap. Bob Erwin, who was married to Joiner's fiancé's niece, hated to have lunch with him when he came to Kotzebue because Joiner would "eat all the crackers. He would drink the cream out of the cream pitcher and he'd try not to pay for soup. He'd ask for bread and butter if it were free and wouldn't leave a tip to save his life."

However, there was one thing Joiner was not. He was not stupid. He was an incredibly intelligent man. A voracious reader, he had the best library in the Arctic, more than 3,000 volumes, some being rare books that he had bought on his travels around the world. He even owned a Bible from the Gutenberg era. His collection was so impressive that 25 years later, Pasquale Spoletini, the Catholic Priest in Kotzebue from 1959 to 1967, instantly remembered Joiner as the man with "all those books," a phrase he said almost reverently.

Additionally, Joiner had close to a photographic memory. Occasionally he stunned his friends by referring to select paragraphs in books and magazine he had not seen in years and went so far as to "come damn near quoting them word for word," Ray Heinrichs remembered.

Further, Joiner's speech marked him as a man of education and, though it was hard for many to believe, culture. He had a myriad of maritime licenses, both foreign and domestic. He had produced documentaries for a film company in Newfoundland, Canada; taught college at Stanford; and, during the war, had been a military flight trainer.[126]

Joiner's sterling background gave no clue to the source of his eccentricities. Born into a rich family in Boaz, Alabama, in 1912, he watched as his family went from being one of the richest in the community to one of the poorest. Even though the family was in financial distress, he was able to find the money to go to college and graduated Phi Beta Kappa from Auburn University with a degree in mechanical engineering. Right out of college, in rapid succession, he married, moved to Montana where he taught at a small college in Billings, had a daughter, a very bitter divorce and spent the war teaching flying to United States Army Air Corps cadets.

"My dad was always an adventurer," Joiner's daughter remembered. "He probably had always wanted to go to Alaska"[127] and, in June of 1945, he went north. There was another reason he went north, Erwin recalled. Joiner was absolutely convinced that the "bureaucracy of government was going to destroy America" so he moved to Kotzebue, as far north as he could get, to evade the line of fire.

Even his arrival in the Arctic was pure Gene Joiner. Robert Jacobs recalled that Joiner landed in Kotzebue flying the "most beat-up airplane I had ever seen in my life." That, Jacobs said, was "the story of Gene Joiner's flying operations."

Joiner's "flying operations" were a lot like his lifestyle. He worked on the engines but he could have cared less about the outward appearance of the plane. As long as the aircraft flew, he was satisfied. His particular plane was a Ryan (B-1 or B-5), the same kind of a plane Lindbergh flew and, interestingly, made at the same factory in San Diego. But Joiner's plane was hardly of the pristine quality of Lindbergh's **Spirit of St. Louis**. It was riddled with holes. Joiner eventually flew the Ryan to Seattle where it went into storage. The rest of his time in Alaska he either flew a PA-12 or a twin-engine Cessna—which he called the "Bamboo Bomber."[128] The "Bamboo Bomber" had originally been owned by Gene Autry. It had a number of owners, including Archie Ferguson, and was finally bought by Ray Heinrichs who turned it into an airboat. Joiner, when he owned it, was not certified to fly the twin-engine aircraft so he used it as an airboat, zipping back and forth across Kotzebue Sound. As long as he knew he was under the watchful eye of the CAA, he limited his flying to using the plane as a water taxicab. But the instant the CAA was out of Kotzebue, Joiner took to the sky.[129]

Joiner flew his planes until they became "too ratty to repair," Mary Oldham recalled. His repairs were sometimes unconventional. Once, when he needed some fabric to recover a wing of a PA-12 Super Cruiser, he used the soiled sheet from off his bed. Forty years later, those who remembered Joiner chuckle over his off-white, bed-sheet wing. Randy Acord remembered Joiner's plane as being made up of "a whole bunch of different colors because he kept cannibalizing old planes to repair his and never painted anything."[130] Rose Marie Lauser, a good friend of Joiner's, also remembered Joiner's plane as being a dangerous aircraft in which to fly. Not only was it always full of groceries and spare parts for his customers in various villages but there was "gas in the back" and Joiner advised her to be careful when she smoked.

Joiner was unsafe in other ways as well. Alice Osborne, whose husband ran the Nome Miner's and Merchant's Bank Kotzebue branch, remembered watching Joiner try to unfreeze his plane's skis from the ice covering Kotzebue Sound. Joiner got into his plane, rammed the throttle forward and then got out and tried to kick the skis loose. If he had succeeded "he would have wiped out half of Kotzebue." In all fairness, Rose Marie Lauser commented that Gene Joiner was "intelligent enough to have thought about that before he got out of the plane."

As a pilot, Jim Hutchison remembered Joiner as someone who never did anything according to the CAA. "He flew this old airplane and he would never have a 100 hour [inspection] on it. Never do any work on it. Never had it licensed. Why [the CAA] never stopped him from flying I'll be damned if I know."[131] The answer to that question was that Joiner was stopped from flying on frequent occasions. But the CAA could only keep him on the ground for so long. Then he was up in the air again. (It should be pointed out that Joiner was an engineer with an A&P license. He did his own inspections.)[132]

To the same extent that Archie was easy to get along with, Joiner was cantankerous. That was his hallmark. He worked for Wien for only three days before they fired him and gave him his airplane back. After that he flew to places no one else would go, like Little Diomede and many of the smaller communities where it was almost impossible to show a profit. He also competed against Archie for cargo and passengers, which did not engender a lengthy friendship between the two men.

It did not take long for the bad blood existing between Archie and Joiner to come to a boil. Gene Jack, a local bush pilot, had left Kotzebue prior to Joiner's arrival and had requested that the building he owned be auctioned off. "For the first time since anyone could remember," Edith Bullock recalled, "Archie and Louie [Rotman] got together" and bid on Gene Jack's building against Joiner and another group of investors. Up and up the price went until Archie and Louie got the structure for more than Archie had ever wanted to pay in the first place. When Archie finally got the bid, Joiner laughed and told Archie he had purposely driven up the price so

Archie would have to pay more for the building. Archie was furious. Thus the feud between the two was initiated.[133]

However, Don Ferguson, Warren's son, remembered that the friction between the two men went back even further. He recalled that Archie had brought Gene Joiner to Kotzebue to fly for Ferguson Airways in 1945 but the relationship had been so strained that Archie fired him.[134] In either case, it could never be said that Archie and Joiner were friends by any definition of the word.

In the Arctic, Joiner's primary source of income was his ownership of jade claims on Jade Mountain. But his rights had come a long way. The first claim had been made by Tom Berryman who sold out when he couldn't make a dime off the mineral. It was bought by Walter Cohen who sold to B. Hanson in 1925. It sat unworked until 1943 when Muktuk Marston took a 165-pound boulder out. That boulder was eventually cut up and distributed to servicemen. In 1947, the claim was bought by Arctic Circle Exploration Company. The company's president, Russell Havenstriff, came north to look over the claim with, of all people, Walt Disney "and some of his bankers."[135] Ozrow Martin recalled that after a barge load of the mineral went down in the Bering Sea, this "dulled their enthusiasm for jade mining." That, in addition to theft of what was reported to be have been a $1 million worth of jade in a transfer company terminal in Seattle, probably encouraged Havenstriff to get involved in oil exploration in Cook Inlet. As he was selling off his Arctic assets, Joiner was able to buy the Havenstriff claim for a fraction of its initial investment. This undoubtedly infuriated Archie who also had a handful of jade claims in the area.[136] For the next twenty-five years, Joiner was to sink a mammoth effort into mining that jade. What money he made flying was swallowed by the jade venture – not that he spent a lot of money buying luxuries.

In the beginning, every activity relating to jade was done by hand as Joiner had neither the money nor the equipment to run a top-notch professional operation – not that he *would* have or *could* have run such an operation had he *had* the money and equipment. He started with a collection of hand-made hammers and wedges that he used to cut the jade into blocks. Then he would wrestle the jade slabs onto small, flat sheets of metal that had been cut from a fuel tank, which he called "go-devils," and drag them with a small Cat overland to the banks of the Kobuk River. From there he would load the slabs onto one of the barges that plied the waters during the ice-free seasons and have them floated downriver into Kotzebue.[137]

Edith Bullock

Even then it wasn't easy. Edith Bullock, who was running Bullock & Rotman Barge at the time, remembered trying to get one of Joiner's jade boulders on board her barge. No one had ever tried lifting something of that weight and Kotzebue, at that time, was a maritime community without a crane. It was, to say the least, a "learning experience," she recalled.

Archie didn't make it any easier. As Joiner, Jack Bullock and a handful of Inupiat were struggling to winch a boulder weighing several tons up a 10-foot incline, Archie came sauntering by as if he just happened to be in the neighborhood.

"How yuh don' Gene?"

"Mind your own business, Archie."

Archie kept sauntering back and forth in front of the barge as everyone else was sweating. It was if he had nothing better to do but watch Gene Joiner sweat over the jade boulder.

"You're never going to get that thing on the barge, Gene," Archie said with a whine and cackle. "It's too heavy."

"Shut your mouth, Archie."

"Looks like it's r-e-a-l heavy there, Gene, real heavy."

Joiner continued to mumble, grunt and curse at Archie as he and the rest of the crew heaved the boulder aboard, an inch at a time. [138]

Joiner, it should be added, was not above a little needling of his own. When Kotzebue big game guide Nelson Walker's wife, Myra, was in labor, Joiner along with Harold Little and another polar bear guide, Gene Starkweather, walked all over town passing out cigars as if they were the proud fathers. Walker was not pleased with the insinuation and went out looking for the two men loaded for bear. He later filed suit against Gene Joiner and "miscellaneous DEW site workers."[139]

While Joiner's jade had great potential, it brought him great difficulties as well. Alaskan jade did not have a good reputation worldwide and when Joiner tried to attract buyers to come to Kotzebue for an auction, no one showed up. There may have been a good reason for this. Some Chinese buyers claimed that the Alaskan jade was "unripe" in the sense that it hadn't matured. Much of it was "splintery green" which meant it would fall apart if cut too thin. Joiner guaranteed to replace any defective stone, but that would take time, possibly months. As a result, many jade buyers were apparently unwilling to take the risk.

In his own way, Joiner was a jade pioneer. He was doing something that had never been done in the Arctic before. While his crude tools were adequate for hewing the slabs, they were not usable for more delicate work. For that reason, the first slabs of jade were sent to East Germany where they were cut, worked and later sold.

At that time there was not a large market for jade in the United States. While today one can buy a spectrum of jade products, in the 1940s and 1950s jade did not have the popularity it does today. So Joiner contracted to produce the one jade product he knew he could sell: ashtrays.

But there was a problem. "Ashtrays" were on the embargo list for East Germany. For three years Joiner fought with the United States Customs to get his jade product into the country. Finally he hit on a new angle. He called the product "paper clip holders" and found they were able to come through the trade embargo easily.[140]

As his inventory grew, Joiner traveled all over the world looking for markets for his jade. According to his almost step-son, Bill Boucher – "Boucher" is pronounced "Boo-Shay"—whenever Joiner went to the Far East, he always had a pocket-full of jade stones. Instead of passing out tips in the local currency, he would give small pieces of jade that the Asians treasured very highly. To Joiner, they were just stones he picked up in the Kobuk River. To the Asians, the stones were better than cash. In fact, he claimed that just having the stones allowed him "into parts of Asia no white men had seen, primarily areas of jade production."[141]

While this is a great story, it may not be true. There are two kinds of jade, Jadite and Nephrite, with Alaskan Nephrite being noticeably different. It is so noticeably different that people who know jade would be able to spot the difference immediately. Edith Bullock felt that this story was "pure Joiner" and was probably something that Joiner *said* rather than something he had done.

Like Archie, Joiner was a great storyteller. For the most part, his stories were not as tall as Archie's, but they did tread on the very edge of believability. One evening Joiner, Dr. Neilson and his wife were having dinner with Dr. Fraser, the Episcopal priest, Tom Osgood, his wife, and three or four other friends of Dr. Fraser. "Gene went into this long dissertation about the Abominable Snowman that was up at Jade Mountain," Dr. Neilson remembered. The Snowman, according to Joiner, had come right into his cabin and confronted Joiner. "'It was like he had on this leather outfit with hair on it,'" Neilson remembered Joiner saying. For the next half hour, Joiner continued to repeat how this Snowman looked as though it was dressed in a leather outfit with hair. Finally the Episcopal priest could take more and leaned forward and asked in mock seriousness, "Did it have on motorcycle boots?"[142]

But unlike a lot of stories that Archie told, many of Joiner's stories were true. But this did not stop the locals from continuing to believe that Joiner was exactly as he appeared: an eccentric. Once after he returned from a trip to India, Joiner was having lunch in Rotman's when he told two Inupiat, Rodney Lincoln and Art Fields, that they should have more respect for him. After all, Joiner said, "when I was in India, everyone called me King Joiner."

Lincoln quickly retorted, "Why didn't you stay over there and be King Joiner instead of Bullshit Joiner?"

Lincoln wasn't the only one who felt that way. Jack Lee of Lee's Flying Service, who ran a polar bear hunting guiding service out of Kotzebue for years, noted dryly that "everything [Joiner] said was bullshit." It wasn't much use talking to Joiner because, Lee said, "he never said anything anyway."

Part of the legacy of Gene Joiner sat in Kotzebue for years. In the early 1950s, Joiner was able to negotiate a sizable deal with the Peron government of Argentina. Eva Peron had just died and her husband Juan, President of Argentina at the time – for the first time – decided to honor her memory with a life-size statue from a single slab of jade. Peron placed an order with Joiner who was more than pleased with the opportunity to take advantage of what was undoubtedly the largest jade deal he had ever consummated: $100,000.

He cut a 20-ton slab of jade from Jade Mountain and had it transported the 200 miles to Kotzebue in time to take advantage to the brief window of opportunity when Kotzebue Sound was ice-free. With great effort, the slab was finally moved into Kotzebue to await the ship that would carry it across the equator and around South America to the other side of the hemisphere.

While Joiner had correctly adjusted his schedule for all Alaskan conditions of weather and season, he could not take into account the stormy nature of South American politics. By the time the jade monolith was in Kotzebue, the Peron government was no more. So, for the next two decades, the boulder sat in Kotzebue by the airport, surrounded by a rusting wire fence, covered with a decaying tarp with a hand-painted sign that read "Keep Out."[143]

Joiner was also different from Archie in that Joiner knew how to handle money. Archie made a lot of money but managed it very poorly. Joiner made very little money but invested it wisely. Archie was a nickel-and-dime man while Joiner looked to the long run. But Joiner wasn't trying to make a living;

he was anticipating making a killing. "Always trying to hit a big lick," Martin remembered, and occasionally he did. One of his larger successes was the sale of several tons of jade to some Arabs, but he failed in convincing a collection of Hollywood stars to plate their swimming pools with jade tiles.[144]

Though Joiner may not have been a very rich man in Kotzebue, he acted as though he had made a killing in the jade business when he visited Anchorage. But he could not bring himself to clean up before he went to the big city. He would fly into Anchorage and walk into the best hotel in town, the Westward, (today the Anchorage Hilton), dragging filthy gunny sacks full of jade and invite people to come up to his room and party.

Then there were his schemes.

While some were within the realm of reasonable, others were so bizarre they seem far-fetched even today. In 1960, Bob Erwin who was the Prosecutor for the newly-admitted State of Alaska in Nome, received a wire from the Justice Department in Washington D. C. that a "known Communist sympathizer" by the name of Gene Joiner had struck a deal with the Soviet Union. When Erwin questioned Joiner, he was told a story that stretches the imagination.

As the story was revealed, Joiner was planning on traveling to Wrangell Island in the Chukchi Sea – an island in the possession of the Soviet Union – where he was going to claim, "all of the sailing ships which had been interned during the Russian Revolution." Joiner had even bought an old "whaleboat" in which he intended to make the trip to Wrangell Island, a risky voyage at best.[145]

(Of historical note, Joiner did have an historical leg to stand on. There had been an American colony on Wrangel Island. Four white men and an Inupiat set up an outpost in 1923; three of the men died trying to reach the Soviet mainland the last one died of scurvy. Only the Inupiat cook survived. She, Ada Blackjack Johnson, was rescued by another expedition of one white man, Charles Wells, and a dozen Inupiat. But that colony did not last long either. It was removed by the Soviet ice breaker **Red October** and Wells, according to Carl Lomen, one of financial backers of the scheme, was "murdered by the Soviets" in Vladivostok. Wells' Inupiat helpers were "driven into northern China" and had to be re-patriated by the Red Cross. Carl Lomen filed for damages with the State Department but never received any compensation.[146])

"If Gene Joiner was a Communist, I'm a Martian," Erwin declared. "But he had legitimately bought up the rights to some of those ships. He figured that the way the Cold War was going, that if he could get himself to Wrangell Island the American government could not afford to leave him there to die and that he might be able to make something commercially out of it."

Former State Legislator Richard Foster also remembered that Joiner was intent on moving to Siberia. The Soviet Union, however, was not very keen on the idea. Joiner applied and was rejected. When he got his rejection he was furious. "Even the Russians don't want me."[147] Joiner, like a lot of other old-timers, felt that the frontier was better off "without the rules and the bureaucracy," Richard Foster said of Joiner. "If there hadn't been a Cold War, I'm sure Gene would have lived in Siberia on the Chukchi Peninsula."[148]

Also like Archie, Joiner spent few winters in Kotzebue. As soon as winter's sub-zero temperatures arrived, he'd fly into Fairbanks, park his plane at Phillips Field and then drive outside. In the early days when he had very little money, he used to live in a little camper that fit over the bed of his pickup. It had a tall shell and Joiner lived there the entire winter, even when visiting his daughter in the San Fernando Valley in California. When he returned to Fairbanks in the spring, he would just park the truck, get in his plane, and fly to Kotzebue.

Though he did not get along with his ex-wife at all, he saw his daughter, now Linda Drohman, frequently. Drohman remembered her father well and recalled quite vividly coming to Kotzebue in December of 1950. Joiner had built her an ice-and-snow igloo – because she expected to see one in the Arctic – and proudly wrote the incident up in his paper, the *Mukluk Telegraph*, noting gleefully that the Inupiat of Kotzebue were fascinated with the structure. Some of them had even taken photographs of this strange creation of ice and snow, a structure they had never seen before.[149]

Most winters, however, Joiner spent in Southern California near his daughter. When his income from the mine increased, he bought a small home in the California desert where he lived during the cold season. But having a home in Southern California did not change his lifestyle in the least. He would arrive in Los Angeles in the same clothes he had been wearing all summer on the jade claim. While he no longer needed a camper in which to live, he still needed transportation. Being parsimonious, rather than rent a vehicle while he was in Southern California, Joiner would buy the "most horrible cars," his daughter shuddered, like Nash Ramblers with one side caved in, for $100 or $200. He would drive these junkers until they gave out or he left for Alaska, whichever came first. In either case, the cars were abandoned in Southern California.

While Joiner may have been both eccentric and slovenly, he was not without defenders. For the young whites and Inupiat, he had a heart of gold and took great pains to spend time with them and teach them what he had learned. Rose Marie remembered him as a very intelligent man who was friendly and talkative. Neil Bergt also recalled him warmly as someone who would have taught a young person "everything he knew about the Arctic." Bill Boucher remembered Joiner tutoring him on literature, engineering, mechanics, flying and mining. While Joiner was indescribably cantankerous to those his own age, he was easy to get along with if you were young. All you really had to do, Boucher recalled, was "let him be what he wanted to be."[150]

He could also be incredibly generous. When Dr. Neilson and his wife were leaving Kotzebue in 1966, Joiner showed up at the going-away party. Surprisingly, Joiner was wearing a "dress shirt with jade cuff links." Mrs. Neilson admired the cuff links and commented how beautiful they were.

"You like them?" Joiner asked. When Mrs. Neilson said she did, Joiner promptly took out his pen knife, dug the stones out of their settings and handed them to her.[151]

Joiner was also open to new experiences, even if it was the young who opened that door. Seriously ill one day, Joiner practically begged Dr. Neilson to come to his home, which the Doctor did. Several weeks later Joiner came to the Neilson's house and said he wanted to give the doctor "a little something" for taking care of him.

"He gave me this handful of dried mushrooms," Dr. Neilson remembered. "Then he went on in some detail of what a trip you could really take by chewing on these things."

Dr. Neilson thanked Joiner very much but never partook of the gift.

One of the few people his own age with whom Joiner had a personal relationship was Emily Boucher, Editor and Publisher of the *Nome Nugget* and daughter of the famous Nome pioneer merchant Antonio Polet. Joiner met her during the time he was publishing the *Mukluk Telegraph* and the two hit it off well. Twice a month he would fly into Nome to have the *Nome*

Nugget print his paper and then sit in Emily's office and wait for the tabloid to come off the press.[152]

One of the two great marital mysteries of the Western Arctic was why Emily Boucher decided to marry Gene Joiner. Emily, a newspaper entrepreneur with three children was living a quiet, aesthetic life in Nome. Bright, cheerful and outgoing, Emily was a sociable person as opposed to Gene Joiner's cantankerous outlook on humans in general and certain individuals in particular. Considering that everyone in the Arctic thought that they knew what Joiner was, they were fairly certain that Emily Boucher would never put up with his lifestyle.

On the other hand, those who knew Emily well, remembered that she was attracted to Gene because he was very literate. Second, he seemed unaffected by the passage of time. He was a Renaissance man in the purest sense of the word. He could do everything and do it well, from music to engine repair and poetry to flying. It was rare to find these qualities in a man anywhere, much less in the Arctic.

Emily did agree to marry him and Joiner treated her children as though they was his own. The courtship lasted ten years until the early 1960s, but a marriage was never held. In November of 1963, Emily went to Seattle for an operation and died as a result of surgery. Joiner furnished and had engraved a solid jade marker for her grave in Seattle.

Joiner wasn't "cheap," Bill Boucher said in defense of his almost-stepfather. He was "thrifty. He lived out of his pocket." Boucher remembered that while Gene Joiner certainly had his faults, lack of thinking was not one of them. "He was an incredibly intelligent man. He always thought ahead. He would cache gasoline near where he would be flying. Then, if he ever needed aviation gas, he could land and fuel up. I'm sure a lot of it is still out there."

Like Archie, Gene Joiner *hated* the government and anyone associated with it. But he was different than Archie. He didn't mumble about it in private and then dodge the CAA. He published what he thought. Between June 15, 1950, and February 28, 1952, Joiner published 20 issues of the *Mukluk Telegraph*, a tabloid that told all of the happenings in the Arctic. It was the scandal sheet of the north and a hoot to almost everyone in the Arctic who could read. Those to whom it was not funny were usually those whose names and antics were included in the newspaper.

While the *Nome Nugget* was read throughout the Arctic, it focused on Nome. The *Mukluk Telegraph* concentrated on those areas the *Nome Nugget* neglected: Kotzebue and the scattered Inupiat villages in the western Arctic. These included such booming metropolitan areas as Wainwright, Elephant Point, Wales, Kiana, Kobuk, Mary's Igloo, Diomede, King Island, Anaktuvik Pass, Point Lay and others where Joiner flew.

The *Mukluk Telegraph* was an instant hit. Libelous, scandalous, irreverent, outrageous, lambastic and sarcastic, it was widely and joyously read. Laughter proceeded every issue. Joiner had the audacity to say things in print other people didn't have the intestinal fortitude to whisper in the privacy of their own home. In every issue, Joiner preached from the only tenet of the Harry S. Truman School of Journalism: he didn't give anyone hell, he just told the truth and they thought it was hell.

Topping his list of targets was anyone who had anything to do with the federal government. In the March 17, 1951, issue he noted since United States Marshal Burt W. Neily "was incompetent" in dealing with people who were stealing emergency equipment from bush planes, the pilots had banded together and decided to take matters into their own hands. According to the report in the *Mukluk Telegraph,*

> *The local pilots recently agreed to work together and chop the fingers off anyone caught stealing emergency equipment from any of their airplanes. One pilot has been putting poison in some of his emergency food in an effort to kill off the thieves but to date has met with no success.*

With regard to the game warden, on July 29, 1950, Joiner reported that Aukouk, the "Eskimo Medicine Man," had put a curse on the Game Warden's head. The Game Warden, according to Aukouk, had been killing caribou, mink, fox and other animals with the poison he has been setting out for wolves. Aukouk placed the curse and allowed Touauk, "the Eskimo Devil," to do his worst. The curse was immediately felt by the warden's house catching fire, his wrecking his airplane, developing considerable engine trouble, falling from his plane into the deep icy water, having equipment stolen from his airplane, his wife leaving him, and trouble with his girlfriend.

With pithy comments, he delivered mighty messages in few words. There was, for instance, a reference to Jack Whaley, "vice president of the C.A.B. breast-fed scheduled airline at Kotzebue," in short, Wien Airlines, and a short item on Robert K. Baker, the local game warden who, when he got married in September of 1950, had "both friends of the groom" in attendance. The headline for the wedding read "HUNTING SEASON CLOSED FOR GAME WARDEN."[153]

While Joiner had a plethora of targets, his favorite was the CAA. Fully realizing the government could not sue for libel, he had a journalistic field day. On the front page of the August 31, 1950, edition was the headline in all capital, bold letters: **14 BABIES MURDERED.** Immediately beneath that was the tag line, "Civil Aeronautics Board Prevents Bush Pilot Flying Serum to Stricken Area. All Babies in Wainwright Die in Whooping Cough Epidemic." According to the story, the nurse in Wainwright could not get serum flown into the village because the regularly scheduled airline was out of operation and "a local Bush Pilot who usually flew her on much [sic] emergency trips was being held for investigation by the Civilian Aeronautics Board for having flown passengers parallel to the local scheduled airlines." That pilot "under investigation" was Gene Joiner. In the column opposite the headlines, Joiner made this fact clear in an alleged news tidbit from Barrow, written as if an Inupiat had scribbled it, "We sorry to hear Gene Joiner have more trouble with C.A.B. in Kotzebue. Maybe many more people die if Bush pilots have to stop flying."

But Joiner was more than bold. In a daring headline he brazenly stated that CAB officials were "Accepting Bribes." In this case, "12 white fox skins" which had been paid to one of the "petty, bribe-hungry maladjusted failures in the Anchorage [CAA] office."[154] The reference to "white fox" here was aimed directly at Archie for it was widely believed – and quite possibly true – that Archie had never really passed his certification for his pilot's license but he had bribed the CAA Inspector with "white fox" furs.[155]

Under another bold headline entitled "Working for Moscow"[156] Joiner attacked the CAA for their relentless battle against the small bush pilots represented by, so stated the *Mukluk Telegraph*, Gene Joiner. Another time he ran a story whose headlines read "C.A.A. Inspector Lands Safely."[157] Once he went so far as to state that the CAA was hiring but only those applicants with "unmarried parents" need apply.

Not one to pull in his horns, Joiner hit the CAA again and again. In the June 9, 1951, diatribe, Joiner stated that a CAB official had "physically beaten a witness at the hearing to make him change his statement [and] had offered bribes in the courtroom to have testimony changed." Then, Joiner alleged, the court transcript had been "altered" so that these alleged offenses did not appear in the official court record. Apparently, Donald W. Nyrop, the new head of the CAB in Washington D. C., had

> put on his rose-colored glasses and joined his fellow murderers, grafters, and reptiles behind the CAB's iron curtain of bureaucracy, feeling secure that, come what may, the Civil Aeronautics Board can do no wrong.[158]

Needless to say, Joiner's popularity with the CAA and associated government agencies was very low. It was so low that once, while he and Bill Boucher were examining some claims at Hunter Creek outside of Buckland, Marshal Neily flew in by helicopter to issue Joiner a summons to come to a CAB hearing in Fairbanks.[159] "[The Federal government people] loved to do stuff like that to Gene," Boucher said, so it was not that unusual for Gene Joiner. For anyone else this would have been grounds for charges of harassment.

Sometimes Joiner tried humor. In the September 16, 1950 edition, he printed the following in phonetic Inupiat:

Toota Yoogaht

Ooploopuk, oovah, ahnook lik pooru – took, ooloot it poorak gooni loo, si la gik poo ruh lissook, oopluk koon, kooyaroogook, ooh ay nee ruk mun, nun gak too goot to ahseen, ahtee gitch choy gota ahseeno.

[Translated, this reads "Now hear this! Today, here, it's very stormy. There is high water in the lagoon. We pray that tomorrow the weather is better. To stay alive we must dress in our parkas and keep warm."]

Former Governor Jay Hammond who had been in Kotzebue during the winter of 1950-1951 as a United States government Fish and Wildlife wolf hunter remembered articles from the *Mukluk Telegraph* verbatim.

He also had good reason to remember Joiner very well.

During a fierce storm in the early weeks of 1951, Joiner had come stumbling into Hammond's cabin in Kotzebue desperate for assistance. All of the planes in the community – except Joiner's – were facing into a 90-mile an hour wind. If Joiner could not turn his plane around, it would be ruined beyond repair. But he could not do it alone.

As Hammond recalled, Joiner fought his way through into the blizzard to the Fish and Wildlife cabin and "came pleading" for the government people to help him move his aircraft. Considering how much Joiner hated anything remotely associated with the United States government, he must have been truly desperate. With *great* difficulty, Hammond and his partner ran a rope line down to the landing strip so they could find their way back in the whiteout. Working together, all three men were able to turn Joiner's plane into a protected position and tie it down securely. Then they fought their way back to the Fish and Wildlife cabin.

Joiner left and later than night the wind direction changed by 180 degrees and blasted at 100 miles an hour. There was nothing anyone could do but wait out the storm and accept what damage the wind had wrought. When the storm cleared, Hammond discovered that almost all of the airplanes had their wings crushed.

"Archie had an old Waco and the fabric had been stripped completely off," Hammond said laughing. "It was totally denuded sitting there on the ice. The only plane that had been virtually unscathed was Joiner's."

But that wasn't the end of the story.

Several weeks later, while working in Dillingham, Hammond was told by a friend that he and his Fish and Wildlife partner had been written up in the *Mukluk Telegraph* –and it had been a scathing reference. When Hammond read the clip, he was outraged. The article, which appeared on the center of the front page in the March 17, 1951, edition, had the headline, "TAX PAYERS LOSE $5,000 IN CHESS GAME." The article stated that Hammond and his partner had "sat in the hotel playing chess while their airplanes were being torn to pieces by the storm."

The article concluded with the stinging paragraph,

> *The game wardens, however, having plenty of planes and an almost unlimited supply of taxpayers' money to buy more, did not feel it worthwhile to interrupt their chess game and go*

outside for a few minutes to give their equipment the attention
it needed.

Hammond and his partner were furious and took a "blood oath to knock Joiner out from under his hat next time we saw him." [The next time Hammond saw him was 25 years later – Joiner was in the Alaska Native Hospital recovering from his celebrated survival trek.]

Gene Joiner in the 1950s.

Then there was Archie. Joiner did not simply enjoy taking editorial pot-shots at Archie; he relished it. The fact Archie had abandoned his wife Hadley in 1944 and was openly living with his mistress made Archie fair game and an easy target. Hadley and Warren's children – whom Archie had adopted by then – were living in Fairbanks at the time, giving Archie the run of Kotzebue.

In the June 1, 1950, edition of the *Mukluk Telegraph*, Joiner hit hard: "Archibald Furguson [sic], local windbag and buffoon, is on a business trip outside, accompanied by his combination partner and mistress – we assume he is having a pleasant trip." When Archie made it back to town and learned he had been written up in the *Mukluk Telegraph*, he was furious! But there wasn't anything he could do.

The needling continued. In the July 29, 1950, edition, Joiner reported Warren's sons – Don, Ray and Frank – were in Kotzebue for the summer and staying with their uncle, "and having a swell time speeding around town."

Their mother, "guardian ... [and] legal wife of Archie Ferguson refused to come to Kotzebue" and "does not intend to come back as long as Archie keeps that woman of his around." Everyone knew who "that woman" was.

Two months later, on August 19, 1950, Joiner reported, sardonically, of a maritime accident involving the loss of some freight off a barge. However, "the nearest thing to a disaster was the loss of a large quantity of furniture for Archie Ferguson's Harlot Den. The furniture was not insured."

But the *piece de resistance* that issue was the front page, center article entitled "**FERGUSON OPERATING ILLEGAL RADIO.**" Joiner reported that the chief of the local airways, Mr. Robbins, "stated under oath he had on many occasions seen Archie Ferguson operating a powerful illegal radio transmitter in Kotzebue, sending illegal messages and planting false information in the local communication station records."

Why was Archie not subject to the $10,000 fine and ten years in prison, Joiner asked? Because, it was stated editorially, "Mr. Ferguson . . . had turned informer and was working with the C.A.B. in obtaining evidence against the defendant in the hearing." That defendant may very well have been Gene Joiner himself. Archie however, was not in town to comment for, in the words of Gene Joiner, "Mr. Ferguson made a hurried departure for Seattle."

In the next issue, August 31, 1950, Joiner struck again with a small note in the newspaper:

> *A little bird tells us that if the insurance company will fish out the 215 barrels of fuel oil lost near Point Hope the other day, they will find that most of them were filled with saltwater before they were "lost" overboard.*

(Archie was the only fuel dealer at the time.)

Later, in December, on the 28th, came another jab. Joiner printed that Archie, "well-known indoor sportsman, left for Seattle last week accompanied by his girlfriend." The two were expected to be touring the United States "in their new super deluxe Cadillac which they will pick up in Seattle" while Mrs. Ferguson will be "keeping a close watch on the trading post" which, if her luck holds, will allow her "to get the children some shoes this Christmas."

In the March 17, 1951, edition Joiner noted that Willie Foster had bought Archie's Kotzebue Grille and "all the customers that Archie Ferguson has kicked out of the place have been invited back." Foster "who, until the CAB put him out of business," operated a flying service out of Nome. (Later, Willy Foster founded Foster Aviation, now defunct.)

Probably the one article that infuriated Archie the most appeared on June 15, 1950. It became common knowledge about Kotzebue that on at least one occasion – and probably on many – Archie and Beulah had been having sexual intercourse with the curtains up. The whole town knew because, on at least this one particular occasion, Warren's three boys were watching the entire performance through the window. Soon thereafter, Archie put up some Venetian blinds. But this was too good a story for Joiner to ignore – and he didn't – but took great delight in printing,

> Archibald Furgeson [sic] and Company is back in town. His establishment is again operating full force, but is now equipped with Venetian blinds. This has been a big help in keeping spectators, especially children, off the roof of Pete Lee's Pool Hall.

Joiner "delighted in driving to the point of insanity" and he was very good in this calling.[160] When it came to Joiner and the *Mukluk Telegraph*, Archie was livid with rage. How could Gene Joiner do that? How could he? Archie was so mad he actually went to the local attorney, Fred Crane, and tried to take Joiner to court.

Fred Crane, the only Nome-based attorney, who probably thought the paper was as funny as everyone else in Kotzebue, basically told Archie that Joiner could, in fact, do exactly what he was doing. It was a protected industry. The *Mukluk Telegraph* was a paper and it really couldn't be sued – particularly if what the paper was saying happened to be true. So Archie stewed on high boil. After all, that was all he could do.

ARCHIE FERGUSON,
THE CON MAN OF KOTZEBUE

Mr. Paul Spurlock, manager of Alaska Airlines at Nome, says he will not buy the Kotzebue Grille and Midnight Sun Theater from Archie Ferguson at Kotzebue as rumored. Mr. Spurlock said the price is satisfactory, but Ferguson cannot be trusted. He would probably turn right around and put up another restaurant and show, and claim it belonged to Beulah or Bill [Billy Levy].

Look at the deal he pulled on Blankenship in Kiana. He sold his store to Blank and agreed not to go back in business there for five years, then turned around and built a bigger store than the one he sold. Then when he sold his airline to Wiens he bought a bunch of planes and started right back in the flying business. Now there is the same thing with Hanson at Kotzebue. After selling his store to Hanson, he starts another store under a phoney [sic] name.

No, Archie seems to double-cross everybody that deals with him, and knowing him as I do, I think I'll just pass up the deal.

Gene Joiner, *Mukluk Telegraph*
November 25, 1950

By 1946, Ferguson Airways was out of the aviation business as a regularly-scheduled airlines. Sort of. It was "sort of" out of the flying business because, as a legal entity, it had been bought out by Wien. In reality, it was still flying over the same route and competing with the airlines that had bought it out. In other words, all Wien had bought was the CAA-approved route. That was the way Archie did business. What someone *thought* they were buying was substantially different from what Archie actually sold them.

In this particular case, Wien – called "Wiens" by the locals because most travelers in the Arctic knew the four Wien brothers personally: Sig, Ralph, Fritz and Noel – might have been buying Archie out more to keep him out of the hands of their competition than for any assets Ferguson Airways might have brought them. The talk among the bush pilots was that the only reason Wien bought Archie out was that they were afraid that "somebody else was going to buy him."[161]

But Archie was unbelievably shrewd. He would not have sold an asset that would have made him a dime unless he had figured how he could recoup that dime with an additional nickel as well. What Archie saw, that many other bush pilots in the Arctic did not, was that the Second World War had altered the face of the Arctic. More and more people were coming north and staying. That meant that the dollars being made carrying people would stabilize.

What would increase were the profits from carrying cargo. By selling his airline route, Archie was getting the best of both worlds. He was out of the passenger service business at a profit while still having the option to carry passengers over the same route at his convenience rather than a schedule. And he was free to carry cargo that would pay him more – particularly when that cargo was destined for his own stores in Kotzebue, Kiana, Selawik and Shungnak.

Little did Archie know how correct his assessment of the future was. The ink on the Japanese surrender in August of 1945, was not dry before the first icy blast of the Cold War hit Washington D.C. As General George Patton predicted before his untimely death, our Soviet allies became our global adversaries. An iron curtain dropped across Europe and, in the Arctic, an icy curtain came down as well.

To freeze the Russian bear in its tracks along America's northern frontier, the United States military began building a network of military bases and support facilities from the Bering Sea to the Atlantic Ocean. Sprinkled along the coastline of the Arctic Ocean were Distant Early Warning (DEW) sites. These radar-equipped bases kept a 24-hour-a-day vigil on the northern horizon ready to report any incoming Soviet Intercontinental Ballistic Missiles (ICBMs). Since these bases were built as far north as possible, they would be the first to spot the incoming ICBMs to give the United States military enough time to launch its missiles from bases in the American Midwest. DEW stations had a range of 3,000 line-of-sight miles and could pick up incoming missiles "five minutes after launching." With the DEW Line sites, the United States military was basically buying a 20-minute early warning.[162]

Further south, running along a latitude just north of Fairbanks, was the North American Air Defense (NORAD) line, a string of Air Command Warning System (ACWS) bases. These bases were also radar-equipped and were specifically designed to report the intrusion of Soviet fighters and bombers into United States air space.

A NORAD site; Note the radar bubbles in the rear.

While a report from a DEW line site would send missile crews to alert in the American Midwest, an alarm from an ACWS site would scramble fighters from the newly-established Elmendorf Air Force Base in Anchorage and Ladd Air Force Base in Fairbanks – Elmendorf has since been combined with the adjacent Fort Richardson Army Base into JBER and Ladd is now Eielson Air Force Base – as well as Galena in the interior of the Territory. Naval intelligence units were also being established in Alaska, primarily along the Aleutians, and the United States Coast Guard established Long Range Aid To Navigation (LORAN) stations along the Alaskan coast in the late 1950s and early 1960s. Publicly announced to be for the safety of aircraft and ships with LORAN gear, the primary, unspoken mission of the LORAN bases was to allow the submarines of that era to triangulate their position for navigation purposes.

But with the establishment of these bases came a significant problem: communication. As this was before the age of earth stations and geostationary satellites, the most advanced technology was line-of-site microwave transmission. To keep in direct contact with all of the DEW, NORAD and LORAN establishments, the United States military established yet another network known individually by a variety of names including WHITE ALICE, ACS (Alaska Communications System) and RCA (Rural Communications of Alaska). None of these systems currently exist. WHITE ALICE has been dismantled while ACS was bought by RCA that, in turn, was purchased by Alascom that was absorbed into Pacific Telecom, Inc. and is now AT&T Alaska.

What this Cold War paranoia meant to the Arctic could be summed up in a single word: construction. This, in turn, meant transportation of men, women, food, supplies, tools, equipment and building material into remote areas. Someone had to airlift those supplies and every entrepreneur in the Arctic saw that there was a substantial slice of the pie for everyone in the transportation business.

Archie saw the future clearly. He would make more money hauling mail by air and cargo by water than he ever would running passengers back and forth between Fairbanks and Kotzebue on a CAA-regulated route. The shrewd entrepreneur that he was, Archie sold that which was no longer of any value to him, (his certificated route,) and proceeded to compete against the very company that bought him out on a piece-meal basis using two of his sons as his pilots. Then he spent his own time building up his barge fleet and fulfilling a mail contract by boat between Nome and St. Michael with intermittent stops in Unalakleet, Golovin, Teller, Wales, Shishmaref, Deering, Keewalik, King Island and Diomede.

In his barge and lighterage business, as in all other ventures, Archie was unbelievably slippery. "The shrewdest man I ever met," noted Shafsky graciously. Others said it differently. "Archie would rather steal a nickel than make an honest dollar," Reverend Miller of Kotzebue said of him sadly. "He should have been a millionaire" but he didn't know how to handle money. It slipped through his fin-gers as fast as it came into his hands. But Archie didn't care; it was all part of the game.

Archie wasn't particular about who he conned. He was a man completely without prejudice. He would short-change *anyone,* white or Inupiat, tourist or sourdough, man or woman. It was a battle of wits and Archie would almost always win. When he didn't, he figured out a way to turn the tables even if it meant breaking the law. One of the ways Archie was able to cut fiscal corners was the printing of "bingles."

While the currency of the United States had been the official tender in the Territory and State of Alaska for almost a century, early Alaskan merchants had always had trouble dealing with low-ticket

Bingles

items. Take Kotzebue as an example. Most people lived on credit at the store. An Inupiat might sell his furs and take his payment in credit. Every time he or his family made a purchase, their account would be adjusted in the store's ledger.

But there was a problem. If the merchants had to adjust the customer's credit every time a child wanted a candy bar or a stick of gum, the book-keeping would have been a nightmare. So the merchants printed their own money. Called "bingles," there were usually made of tin or aluminum and looked like play coins. What made the coins legal was that there were only **supposed** to be used in the store which issued them.

However, it was not unusual for merchants to accept bingles from another store. Although this was clearly illegal and in any other part of the country called counterfeiting, Alaska was a long way from Washington D. C. and the Secret Service had better things to do than slap the wrists of merchants in the Arctic who were wheeling and dealing with $30 or $40 worth of bingles.

But Archie was dealing with quite a bit more than $40 or $50 worth of bingles. The way he viewed it, he could <u>underpay</u> with bingles that were only negotiable at his store and then <u>overcharge</u> for his goods that were bought with bingles. (Archie had no prices listed in his store so he could charge different prices to different people for the same items.) So Archie went out of his way to use the bingles in lieu of cash as much as possible. When he had his jukebox working in the Kotzebue Grille, he was charging a nickel a song. Pretty soon he had all the nickels in town and he replaced them with bingles. Another scam he worked with bingles was offering to pay the Inupiat more than any other fur trader for their furs. After they made the commitment to sell to Archie, he paid them in bingles.

But the story of Archie's profiteering went deeper than just a skim on the bingles. Archie was regularly selling goods he got for free. Each year he would go to Seattle and make a purchase of $50,000 or more for groceries, hardware and supplies and pay with a check. The merchandise would be loaded on one of the ships headed north and that would be the last contact that merchant had with Archie. Archie never honored his bills and dodged collectors and legal writs for years. When Harold Little was buying food and supplies for his construction projects in the Arctic in the 1950s, he found wholesale grocer after grocer in Seattle who had been stung by Archie. Everybody knew Archie, Little remembered. One at a time he had burned them all.

Thus, when Archie confided to Burleigh Putnam that "If you didn't make a 100 percent markup on your trade goods you were crazy," it would be fair to say that Archie knew what he was talking about. Except Archie had figured an even better rule: sell all your goods for twice what they would have cost you if you had paid for them in the first place. Archie's store was also full of canned goods that were hardly top of the line in the Lower 48, like #3 green beans, canned figs and okra. Archie probably received cut rates for these slow-moving food items and then foisted them off in the Arctic on his captive clientele.[163]

When it came to dealing with the Inupiat, Archie was just as under-handed as with whites. This was a game he had been playing for a long time. He'd hire Inupiats to work and then pay them in credit at his store. Or pay them in bingles. Sometimes he didn't pay them at all. But many of the Inupiat didn't seem to mind. Wayne Hawley from Kivalina was working for Archie on The Eskimo Building and Ray Heinrichs asked him why he didn't quit because he wasn't getting paid.

"'Archie never pays me,'" Hawley complained loudly, "'but I sure like to work for him.'"

On the flip side of the coin, people tried to skin Archie as well and occasionally they did. For a while Archie was collecting copper from around Kotzebue and selling it for scrap in Fairbanks. Actually, Archie was looking for a product that he could back haul with his barges. His barges would come north loaded with merchandise but had to go south empty. Taking the copper south was his way of making money off scrap in Kotzebue. There was quite a bit of copper lying around at the time because the ACS site was being built and all the copper tubing that was not used was just tossed aside. Archie, smelling a profit, hired children to collect copper scraps for which he paid a pittance. One child, Al Adams, figured a way to get the propeller and drive shaft off Archie's boat and sold it as scrap.[164] [Al Adams later became a legislator and for years was the highest-paid lobbyist in Juneau.]

But some of the children were smarter than Archie. They would sell him a handful of copper and wait for him to put the scraps in storage in his old warehouse next to Hanson's store. As soon as Archie locked the door, the kids would worm their way into the building, steal the copper they had just sold Archie and then re-sell it to him.[165] Archie was not pleased when he discovered the scam but undoubtedly had a good laugh over it.

Archie himself was not above outright larceny. Until the 1950s, he owned a generator and turned it off and on as he pleased. Since he got up early, about 4 am, he went to bed early. When Archie went to bed, usually about 9 pm, everyone had to go to bed because that was when he shut off the generator. It was either sleep or sit in the dark.

One evening there was an uproar at the ACS site when it was discovered that Archie had surreptitiously attached his electrical wires to the ACS's system. While everyone in Kotzebue was paying Archie for the power he was supposedly generating, it appears that a certain amount of that power was actually being produced by the United States government. Archie swore he didn't know anything about the errant wire and claimed it must have been put up by someone working for him. Nobody believed him but there wasn't much that anyone could do about the theft. In all fairness it should be pointed out that the ACS site did allow some people to use the power from the government installation but that was for lighting and heat, not for running several businesses <u>and</u> charging for electrical services not rendered.

Archie's personal life changed significantly after the Second World War. After a bitter confrontation with his wife, Hadley, on June 19, 1944, or so divorce papers claimed, he abandoned her.[166] Hadley left Kotzebue and returned to her parents' village of Selawik with Warren's three children. There she remained for a few years until she moved to Fairbanks. Hadley made at least one more appearance in Archie's life, on June 7, 1958. The meeting took place in the Ferguson Restaurant and became so heated that Hadley was arrested for "disorderly conduct." The charges were dismissed before the case went to trial.[167]

Once Hadley was out of the picture, Archie moved his long-time mistress, Beulah, into his apartment. He had just opened his restaurant, the Kotzebue Grille, and Beulah conveniently fit into his business life as well as his personal affairs. As the Kotzebue Grille was the only restaurant in town, Archie got the pass-through clientele as well as the business in town. Everyone, of course, had to eat. Entrepreneurially speaking, it was an ideal situation for Archie. He ran the store and Beulah ran the restaurant. The businesses were close enough that Archie could run back and forth all day, as was his habit, and keep an eye on his cash drawer and on Beulah. She was also personally close enough to Archie but not married to him which made it easy for him to shift assets from his name into her name and thus hide those assets from his creditors.

But, while Archie lived with Beulah, he felt no compunction about being faithful to her. Archie rarely resisted temptation. Beulah didn't complain when Archie went philandering because, from her point of view, what was good enough for Archie was good enough for her. Archie didn't look at it that way but there was nothing he could do about it. Whenever Beulah would disappear for a while, Archie would "go crazy" in the Kotzebue Grille, Edith Bullock remembered. Anyone coming into the restaurant would know even without talking to Archie that Beulah was out on the town. Customers could see a string of half-empty coffee cups stretching down the counter denoting that the ego-wounded Archie had drunk half a cup, left it on the counter while he went to see if he could find Beulah, returned, got another cup of coffee, left again *ad infinitum*.[168]

In addition to its reputation for having incredibly tasty reindeer steaks, the Kotzebue Grille also had the only ice cream machine in the Arctic – for a while. Archie found an ice cream machine in Seattle and had it sent to Kotzebue where he made a killing selling ice cream to the Inupiat. In fact, he was making so much money that he had the machine working overtime and still the demand for ice cream continued to rise. But rather than buy another ice cream machine, Archie kept turning up the dial on the machine. While Archie had read "Do Not Set the Machine Above 10," he did not believe the instructions and set the machine for 15. The machine got so cold and the mixture so thick and heavy that it snapped off the mixing shaft. That was the end of ice cream in Kotzebue for years.[169]

Archie and ice cream machine courtesy of the
Southwest Museum in Los Angeles

With the end of his ice cream enterprise, there was no longer any use for the 24-door ice cream freezer Archie had purchased for his wares. So he unplugged the freezer and used it to store what records he had.[170] When Burleigh Putnam asked to see Archie's aviation logbook, Archie had to go digging through a dozen freezer drawers before he found the drawer where the log book was buried.

As far as receipts for his store were concerned, Archie used to do his accounting with a pencil on his store wall.[171] Archie also had very little use for a cash register. He once had a cash register flown in from Fairbanks, but he rarely opened it. He simply cut into the side of the machine and stuffed money in through the crack.[172]

In dealing with Archie, customers had to be prepared for anything because anything could happen. One of Archie's larger customers, a couple who been in Candle mining for a number of months, came back to Kotzebue to discover that Archie had been slipping charges against their account while they were gone. When they complained, Archie refused to listen and went so far as to garnish the husband's wages and took the family to court. The Commissioner ruled in their favor but they still had to live in the same town as Archie and at some point deal with him. After all, sooner or later everyone had to buy something from Archie.[173]

No amount of money was too small for Archie to grab. He would short-change a customer whether he thought he could get away with it or not and always "tried to wipe up your change on the counter," Erwin recalled. "Archie used to say, and these are his words, that 'It's more fun to steal a nickel than to make a dollar honestly.' Then he'd cackle in that Donald Duck laugh."[174]

Even among his friends, Archie could not be trusted. Archie was, like his brother Warren had been, a boxing enthusiast. He was such an enthusiast that one of the few things that Archie read other than *Trade-A-Plane*, the Bible for aviators looking for used aircraft, was *Ring Magazine*, a boxing magazine. He and another boxing fan, Art Fields, were looking forward to the July 28, 1952, bout between Rocky Marciano and Harry "Kid" Matthews and deciding how they were going to bet. On the day of the fight, neither man had decided where to place his money.

As the fight was about to begin, Archie suddenly decided to bet $40 on Marciano. Fields took the bet and sure enough, Marciano won. Later Fields found out that Archie had already heard the results of the fight on his airplane radio – before the fight was broadcast in Alaska.[175] Fields, a well-known guide and former city council member in the 1980s, also remembered Archie borrowing money from him. Then Archie paid Fields back in bingles. Another time, Fields ran Archie's store for 10 percent of everything that sold but Fields "never seemed to make any money."

Archie was also good at taking advantage of others misfortune if their path happened to cross his. In the summer of 1949, Graham Mower was flying into Kotzebue in a Goose when he discovered there was no place to land on the water. There were set nets everywhere so he decided to land on the runway in town. He didn't know the condition of the short runway which ran at a right angle to the main landing strip. Mower raised Archie on the radio and Archie said "Aah, that strip's real good. You won't have any trouble, go ahead and land. No problem at all."

Mower knew the runway was going to be short so he took advantage of every foot he had. He was lucky he had been cautious. "As soon as I went across the good runway, the Goose went up on its nose. There was mud all over the windshield and the wheels sank into the tundra six inches deep." Mower came out of the cockpit with murder in his eye. He stormed into Archie's store yelling "What did you tell me that runway was good for?!"

"Oh, wow," Archie whined. "I've always been wanting one of those airplanes to make a good boat."[176]

Archie was also adept at cheating insurance companies. He was, after all, in Kotzebue and the nearest insurance investigator of any kind was, at best, in Nome and more likely in Fairbanks or Anchorage. Later in life, Archie bragged that he had occasionally flown one of his planes into a remote area, walked out and claimed that his plane had crashed. After he collected the insurance money, he would retrieve his "wrecked" plane with no one the wiser.

Another insurance swindle he frequently pulled was to wait until one of his barges went ashore in a storm. Then he'd wire the insurance company to insure the barge, wait three days and then claim the barge was aground. There would be an investigation and, sure enough, the barge was found beached. Then Archie would offer to buy the barge back from the insurance company at a fraction of its real cost. Since he was the only one in the area who could retrieve it and thus the only one making the offer, the insurance companies usually took his bid.[177]

While Archie may have been a master con man, he was one other thing as well: sharp. He was sharp enough to know that he needed a good lawyer. Fortunately for Archie, he didn't have to go looking for a crafty lawyer. Fred Crane came to town.

Fred Crane was yet another of the colorful characters of the Arctic. Crane, who spent as much time seducing Native women as he did assisting men like Archie Ferguson sidestep the law, was widely regarded as one of the craftiest – if not <u>the</u> craftiest –legal mind in the Arctic. But this was not his standout characteristic.

If someone had to describe Fred Crane in a few words, most people who knew him would say he was either "crafty" or "drunk." He was both. At each he was a master.

Fred Crane, MOST HIGH LOUNGE LIZARD, 1945,
courtesy of the Anchorage Museum

Disbarred for life in the late 1930s for drinking his way through several trust funds, none of them his own, he spent the next 20 years searching for gold in the Arctic. By the time he settled in Kotzebue, he had lived in every community in the Arctic from Nome to Demarcation Point on the Canadian border with the exception of Barrow, a community he claimed to dislike intensely.

Crane was the most unlikely of frontier lawyers. He came from a very unusual family in which his father, a close relative of Senator William Borah of Idaho, had maintained three, concurrent careers as a lawyer, banker and miner. The family was very political and Fred grew up in a world where political connections were just a handshake away.

Crane's introduction to the law came early. As a young man in 1907 he watched his father assist William Borah, not yet a Senator, prosecute William "Big Bill" Haywood along with Charles H. Moyers and George A. Pettibone for conspiracy to assassinate the former Governor of Idaho, Frank Steuneberg. The man who had initially confessed to the murder, Harry Orchard, claimed that he had done it on orders from "Big Bill" Haywood. Clarence Darrow was the defending attorney and while Orchard went to prison, Haywood and the other defendants were found not guilty.

Intent on becoming a lawyer, Crane received his degree from Cumberland University in Lebanon, Tennessee. He was licensed on December 7, 1915, and began building a practice with the mining companies in Idaho. But the tide of world events was against him. America entered the First World War and Crane served as an officer in France. When he returned to Idaho, Crane began where he left off and established himself as an attorney of no mean qualifications. The highlight of his legal career in the Lower 48 was his appearance before the United States Supreme Court to successfully argue the "Law of the Apex" case which established that the highest claim on the mineral vein had the right to excavate and extract all the minerals even if those minerals were in someone else's claim. Maintaining his political ties, through now-Senator Borah, Crane attended the Republican National Convention in 1920 that nominated Warren G. Harding.

Greed getting the better of him, he abandoned his law practice in 1924 and sank his entire fortune, $100,000, into an oil well in Eastern Montana. Prospects for a gusher looked so good that a larger company offered to buy him out. Crane turned them down because he believed he would find the bonanza the next day. With the dawn did come a gusher but, unfortunately, the liquid was salt water, not oil.

Flat broke, Crane headed back home. On the way he met Senator Borah in Butte, Montana, and asked for a job. Borah told him that the only patronage job at his disposal was the Assistant Federal Prosecutor in

Fairbanks, Territory of Alaska. "Any port in the storm," remarked Fred who borrowed enough money from Borah to make it north.[178]

In Alaska, Crane served with distinction and was able to quickly ferret out culprits who were stealing money from the United States mail. "Sums of $30,000 and $40,000 were disappearing from mail bags, being replaced with magazines and other forms of bulk material," the newspapers of the era disclosed. But talent was not a determining factor in staying employed with the Federal government and, in 1932, when FDR, a Democrat, was elected, Crane, a Republican, was out of a job once again.

He spent the next three years living "high, wide and handsome," as he said of this era of his life, until his alcoholism got the better of him. "He always told me," recalled C. R. Kennelly, an old law partner of Crane's, "that it was someone else's fault that he got suspended, that [he was] blamed [because this other lawyer, then dead, had] not cover[ed] something. Then [Crane] got suspended for it. He'd paid another lawyer to cover it and the lawyer didn't." While that may be true, the fact still remains, as Erwin reported, Crane "used money out of his trust funds and was disbarred for life."

For the next 25 years Crane wandered the Arctic, mining and drinking. Sometimes living in a whalebone and sod hut and other times in a tent, Crane learned to speak Inupiat and developed a network of friends – white and Inupiat – across the Arctic. He made very little money and was so broke that in 1941 he slipped out on a hotel bill in Anchorage and had to be arrested telephonically.[179]

By the time Crane moved to Kotzebue, he was well-known in Alaska's legal circles. Anyone who wanted to start a business in the Arctic knew of Crane and put him on retainer immediately. That was considered a business expense because "it was better to have Fred <u>with</u> you than against you." Even the City of Nome had him on retainer – for $50 a month.[180]

While he could not <u>practice</u> legally – which did not stop him from portraying himself as a practicing attorney – Crane was excellent at working with a jury. Not only did he know all the fine points of being before a jury, there were few juries in the Arctic which did not include his friends or relatives. One time, Erwin remembered, a woman on a jury was asked if she knew the defendant or any of the others in the room. "Only Fred Crane," she said and admitted that she had not seen him since the time she lived with him for three years.

His courtroom presence was stunning. Bob Erwin remembered that Crane "knew a thousand tricks and would reveal them one at a time." It didn't bother Crane to come over after the trial and give the young Erwin a few pointers. "He would talk to me and tell me what I did wrong or how I could have improved my presentation. I and [and many other young Alaskan attorneys] learned quite a lot from Fred."

To have called Fred Crane crafty would have been a gross understatement of the man's talent. Not only did he have a firm grasp of the law, he also had a quick wit and a superb sense of timing. Once, while defending Art Fields in Kotzebue on a charge of bootlegging, the prosecutor noted that Fields had been caught with the "tool" of his trade, i.e., a bottle of booze. Crane snapped at the Commissioner that Fields should be charged with rape as well because "he has the tool for that too."[181]

Crane's reputation with the ladies and the law was well established by the time he moved to Kotzebue in the early 1950s. He always had a "bevy of teenage girls," the Baptist Minister recalled, that were living with him.[182] Bush pilot Ray Hawk remembered the one time he was in Fred's house with some homebrew he found "half a dozen young girls in there, from 13 to 16 or 17. They apparently lived there when they wanted to. Their attitude was kind of like when you have nothing to do, you go to Fred's place."[183]

"K" Doyle said that Fred "must have really loved" the woman he was living with because his honey bucket was in a peach crate with a carved seat.[184] Little did she know that she should have referred to Fred's "woman" as "women." Edith Bullock said she never went to Fred's apartment in Kotzebue because she was "afraid of what she might walk in on."

But rumors are a far cry from the truth. It was widely reported and possibly true that Crane had "many, many children" though the most frequently used number, "500," is probably widely exaggerated. When Crane was older and asked about his sexual prowess, he replied candidly that "if I had done half of what people are saying I've done I'd have to have found a fountain of youth somewhere."

Crane was still a heavy drinker in Kotzebue but by the mid-1950s his body was no longer as forgiving. He could no longer drink continuously and when he went on a bender, "every six months or so," it was one for the record books.[185] Harold Little, who kept the books for Crane in Kotzebue for years remembers many times when he had to fly to Nome or Fairbanks and pick Fred up from a bender.

But for all the negative comments of Crane, one of his greatest attributes was his compassion for the Inupiat. He never made a lot of money as a lawyer but this did not dissuade him from defending Inupiat who could never pay him back. This was fortunate for most Inupiat defendants did not understand the court system and Crane, as later Federal Judge von der Heydt noted, "made a lot of decisions as a lawyer that ordinarily would have been made in consultation with a client."[186]

He was also incredibly crafty, noted polar guide Ken Oldham. When he had the Game Warden on the stand, under oath, he asked him if he was going to be back in the spring. The question was significant since everyone in Kotzebue looked forward to spring and the return of the ducks. All that stood between the first fresh meat in eight months and many Kotzebue residents, some of them on the jury, was the Game Warden. By asking of the Game Warden's whereabouts in the spring, Crane was moving the jury in the defendant's favor and, at the same time, letting everyone know where the Game Warden was going to be in spring. If the Game Warden had said "No," and then showed up, it could have led to legal ramifications which, no doubt, Fred Crane would have exploited fully.

Joiner, too, understood what spring meant to the Inupiat and on the front page of his June 9, 1951, edition of the *Mukluk Telegraph*, he wrote a warning, translated from Inupiat:

> *"The Kotzebue-based Game Warden is observing the taking of birds from Nome north. [He is doing it] there because everyone is in need of food. It is the Native [who are] especially are targeted. There is talk of taxing the taking of animals."*[187]

Everyone was hunting ducks. Even Archie. But with Archie, as usual, it led to hilarious results.

Archie and Walter "Blank" Blankenship were illegally hunting ducks near Kiana when the game warden stopped for an inspection. First the warden went into Rotman's to re-inform the residents that duck hunting in the spring was illegal.

Archie and Blank spotted the warden before he entered Blankenship's store and quickly tossed their gunny sacks full of ducks under the bed. The game warden came into Blankenship's backroom and proceeded to lecture the two men on the illegality of duck hunting in the spring. Unbeknownst to Archie and Blank, one of the ducks they thought they had killed was actually only stunned. It came back to its senses in a bag full of its dead brethren and proceeded to wiggle its way out of the bag. Just as the Game Warden was finishing his lecture, out from under the bed waddled the disoriented mallard.

There was dead silence for a moment and then Archie remarked casually, "That's my pet duck."[188]

Archie Ferguson and Fred Crane were like peas in a pod. They got along famously. "Fred, in one way, was as much of an anarchist as Archie was," Bob Erwin recalled. "He had never seen the organized way of doing things [to be of any value] and that was probably one of the reasons that he and Archie got along so well."

For the next decade, Fred Crane and Archie devised a series of interlocking yet independent corporations. Using Crane as his mastermind, Archie came up with legal stumbling blocks to collection that would be a marvel even today. With his corporations in place, Archie felt he would never have trouble with the IRS. Paraphrased, he once told Fred Goodwin that "it takes the IRS a year to penetrate a corporation and I have enough corporations to keep them busy as long as I'm alive."

But Archie's scheme was not foolproof. He succeeded primarily because he was usually dealing with people less shrewd than he was. Archie could be taken but it was difficult. But Harold Little was shrewd too and, in the tradition of the classical sting where the victim never knows when he's been taken, Archie went to his grave never knowing that he'd been snookered by Harold Little.

In the mid-1950s, Little realized that there was a need for a hotel in Kotzebue. While several so-called hotels were operating – Archie's, Rotman's and Wien's – none of them was a real hotel. (Wien also had a hotel for its passengers – primarily because Wien had learned the hard way about doing business with Archie.) Little decided to take a chance and open a hotel in Kotzebue, which later became the Arctic Inn. He knew he could rent rooms to polar bear hunters during the winter and tourists coming up on Wien and Alaska Airlines during the summer.

But he had a problem. Since he would have to build the hotel on a shoestring, it was going to take him a number of years to complete the project. This would not have been difficult in any other community, but in Kotzebue he had to contend with Archie. The minute Archie thought someone else was making a dollar on anything, Archie would try to crowbar his way into the deal. If Archie knew that Harold Little was building a hotel, Archie would build one right next door. Archie could build his structure cheaper because he could con the lumber out of a lumberyard in the Lower 48, or he could just steal the building.

Archie was remarkably adept at stealing buildings. But he did not steal a building in the sense that he found an abandoned building and absconded with it one timber at a time. He stole buildings in the sense that he would find a collection of structures in a remote location, like along the Aleutians or at Port Clarence where there was an abandoned United States Army Air Corps base, and dismantle all of them. Like a William Randolph Hearst operation – but on a much smaller scale – Archie would pull buildings apart as if they were pre-fab homes, stack the walls and roofs on his barge, and float them to Kotzebue. In his career he had stolen, in the words of Harold Little, "dozens of them." Willie Hensley believes that the number of buildings he stole was more likely around 30.

Probably the largest buildings Archie ever moved was the Federal Building in Nome. He put money down to buy the structure, took it apart and loaded it onto a barge. On the way to Kotzebue, a storm came up and the barge went down. Shortly thereafter, what was left of the structure in Nome burned. Harold Herning, who knew Archie well for decades, believed that Archie made the initial payment but "never paid anything else after that."

Fearful that Archie could steal his way to a hotel faster than Little could build one legitimately, Little slyly suggested to Archie that he build the "largest building in the Arctic." Little knew full well that Archie would probably like the idea but it would take him at least two, maybe three seasons to complete the structure. By that time, his Arctic Inn would be completed.

The first year Archie put in the foundation with the help of Harold Herning. While Archie claimed for years that the structure had been built from "plans drawn on the back of a sheet of cardboard"—and Archie was usually quick to produce the cardboard – he did have help at least in the construction of the foundation.

Once the foundation was completed, Archie set steel girders to provide an anchor for the walls and cross beams to support the second floor. However, while the second floor was supposed to have been secured with steel girders, the girders Archie used could not reach across the entire width of the structure. Archie solved this problem unconventionally by welding one end of the support girder to an upright and then using a wooden beam to bridge the gap between the end of the short support girder and the upright on the other side of the building.[189]

Just as Little had anticipated, Archie didn't put a dime in the building. Some of the wood that went into the structure was booty from a raid on Port Clarence. The rest came from a lumber yard in Seattle whose invoice Archie neglected to pay. But it took Archie years to complete the building, almost a decade as Willie Hensley remembered. "Everyone in Kotzebue who could pound a nail worked on that building," he said, and, as both Bullock and Heinrichs commented wryly, "not many of them got paid."

Though the outside of the structure was weather-proof, the inside was extremely cold. That was because Archie did not bother to put in much insulation. What insulation Archie did use was poorly installed and dangled from the ceiling. Other insulation was a bit more unconventional. Edith Bullock recalled watching Archie shoving hay into the wall.[190] Harold Herning remembered that Archie brought a barge load of sand from the Kobuk Sand Dunes which he used for insulation.

But, to Archie's credit, he used virtually all Inupiat labor. He didn't pay all the Inupiat labor, but it was nonetheless one of the largest building in the Arctic (96' x 125') and possibly the largest building ever constructed with Inupiat labor up to that time. Since it was in the Arctic and put up by Inupiat labor, Archie christened the Arctic skyscraper "The Eskimo Building." When it was completed, the buildings' upstairs was dedicated to apartments. Archie didn't construct a hallway, in the sense that someone could walk down a corridor past doors indicating empty rooms. Rather, he constructed apartments as needed. When a renter went upstairs, it was like an open loft with apartments set along the sides.

The largest apartment, naturally, was Archie's. It had a bedroom in the back and a huge living room with a "livid orangy rug." The main room was vacant except for a "huge, sexy S-shaped sofa" that was a "purple color." Archie loved to pace and at least one person was amused to watch Archie pace back and forth across his spacious living room with a 30-foot cord on his electric razor dictating to his secretary, Marge Bogard. The sofa did not stop Archie pacing; as he crossed the room, he just stepped up and over it.[191]

Gordon Osborne, who headed the first bank in Kotzebue, and his wife Alice lived upstairs in The Eskimo Building and remembered that they could peek through the cracks in the floorboards to the pool hall downstairs. The sound of the jukebox pierced the plywood easily and kept the Osbornes awake until midnight when the generator was turned off. (Alice Osborne remembered that Archie was not using his generators by the time she and Gordon lived in The Eskimo Building. At that time, all power in Kotzebue came from the REA and Archie was the largest user of electrical power. But Archie was Archie, and he would start up his generators from time to time as a "threat to REA that he might cut them off.")

For heating, Archie installed a network of heating ducts through which hot air was supposed to circulate. This did not occur because Archie never turned on the heat. Archie also had an escape pipe for the grease and steam from the stove in the kitchen. But this pipe could be used for other purposes as well. Since this pipe started right over the stove, in the mornings Gordon Osborne would walk out into the open loft area, open up the escape duct, stick his head inside and yell down to the cook to order breakfast. On those days when the cook came to work with a crashing hangover, Gordon, prankster that he was, would lower a large plastic spider down the pipe so that the arachnid would suddenly appear before the swimming eyes of the cook sweating over the hot stove.

When Gordon complained about the coldness of the building, Archie said he would turn on the heat. After the heat had allegedly been turned on, Archie placed a calendar in front of the heating duct whereupon the paper gave a little flutter.

"Maann, look at the heat coming out of that," Archie said with an impish smile.

"Archie," snapped Gordon. "The only thing that's ever come out of that was a cat!"[192] This was true. The only other perceived use for the duct system was to provide Archie's cat, Hercules, a way to prowl around inside the building. Hercules was adept at traveling in this manner and wandered in and out of apartments at will.

Upstairs, the insulation was so poor that condensation gathered in the attic and dripped into the upstairs rooms. Mary Oldham, who spent 11 polar bear seasons – from January to May – in The Eskimo Building routinely tacked Visqueen from corner to corner on the ceiling. One corner was lower than the others so the drips ran into the sink. All night long she and her children could hear the steady drip-drip of water falling onto the plastic and, regularly, a cascade into the sink. Another clear memory she had of The Eskimo Building was the rusty water. "You were cleaner before a shower than after," she recalled.

The Eskimo in 1945 courtesy of the Alaska and Polar Regions Dept, UAF

On the ground floor were four establishments: Archie's store, the post office, the Midnight Sun Theater and, in the back, a pool hall. The pool hall was a gathering place for the community and, like many other of Archie's operations, it was slip-shod. State Trooper Ed Dankworth, who spent some time in Kotzebue in the early 1960s, had vivid recollections of the pool hall. "These guys were playing with two or three balls missing, the pool cues didn't have any tips," he recalled, "and the felt [on the tables] was all ratty."

The best definition of Archie's store – his original store in a separate building and the newer one in The Eskimo Building – came from former Governor Jay Hammond. "Archie's store was a lot like Archie," he said. "It was dark and dingy and there was stuff piled all over the place. It was organized chaos."

But Archie did take full advantage of his role as a store owner. Not only did he made a profit on what he sold, he made certain that his family had those special food items they craved. Archie's adopted son Frank was known by his nickname as "Bananas" because he raided every Ferguson plane that came to Kotzebue for bananas, eating the fruit in the plane rather than sharing it.

Archie liked watermelons but he loved tuna fish. Ed Yost remembered that Archie kept his tuna fish under lock and key. "He was a real nut about canned tuna fish and he had it in the basement locked up. If he really liked you, after dinner in the evening he'd go down and open up a can of tuna fish and share it with you. But he wouldn't sell it in the store."

But the talk of the town and Territory was Archie's Midnight Sun Theater. Originally, before Archie had completed construction of The Eskimo Building, the theater had been across the street in an old cold storage building the government had once used in Candle for storing reindeer carcasses.[193] That building had been a fire trap. In addition to its tinderbox walls and ceiling, the theater's single **Emergency Exit** opened up to a 20-foot drop out of the back of the building. Archie operated the older theater for almost a decade before he moved it into The Eskimo Building.

The origin of Archie's movie-making venture was both hilarious and vintage Archie. Just before Warren died, Archie was in Seattle on a buying trip and he saw his first cowboy movie. He was so thrilled with the silver screen that right in the middle of the presentation he went up to the projection booth and offered to buy the projector right out of the theater. The theater manager, who thought Archie was a bit daffy, refused to sell him the projector but did point him in the direction of a theater supply company. There Archie purchased – promising he would pay for – a projector and a screen.[194] He rented a large collection of films which included every cowboy movie he could get his hands on along with a generator for the projector and headed north.

When it came to films, everyone agreed that Archie's were the best in the Territory. In fact, his were better than those being shown in Seattle. Archie spared no expense in getting top-of-the-line films as soon as they were available, often renting them from major film companies if necessary. But Archie was just as mischievous in his dealings with the film houses and production companies as he was with grocers and lumber yards – long on promises and short on cash. One winter he went south and rented a large load of Disney films by promising the rental company that the films would be back "on the next boat." What they did not know was that the "next boat" out of Kotzebue would not be until a year later.[195]

While Archie's library of films was admirable, his equipment was less than satisfactory. The quality of the movies was good but Archie only had one projector and the movie would stop whenever a reel had to be changed. Sometimes the sound worked and the picture didn't or the picture worked and the sound didn't. If there was trouble with the machine, Archie would immediately close the theater down and tell everyone to come back the next night.

Sometimes, when everything was working perfectly, the entire show would be stopped if Archie didn't like the movie. "Stop the damn film! Bring in another one!" he'd yell and Sam Shafsky and Ed Yost would go looking for another film.

Archie was the one who chose the movie for the evening and he usually made the decision at the last moment. There wasn't a marquee so there was no reason to be in a rush to make a decision. For the audience it was potpourri. Dr. Neilson remembered stopping Archie on the streets of Kotzebue on a couple of occasions asking about the movie that would be showing that evening.

"Hey, Archie. What's runnin' in the movie tonight?"

Archie would answer. "I dunno. But whatever it is, it's a good one."

Even with spotty performance of the projector, the movies gave Kotzebue Inupiat and whites a glimpse of the outside world many had never seen. Sometimes what they saw amazed them. Ida Evern, whose father, "Blank" Blankenship, ran a trading post in Kiana, remembered seeing Bud Costello eating "a crunchy thing." Later, when she went to Fairbanks, she discovered it was celery.

To get the highest possible attendance, Archie would shut down his store when it was time to run the show. He also increased attendance by putting the rows of seats so close to each other that when a large man sat down, he felt as though he were "a pretzel."[196] Sam Shafsky and Ed Yost ran the projector while Archie took the ticket money, a muskrat skin, a mukluk sole or $1.[197] Archie also sold popcorn in the theater which he loaded with salt so the Inupiat would "buy more pop."[198]

Even though he loved watching movies, Archie wasn't any better with the mechanical devices of the theater than he was with aviation equipment. One night he went out to check the generator, the "Disel," [Di-sul], he called it. He stuck the dipstick in while the engine was running and thought the oil was a little low. So he just grabbed the nearest jar of something and poured it in. Then he realized that he had poured a jar of sulfuric acid for the battery into the oil tank. The moment he realized he had made a mistake, he came running back into the theater yelling "Stop the movie! Stop the movie! I've dumped acid in the disel and she's all corrided!" [Core-rid-ded.][199]

Archie didn't heat the theater any better than he heated the rest of the building. He felt it didn't need to be heated and, to a certain extent he was right. During the summer the problem was cooling, not heating; and in the winter, everyone was wearing parkas.

But there was another problem during the winter. The clouds of vapor from peoples' breath rose until it froze on the plywood ceiling and sheets of insulation that were hanging down. Then, as the temperature in the theater heated up, the slick of ice on the ceiling began to melt until it, quite literally, rained inside.[200]

The warmth also brought another problem. As the temperature rose, all of the smells associated with living in the Arctic began to fill the room. During the winter when no one was bathing regularly, the combined smells of dried fish, seal oil, unwashed bodies, poorly scraped parka skins tanned with human urine[201], bad breath and a host of other odorous sources made the theater a shock to the senses of visitors. Graham Mower, who was flying for Fish and Wildlife in 1949, recalled that Archie invited him to the movie theater in a "reserved seat." This special seat turned out to be the top stair of the walkway up to the projector room. But the room was so "hot and stinky

I never did see the movie," Mower recalled. "I got out of there, I was suffocating! And[Archie] laughed about that. It thought it was a big joke."[202]

Archie, never satisfied with only the money he was making, was forever on the lookout for other enterprises. For a while he even tried to profit from one of the most dangerous enterprises in the Arctic: polar bear guiding. Hoping to attract well-heeled clients from the Lower 48, Archie began running advertisements in the *Alaska Sportsman,* the forerunner of *Alaska Magazine.* But Archie did more than just promise a good hunt, he *guaranteed* every hunter a polar bear along with a dog team to bring in the carcass.[203]

While an Archie Ferguson guarantee was worth the paper it was written on, a dog team to bring in the carcass was laughable. First, not a lot of whites or Inupiat ate polar bear so there was no reason to return with the carcass. Second, hunters brought back only the polar bear pelt and skull, the latter a requirement for the United States Department of Fish and Game. Even the largest polar bear pelt could be pulled into the smallest of bush planes. The dog team concept looked good on paper but, in reality, there was really nothing of substance being offered.

Third, and most important, polar bear hunting was one of the most dangerous sports in the world. Hunters are flown scores of miles across a barren ice where the temperatures get up to 20 degrees below zero during the day. When the hunters spot a bear they land and wait for the bear to come to them. (Polar bears do not have to be stalked in the traditional sense of the word.)

But there are dangers. Polar bears move very quickly, even on the ice. They weigh up to 1,200 pounds and have been known to attack humans – or anything else. Ken Oldham once watched as a boar attack his airplane with the engine running! A wounded bear was unpredictable and if the hunter did not deliver a fatal shot, the animal could destroy the hunter's airplane before it died. If the hunting party only had a single plane, damage to that plane could prove to be fatal. (Polar bear guides quickly learned to fly in pairs of airplanes.)

Archie's first foray into the world of big game hunting was disastrous. Flying over the ice with an Inupiat, Herman Tickett, the two men spotted a large bear and landed for the kill. But as the bear got closer and closer – and larger and larger – Archie lost his nerve and jumped into his plane. He revved the engine and began to take off. Tickett, quite concerned that he would be left on the ice alone with a hungry behemoth bearing down on him, leaped onto the plane's skis just as the aircraft passed him. The plane lifted off with a frightened Archie looking to put as much snow and ice between himself and the polar bear as possible and Tickett clutching the aircraft's ski strut for dear life.[204]

Archie and his Bearskin

With such a start, Archie's career as a professional polar bear hunter was not destined to be long. He guided three or four different hunters but never made any money. It was hard to hunt with one airplane and Archie learned why the hard way. In March of the next year, 1947, he went down on the ice with his client, Dr. Wedel, and the two men remained on the ice for three or four days. Seventy planes spent three days looking for Archie before he was finally found 40 miles north of Kotzebue.[205] This experience apparently extinguished Archie's ambition to become a polar bear hunter.

Archie also concentrated on furs: but in the flat, not the round. After all, there was a profit to be made. The fur business, which had been established in the Arctic more than 100 years earlier by the Russians, was well-established. Fur buyers came north regularly where they would buy from anyone who had furs. Usually they ended up buying from merchants across the Arctic who had taken the furs in for credit. Archie, like the other merchants, dealt in furs for which he traded with Inupiat and other times he shot the animals himself.

Dealing with the local Inupiat was easy for Archie. He overpaid for the furs in bingles and then overcharged the Inupiat in his store for the same tokens. Many whites were, understandably, hesitant to accept Archie's bingles. They, like Archie, wanted the best deal for their furs and bingles were not a good trade. Ida Evern remembers Archie talking to her father and demanding to know why Blank had sold his furs from his store in Kiana to a fur buyer instead of to Archie. When Blank said he made more money from the fur buyers, Archie went wild with anger and began cussing at Blank so vilely that Ida, then seven or eight, was appalled that anyone would say such things about her father. In a fury she attacked Archie with a broom. For years after that, whenever Archie visited Kiana, he always waited outside the store until he yelled, "Is your broom hidden, Ida?"

When it came to fur buyers, entrepreneurs who were supposed to know their own industry well, Archie was not above shenanigans. One time, Shafsky remembered, Archie flew into Siberia where he shot some local dogs. The animals had unusual fur so Archie tanned the hides and, when the fur buyers from the Lower 48 asked what these strange items were, Archie replied they were "Makuran dogs." Archie laughed heartily when the buyers left thinking they had bought the furs of an exotic Arctic animal.[206]

On and on went Archie's fiscal transgressions. With one hand he made money short-changing clients and, on the other, he was slow in paying his bills – if he paid them at all. Working for him, as Edith Bullock quickly discovered, was an ethical nightmare. Bullock originally came to Kotzebue for a month in the late 1940s to run the Wien Hotel and booking office while the regular employee took leave to have a baby. While Bullock was there, she and her husband Jack, met Archie. Archie was looking for someone to run his barges, another enterprise of the Ferguson empire, and needed someone to handle his business books. Immediately prior to coming to

Kotzebue, Jack had been a dredge master on the Solomon River and Edith, the bookkeeper for the same company.[207] Archie offered them both jobs in his empire and they accepted.

But Archie was a "terrible, terr-i-ble" boss, as Edith Bullock remembered. He kept no records and he paid no bills. When he had to pay someone, he was a skinflint. He didn't believe in contracts – signing them or following the obligations enumerated therein – and hated tape recorders. The distaste for tape records came because once he let the manager of the Candle Mine tape him and Archie, on tape, agreed to perform a certain number of specific activities. When Archie reneged and said he had never agreed to perform those functions, the manager brought out the tape and played it for him. After that, Archie stayed away from tape recorders.

In every operation, Archie was unbelievably inefficient. While Archie could promote anything and squeeze a dollar out of anyone, Edith was surprised that Archie made any money at all. He would also push his luck. If he had a pilot sitting out a spell of bad weather, Archie was always after him to "get that [plane] cranked up and get back to Kotzebue." Sometimes the pilots tried and at least one, Leo Malloy, died.[208] Other pilots just quit, as did Sam Shafsky and Ed Yost after Archie sent them after a cargo load of film in bad weather in a plane that had oil problems. They were flying an aircraft with a Challenger Whirlwind engine, a "rough son-of-a-bitch to fly," noted Shafsky. Archie had bought another film projector and load of films in Nome and was having Shafsky and Yost pack it for transport to Kotzebue. The projector was going to go in a Bellanca but Shafsky and Yost were to bring the film back first.

"Take everything out of the plane," ordered Archie, "the sleeping bags and all that bullshit (ie., the survival kit) and fill it with nothin' but films." When Shafsky protested that they would be flying with no radio, no survival kit, no snowshoes and no sleeping bags, Archie told the two of them had "nothing to worry about."

Shafsky complied and in Nome used "just about every foot of runway to get up," because the plane was so overloaded. Yost was on the films in the back because there was nowhere else for him to sit. They had not been aloft very long before Shafsky smelled "hot metal." He looked at his instruments and saw that the heat was way up and the oil pressure way down. Yost wanted to land right away, and Shafsky nixed the idea.

"And do what? Freeze to death? We don't have any sleeping bags, grub, snowshoes. We don't even have a coffee pot."

So they opted to crest a mountain ridge and head for a mine that Shafsky knew had a landing strip. They had just cleared the ridge when the engine froze. Then they were in a glide pattern. Shafsky knew he could not make the runway so he headed for a boardwalk on the far side of the machine shop where "Old Man Lee was out and he had this tub and he was stirring these dandelions to cook to use to de-worm the dogs." Lee couldn't hear the plane coming in because its motor was not running and when Shafsky hit the boardwalk, the boards jumped and knocked over the tub. "Where the did you come from?" yelled a shaken Lee.

"Just the other side of the machine shop," shot back Shafsky.

When the Shafsky and Yost got back to Nome, they wired Archie that they had resigned. Shafsky finished the telegram with the words, "I'm tired of flying out and walking back." (Archie kept that telegram on his wall for years.)

But Archie paid those pilots who put up with him very well. They were the only people he paid consistently and without hesitation. He kept his cash in a "big old electric razor case" he always had in his pocket and over-paid his pilots, Yost recalled. "Archie's pilots were the best paid up there." Shafsky agreed, "We were the highest-paid pilots in the Territory."

But with everyone else, Archie was a skinflint. And he was crooked. So crooked it didn't take long for Edith Bullock to have second thoughts about working for Archie. "I didn't do [Archie's bookkeeping] very long because I couldn't go along with some of the things that he expected me to do," she said.

Though Jack Bullock lasted longer, he was appalled by the condition of Archie's barges, the quality of his Inupiat workers, the lack of commitment to quality service and the poor products being sold as top-of-the-line goods. He was also livid with rage when Archie failed to follow through on his verbal commitment to provide Jack with a portion of the profits.

When Archie didn't pay the profit-sharing he had promised and then even denied he had made the promise, Jack became more than enraged. A bull of a man with his strength enhanced by his anger, Jack Bullock seized Archie by his shirt and threatened to throw him out the window of the office in the back of Archie's store. A quivering Archie paid what he had promised, but neither Jack nor Edith would work for him after that. (Jack

Bullock was strong enough to lift full 55 gallon drums of gasoline into his pickup alone.[209])

Jack Bullock and Edith Bullock from Edith Bullock Collection

Jack and Edith both realized that there was a fortune to be made in the lighterage business. They were correct. Almost all cargo came north by ship, from match sticks to gasoline. But it was not a year-round enterprise and timing had to be precise. There were only a limited number of days each year when the Bering Sea was ice-free. For this reason, most maritime companies would not insure ships that were headed north of the Aleutians before June 15th or planned on being in the Bering Sea after September 15th. The further north the ship's destination, the shorter still were the time constraints for insurance purposes.

Where Archie was making his money – and where Jack and Edith decided to compete against him head-on – was in the lighterage end of the maritime industry. None of the cargo ships could approach any closer than about 12 miles from Kotzebue because of the shallowness of Kotzebue Lagoon. Thus all cargo had to be off loaded into shallower draft barges and then barged to its final destination.

For more than a decade, Archie had a monopoly on the lighterage business and not only did he gouge for his services, he and his employees engaged in an ongoing campaign of unmitigated pilferage of goods. Exotic foods like "mixed nuts or mushrooms or mandarin oranges" regularly disappeared. Boxes were opened and their contents rifled. Complaints did no good. Finally, in an attempt to see that some of the specialty foods actually made their destination, wholesale houses in the Pacific Northwest began packing the delicacies "inside other boxes labeled soap or sauerkraut."

Not much care was given in the protection of food being shipped either. Marvin Warbelow and his wife, a schoolteacher, were living in Shungnak at the time, and had ordered some celery. By the time the vegetable arrived, it had gone through so many freezings and thawings that it was nothing but mush. When Marvin reached for the erstwhile vegetable, "he could put his hand straight through it from top to bottom without touching much of anything solid."[210]

With backing from Louis Rotman, Jack and Edith started B&R (Bullock & Rotman) in 1951, with "three cents pocket money and $100,000 in hock" and went head-to-head with Archie. They offered superior service – which was not hard considering the service that Archie was offering – and did not pilfer goods. They were also less expensive than Archie. Gradually they squeezed Archie out of the lighterage business. Eventually they bought him out. (Because of the Bullock's success in the lighterage business, Edith was dubbed the "Tugboat Queen of Alaska.")[211]

The Bullocks were also able to use Archie's lack of business sense to their advantage. One summer Archie loaded a barge poorly and it turned turtle in a small river. All of the light cargo was saved but a bulldozer sank to the bottom and could not be salvaged. Jack and Edith thought they could recover it and Archie quickly sold it to them for $50 "as is where is." Right after Archie sold the machinery, Jack got Doc Rabeau drunk and both men jumped off the Bullock barge into the chilly water and lashed chains onto the submerged bulldozer. Then, while the men shivered on deck, the machinery was pulled laboriously winched aboard. The water didn't appear to have done any harm as the bulldozer was a fixture around Kotzebue for the next two decades "and might be running still."[212]

Then Archie also moved into the cargo transport business. His best-known tug was the **Kotzebue of Nome**, an interesting name, which had been built in Bellingham, Washington. The barge headed north during the ice-free season of 1951 with 400 drums of oil from Standard Oil on board but, unfortunately, the tug had started too late in the year. Shortly before it could reach Kotzebue, it was captured by the ice. The captain was able to get the barge ashore but by that time the barge was filling with water, which subsequently froze, causing the hull to "bust inside."

Once on shore, it stayed for years until it was finally caught by a slab of shore ice and pulled out to sea. Art Fields was the last American to see the **Kotzebue of Nome**. It was 60 miles from Kivalina, headed for Siberia where it is undoubtedly resting today. Ironically, for all of his maritime business, Archie was not comfortable on the water. Quoted in the *Ketchikan Alaska Chronicle* when the ship was built, Archie told a Seattle paper that he didn't trust boats. "If I can't fly, I'll stay home."[213]

At the height of his fortune, Archie had a handful of barges which he used to haul cargo and mail as well as to steal buildings and assorted other goods. Vincent Doran remembered Archie's antics well. Working as Project Manager for Morrison-Knudsen (MK) in 1953, Doran was finishing up the construction of the United States Air Force ACWS stations at Cape Romanzof, Tin City and Cape Lisburne. Archie had approached Doran in Seattle the winter before and offered to barge MK's equipment and supplies north. Doran didn't know better at the time and agreed to Archie's price and authorized the shipment of enough freight to finish up the construction for the three stations.

Next summer, when the barge finally made it into Cape Romanzof, Doran was appalled at what he saw. Archie had gone to a number of other companies for cargo and had overloaded his barge to the point that it was "almost ready to sink." The cargo was stacked so high that when a headwind became strong, it actually blew the barge backwards. The crew was made up of landlubbers and composed entirely of men off Seattle's Skid Road.

The lamentable condition of this barge and its crew was not unusual for Archie. Frank Irick, a maritime businessman, remembered a time when he sold Archie two 1,200-pound anchors in Dutch Harbor. "I went out to that barge and, the only thing holding that thing together were cockroaches and termites. I wouldn't have had anything to eat [on board where I had been invited for dinner.] If there had been an inspector there that barge never would have sailed." It should come as no surprise that Archie never paid for these anchors.

Doran should have been so lucky. It took him a while to find what Archie had pilfered. "It was [not until] sometime later that we found out that half of the insulation was missing. The son-of-a-bitch stole our insulation, had the crew steal it, see, because that's the way Archie was."

This was a critical component of the construction project because un-insulated buildings in the Arctic were useless. Getting insulation at that time of the year meant chartering a cargo plane to Nome and then barging the material back to Romanzof – an expense not in the MK's budget.

But the story of the escapade continued. When Archie's barge crew got to Nome on their way to Tin City, they refused to go any further. They had been on the water so long that they had run out of food. What money they had, they spent on liquor and got royally drunk which did not make dealing with the crew any easier. Finally Doran authorized the NC (Northern Commercial) Company to let the crew have food. Doran remembered that when he authorized food for the barge crew, NC Company officials in Nome quickly told him to put an expiration date on it that was "very soon." If Archie found out that he had credit at the NC, he would have cleaned out the store.

Several weeks later, when Archie did find out that Doran had given his men food and was going to back charge for it, Archie flew into Nome to "chew [Doran] out about it." Archie pulled Doran out of bed at about 5:30 in the morning and griped about how his men didn't need any food. They could have shot their own food. While this may not have been realistic, it was how Archie worked. Once when his boatmen in the Arctic complained about not having any food, Archie gave them a gun and some shells and said, "shoot your food."[214]

Archie did get back-charged and he didn't like it all. But he got over it. After that, Doran and Archie got along very well – so well, in fact that Archie even offered to go into business with MK on a speculative venture. While it may have been the company's lucky day that it did not go into business with Archie, his proposal was nonetheless tantalizing. What Archie suggested was an idea that still has merit today. He wanted to joint-venture with MK in transporting coal out of the Arctic. There was an old liberty ship in Seattle named the **Gadsden** which had been used to haul railroad locomotives to Europe after the Second World War. Now that the vessel had outlived its usefulness, Archie suggested that it could be converted for the transport of coal. After all, it had been reconstructed at government expense as an ore carrier, why not continue to use it as a mineral carrier?

There was one coal seam in particular that interested Archie. It was high enough above water level that the coal could be loaded onto the **Gadsden** by a "conveyor belt operated by gravity."

"Well," Doran said. "The water's only open 45 to 60 days a year. You can't make it pay in that short a period of time."

"You don't have to wait." Archie said. "I've been flying all over the Arctic Ocean for years. I see fleets of Soviet ships going in and around, never stopping, going clear north around Siberia and then going back west again [following an ice breaker.] The ice in this part of the Arctic isn't that deep." It was not a bad idea but MK wasn't interested. They were "dirt movers" then, Doran regretted, and a speculative project like that just wasn't something they would consider.

Forty years later, this idea came to the fore again. In 1992, the Arctic Slope Regional Corporation, the Native regional corporation on the North Slope, was seriously considering opening a coal mine in the Point Lay area on the Chukchi Sea. The project, called the Aluaq Mine, seems to have the numbers to make it a success. According to former Governor of Alaska Bill Sheffield, "half the coal reserves in America are in Alaska and half of Alaska's reserves are in the Arctic. There are an estimated 3 trillion tons of coal on Alaska's North Slope and 3 billion tons in the Western Arctic Coal Field alone."[215] In terms of BTUs, one ton of coal is equivalent to about four barrels of oil. Thus, in terms of energy potential, the coal on Alaska's North Slope is equivalent to 12 times the energy in all the oil fields of the world combined.[216]

Doran also remembered how Archie convinced the NC Company to lend him a D8 Cat. "Archie could con you out of your eye teeth, he was so persuasive," Doran said shaking his head, unable to understand how "a hard-headed outfit" like NC company could part with a brand new D8 Cat to someone they knew was a chiseler. Actually, there may have been a bit of greed involved. At that time Archie had a contract with the United States government to build some landing strips and to move driftwood off the beaches on the coastline in case the stretches of gravel and sand had to be used as emergency landing strips. It is quite likely that Archie cut a deal with the NC Company to use their equipment to move the driftwood and then offered a cut of the contract payment. Whether Archie ever paid or not, of course, is another story.

With the emphasis on construction after the war, Archie saw a wide range of entrepreneurial possibilities. When the Alaska Territorial Road Commission announced that it was paying $5,000 for the construction of dirt landing strips, Archie was at the front of the line. But he didn't have any heavy equipment so he cut a deal with his old friend Jim Robbins to use one of his Caterpillars. Archie agreed to do the work if Robbins would provide the equipment. It was the kind of joint venture Archie liked: he would provide the experience and someone else would provide the capital. When the project was through, it would be the other way around.

Archie showed up in Nome and talked to the Regional Commissioner of the Road Commission to convince him to authorize construction of a landing strip in Koutchak. Archie then produced a petition alleged to have been signed by the people in Koutchak requesting that a landing strip be built in their community. In actuality, the signatures were those of Inupiat in Kotzebue, a fact Archie neglected to share with the Regional Commissioner.

Also included with the petition was a statement by the doctor in Kotzebue declaring that a landing strip in Koutchak would in the best interest of the health of the residents thereof. Unmentioned by Archie was the fact that he had blackmailed the doctor into signing the request.[217] When the landing strip construction was approved, Archie went out and gathered Inupiat labor for the job and paid the men in bingles. And he charged the Inupiat to be flown to and from the construction site.

When it came to Jim Robbins' caterpillar, he put it on a barge going to Koutchak. Archie's arrangement was that he would take the D-8 on his regular lighterage run up the river and drop it off as he passed Koutchak and then pick it up on his way back – after the landing strip had been completed. The two men were to split the $5,000 evenly. So a deal was struck and Archie loaded up the D-8 and headed out.

However, Archie started the construction late in the year. The ground was so wet that the landing strip was more mud than dirt. It looked functional, but it was all mud and the D-8 tracks were filled with water were all over the strip. But Archie still needed the Commissioner to sign off on the landing strip. So Archie devised a clever scheme. He flew to Shungnak and borrowed a team of dogs from Harry Brown and used them to drag poles along the length of the runway thus smoothing it out. When the landing strip looked functional from the air, Archie radioed the Commissioner to meet him in Kotzebue. But before the director arrived, Archie had his mechanic, Peter Lazarus, bleed quite a bit of the air out of his tundra tires. By the time Archie took off, his tires were almost flat.

To collect his $5,000, the Commissioner had to make one landing and one takeoff to make sure it was functional. Archie was going to use this rule to his advantage.

"We'll go on up and land and take off, OK?" Archie said to the Commissioner.

"That's fine, Archie."

So they flew to Koutchak, circled around and Archie started to land. "It looks a little muddy out there," said the Commissioner.

"Yeah," replied Archie, "but good bottom on it, good bottom."

Archie went into final approach and started to land. Just as his flat tires touched the runway he grabbed his microphone and said, "Yeah. Yeah. I'll be right there."

Then he turned to the Commissioner and said excitedly, "I've got an emergency I've got to go into Kotzebue. That was [the doctor who Archie had blackmailed.]" The Commissioner nodded his head and Archie flew back to Kotzebue. Unbelievably, the Road Commissioner signed off on the runway. But then again, he may not have had a choice. After all, he had landed and taken off from the strip. It may have been a touch-and-go but that, technically, was a landing and a takeoff.

And Archie charged the Commissioner for his passage from Kotzebue to Koutchak and back.

At the same time, unbeknownst to his friend and joint-venture partner, Jim Robbins, Archie had submitted another petition for a landing strip at Kiana. After he had finished the strip at Koutchak, he surreptitiously loaded the D-8 onto his tug and brought it down to Kiana where he made a second landing strip. In the meantime, Robbins, who needed his D-8 in Candle, was on the radio with Archie.

"Where the cat?"

"Well," said Archie, "We had a little problem with the **Helen Lee**, Jim. But I'll get her down there. I've got to order some parts. They're on their way. How's the wife and kids?"

Four days later, Robbins had his D-8 cat back, and Archie had another field built. Robbins ended up with $2,500. Archie made $7,500 plus the profit he planned to make when the Inupiat labor brought their bingles into his store. Plus the charges flying the Inupiat back to their villages. And Archie charged the Commissioner again to check the landing strip at Kiana.[218]

Archie didn't treat the clergy any different than he treated friends. They, like everyone else, were simply plums to be picked. But with the clergy, Archie had the added pleasure of teasing. Richard Miller, the Baptist minister in Kotzebue, remembered that Archie was always saying that "he was going to be a Baptist." Miller kept telling Archie that before he could become a Baptist he had to "join the Lord" which, considering all the wrecks Archie was having, might not have been such a bad idea. But the only time Archie was ever serious about religion was when he needed something "from God."

One time Miller remembered that Archie had a barge stuck on a sandbar. "I've got a barge stuck out on the, gotta boat stuck out on the sandbar here. Sure do need some high water. I've been talkin' to the medicine man up there to see if he could get me some, gonna have to have some high water to get that barge off that sand bar or we're gonna lose it. Why don't you see what you can do about this. Why don't you talk to the Lord about this."

"Why don't you talk to him yourself?" Miller asked Archie.

"Well, you're better acquainted with him," Archie returned.

But the first time Archie did anything other than tease Miller was when the Baptist Church decided to buy some land in Kotzebue.

The word "land" in Kotzebue in the 1950s had a nebulous definition at best. No one really knew who owned what because it was all Federal property and it was not until Kotzebue became a townsite that anyone actually "owned" acreage in the sense that they had a title of conveyance. Prior to that, all anyone had were "squatter's rights."[219] This, however, did not stop Archie from appropriating land as fast as he could drag some of his property onto vacant lots. While Archie didn't "own" the land, he certainly controlled it. Then, when the townsite was established, Archie claimed for himself and Beulah, all the land he could seize.

One of the pieces of land next to Archie was that on which the Baptist Mission sat. N. G. Hanson, one of the store owners in Kotzebue and personally well-acquainted with Archie's convoluted thinking, told Miller "if I were you I'd try to claim some land on the north side of the building. There used to be a shed attached to that building you bought." Hanson knew that if Miller didn't claim it, Archie certainly would.

But Archie was already one step ahead of both Hanson and Miller. He was already claiming that property as his. Miller did not fight Archie because, at the time, he didn't need the property.

However, the Baptist Church had been at this location for a number of years and a decision was made by the Church administrators to buy the property on which the Kotzebue Baptist Church stood. Miller did buy the land and the minute Archie realized that the Mission had money, he began urging Miller to buy the vacant lot next door – that which Archie claimed he owned.

But Archie's way of getting someone to buy the property was a bit backwards. Rather than convincing the Church of all of the positive events that would occur by owning more land immediately adjacent to its property, he proceeded to tell Miller all the negative things he *would do* on the property next to the Church if the Church *did not* buy it.

Miller told Archie it was not up to him to make the purchase and Archie, in a fury, began stacking oil drums about 25 feet from the building in hopes that the proximity to a danger would swiftly cut through red tape at Baptist Church headquarters. Mid-summer in 1954, Miller and a teen-age Willie Hensley were in the Baptist Church cooking dinner when Miller noticed Archie "half-raking" the property next door. After it was in a pile, he set it ablaze, undoubtedly hoping that the smoke would be an annoyance to Miller. This was the way Archie kept after those he wished to skin; he annoyed them until it was easier to pay him off than put up with him.

While Archie wasn't watching, the fire ate its way from the pile of rubbish along the ground until it was under the drums of oil. As soon as Archie saw what was happening, he high-tailed it down the street. Just as he disappeared, **BOOM!**, one of the barrels exploded, spewing fuel oil as it arced 200 feet down the beach. Suddenly the whole pile was ablaze, barrels shooting off every which way. Some were going up, others were spinning around on the ground in flames. As the barrels exploded, some of the tops were sent spinning off into the atmosphere, "like flying saucers" while the flaming contents of the barrels poured onto the ground in rivers of liquid fire.[220]

"We'd better get out of here," Miller said to Hensley and the two exited the small building just as a barrel smashed a hole in it. Outside, the entire city of Kotzebue had gathered to watch the fireworks. Though later they all realized how dangerous the situation had been, at that time everyone was enraptured at the spectacle of barrels blasting off into the sky. Had the Baptist Mission caught fire, the conflagration could have spread from building to building until there was nothing left of Kotzebue.[221] By this time Archie sauntered back to the scene acting as if he had nothing to do with the exploding barrels. Miller immediately buttonholed him and suggested the two of them move those barrels that weren't burning back from the Church.

"Not me," whined Archie. "I'm not a member of any church. I'm not ready to die." With that comment, he disappeared.

When the Baptist Church finally decided to buy the property – which had nothing to do with the close call from the burning barrels – Miller had to buy 100 feet of frontage. But he knew Archie well enough to know that if there was a way to squeeze the Church, Archie would. Though Archie claimed Beulah actually owned the property, Miller would not sign any papers until Archie's name was on the Bill of Sale as he knew full well that Archie would come back at some time and claim that he actually owned the property and it had been sold without his permission.

Or he would claim that not all of the property bought was that which he sold.

Or there would be some other angle Miller had not considered.

Since the United States government had still not conveyed land, ownership was still unknown. This meant, in essence, the Church was paying for property not yet conveyed. But the decision had been made to purchase the property and Miller was instructed to consummate the acquisition. It was not until after the Church had paid Archie for the land and the title to the property had been conveyed that Miller discovered that he had paid Archie for 17 feet of frontage the Church already owned.

But this was not the end of this particular land deal.

Just as Miller had suspected, Archie was not content with just selling the property once and being done with it. Even after it was discovered that 17 feet of the sale had been improperly charged for, Archie came back and demanded to re-negotiate the price. The property was worth more, he claimed, and now he wanted to "crawfish" on the deal, the word Miller used.

When the Baptist minister told him the deal had been consummated, Archie threatened to sue. Miller said fine and Archie was infuriated. Archie left in a huff and a few days later, began another campaign of annoyance. Once again, Archie figured that if he caused enough of a commotion, Miller would buckle. Over at his pool hall he convinced a handful of Inupiat to pick a fight with Miller. This kind of violence in Kotzebue surprised Miller and he wasn't sure what was happening until Natividad "Steve" Salinas told him, "Archie's over at the pool hall telling lies about you."

Miller, however, was an old hand at dealing with man's proclivities. He had been in this position before. It was time to "fight fire with fire," he realized with no pun intended. Planning his strategy, he went to a known "loud mouth" in Kotzebue and casually said, "Archie threatened to sue me and take me to court. I wish he would. If he got this skinny preacher into court he would rue the day. I know so much dirt on him that he'd be sorry." After that, Miller never heard another word from Archie about the property deal.

Steve Salinas, who had tipped Miller as to what Archie was doing, was another interesting character/con man of Kotzebue. He came to the attention of the residents in the Arctic in October of 1955 when he was suspected of killing his girlfriend, Betty Mae Braidwood, an Anchorage waitress. She had been found dead in Salinas' apartment in Nome "with a knife wound about one and a half inches below the right ear." (Another news article indicated that she had been wounded in the throat.) She was supposed to have left for Tacoma earlier that week to arrange for her marriage to Salinas.

Though Salinas had blood smeared on his clothing, he explained that the blood had come when he "attempted to help" Braidwood after he discovered her body. That was his story. Bob Erwin, who was the prosecutor in Nome shortly after Statehood, recalled being told by his predecessor, the Territorial prosecutor, that Salinas was "so fastidious that he [had] held [Briadwood's] head over the toilet until the blood drained out and she was in the bathtub when [investigators] found her." The death was ruled a suicide after a lukewarm statement from the coroner who stated that the wound "could have been self-inflicted."

The grand jury felt otherwise. On November 5, 1955, it returned a verdict stating that Braidwood's death had been caused by "party or parties unknown." Steve Salinas, the obvious suspect, it was reported, had "cooperated voluntarily in a lie detector test." Salinas passed the polygraph twice.[222] However, those familiar with the case had their doubts. Bob Erwin said that Salinas was the "coldest man that [he had] ever met in [his] entire life." (Erwin prosecuted Salinas several years later on an arson charge.) The Territorial Prosecutor had called in a polygraph specialist from Anchorage, Ed Dankworth. Dankworth was a graduate of the top polygraph training institution in the country: the Keeler Polygraph School in Chicago. When Dankworth wired Salinas into the machine, the needles ran flat. Dankworth thought the machine was broken. A second polygraph test showed the same results. Thus did Steve Salinas pass his polygraph.

(Salinas' FBI file also revealed that he was involved in a matter of "involuntary servitude and slavery." The case must have involved Mexican nationals for the investigation was conducted by the San Antonio office of the FBI. But it spread from there to Kotzebue where the case became inexplicably tied to the arson charge that was to send Salinas to jail. The case was closed in March of 1958.)[223]

The second of the two marital mysteries of the Arctic was why Clara Rotman, Louis's widow and a multi-millionairess, married Steve Salinas. When he was no longer a suspect in the Braidwood murder, Salinas left for Kotzebue with the "announced purpose of marrying Clara Rotman." No one in Nome believed him. In Kotzebue, Clara's daughters and their husbands were less than enamored with the idea and when Clara did marry Salinas, on at least one occasion one of the in-laws went to the State Trooper in Kotzebue in terror because Salinas had taken Clara alone for a drive down the beach.

Even with his marriage to Clara, Salinas could not stay out of trouble. He ran afoul of the law in Kotzebue when he tapped into the power lines of the newly-established Kotzebue Electric Association. But, unlike the time that Archie tapped into the ACS lines, criminal charges were filed against Salinas. In the legal wrangling, Salinas was defended by Fred Crane who, at that time, was also Archie's lawyer *and* the lawyer for the Kotzebue Electric Association.

The ensuing tangle was vintage Fred Crane. The trial was set before the Justice of the Peace in the Noatak-Kobuk Precinct because the Justice of the Peace and United States Commissioner in Kotzebue, Alfred Francis, had to disqualify himself since he was a board member of the electric utility. Crane subsequently filed a motion for dismissal on the grounds that if the trial was transferred, the Noatak-Kobuk Justice of the Peace would have been out of his jurisdiction. Therefore, stated Fred Crane, for the trial to be held properly, a new Justice of the Peace would have to be brought in. Since Kotzebue already had a Commissioner and "ex-officio Justice of the Peace," it was highly doubtful that another Federal employee would be put on payroll for a single trial. Crane's motion was filed on September 30, 1958 in the a.m. On the same day, in the p.m., the United States Attorney in Nome moved to dismiss Fred Crane as the attorney for Salinas and to dismiss Crane's motion for dismissal since the Justice of the Peace for the Noatak-Kobuk Precinct was going to handle the case. A month and a half later, during which time there was no movement on the case, the United States Commissioner, Alfred G. Francis, petitioned the court to drop the charges because the utility "property had changed hands and all bills owing the Kotzebue Electric Association" had been paid.

Several years later, Salinas ran afoul of the law yet again, this time in Kotzebue. On December 18, one of Archie Ferguson's buildings was destroyed by a "fire of undetermined origin." Consumed in the fire were the Alaska Airlines ticket office and Archie's home. Though it was initially believed that two people died in the blaze, this was not the case.[224] (Archie was never in danger either; he always stayed with Beulah even though he kept his own apartment for appearances' sake.) Salinas was tried and convicted for arson in the second degree in March of 1958 and sentenced to four years in prison. His case was appealed – by Fred Crane – and heard by the new State of Alaska Supreme Court – twice. Salinas lost both times and did spend some time behind bars. However, with Clara's Rotman's money and Fred Crane's assistance, it appears that Salinas was able to have his record expunged.[225] Few of Salinas' records currently exist. Also of passing interest, in addition to the arson charge, Salinas was also charged with and scheduled to be tried for "illegal cohabitation."[226] Nothing came of the charge.

Salinas, like the other colorful characters of Kotzebue, had his own style. He had been born into an incredibly poor Mexican family in Mission, Texas. His early life had been one of privation and one of his bitterest memories was living in a hut with a dirt floor and a sizable collection of kith and kin. He married young, was divorced with a number of children and left Texas to enlist in the United States Army After he was discharged, he headed north.

Among the Inupiat at Kotzebue, he was considered a bit odd as he always wore a "broad-brimmed, fairly high peaked, straw hat in the summer" and boots along with sun glasses.[227] Among the non-Natives, he was considered a man who dressed for the social occasion even in a casual community like Kotzebue. Dr. Neilson remembered a Christmas party which he and the dentist in Kotzebue hosted where Salinas "came in a powder-blue dinner jacket, a complete tux outfit with patent leather shoes. The whole nine yards."

Whites also marveled that in Kotzebue, a community where bathing was a Saturday night affair, Salinas was always physically clean and "perfectly manicured."[228] Every hair on his head was exactly in place and his clothes were always clean. He was also a "clean freak" in the sense that he always had several employees at the store cleaning the floors and counter. Nothing was ever clean enough for Steve Salinas.

Another eccentricity of Salinas were his two Dobermans. They traveled with him everywhere. Considering that most of the dogs in Kotzebue were for pulling sleds, no one could fathom why Salinas would need guard dogs in that town. In the 1960s, Salinas contracted with Ray Heinrichs to have one of the dog's leather collar inlaid with jade and gold nuggets. After Heinrichs finished the job, he and his friends spent years talking about tranquillizing the dog just to see the expression on Salinas' face when he discovered his dog had been "robbed" of its collar.

Another quirk of his personality was that he loved heavy equipment. He spent thousands of dollars on bulldozers, road graders, caterpillars and trucks and enjoyed driving the equipment around, even if there was no work to be done. In an Arctic town full of colorful characters, the sight of a clean, manicured Mexican in a Stetson and cowboy boots with two Dobermans aboard a cat rumbling alongside Kotzebue Sound was a standout memory.

Salinas was also famous for his taverns. When Kotzebue was wet, he had bought a disabled Alaska Airlines Constellation and planned on turning it into a bar known as the "Flying Martini."[229] That never happened but he and Clara did open several bars in Kotzebue, one named the "Top of the Whale" which featured, among other local memorabilia, copies of the *Mukluk Telegraph* under glass at the booths and tables.[230] They also owned the package store.

Ever the entrepreneur, Salinas was also known for his unusual air-freight business. In the early 1960s he was shipping chum salmon in plastic containers to Seattle which were "on restaurant tables five hours after being shipped from Kotzebue." In the summer of 1965, he tried a new product: beluga *muktuk*. The raw product was air-freighted to Chicago where it was cooked, pickled and served as an appetizer. It proved to be a popular item in Chicago and profitable to Salinas.[231] Salinas was also well-known for his strictly illegal high-stakes poker games. Photographs taken by law enforcement officials of the players revealed them to be "Western states crime big wig types" masquerading as polar bear hunters "who never made it to the ice." In those days, it was $25,000 just to sit in.[232]

In all fairness it should be mentioned that Salinas was by no means the only high stakes gambler in Kotzebue. Art Fields and Leon Shellaberger were also well-known for their high stakes poker games. Well-known, comedic Anchorage fur entrepreneur Perry Green was "cleaned out" of all his poker winnings in 1960 in a "crooked dice game" with Leon Shellaberger and another pilot who subsequently left town the next morning. (Green lost $8,000, an average *year's* salary in those days. Today, Perry Green is well-known for his high stakes poker gambling – but today he does it in Las Vegas.) By comparison, Archie was arrested in July of 1941 for "gambling by using [a] punch card." He plead guilty and was fined the walloping sum of $10.[233]

But Salinas was not a whimsical character like Archie. Archie was in a class by himself. Half of the hilarity of Archie was knowing his personality. Although everyone threw up their hands when they had to deal with him, he was still loveable and his antics made everyone smile.

While Archie was famous for not getting along with government agents, upon occasion he did bend his own rules. In November of 1950, for instance, he agreed to let the United States Department of Fish and Wildlife construct a building on his property. When Fish and Wildlife personnel were drilling to find water, they struck oil. Though the find was not significant, Edith Bullock remembered that "Archie was beside himself for days, running around all excited about oil on his property." In the end, the oil strike was minuscule at best, much to Archie's dismay.[234]

In the same year, Archie showed that he was still a con man. He, along with Beulah and "M. J. Bogard," Archie's secretary, were named in a $48,000 suit in Nome for dismantling an Alaska Housing Authority (AHA) boat, the **Hwaka** the previous January. They had allegedly stripped a $50,000 boat to a salvage value of $2,000. The AHA was going after all three even though Archie was the only one who had done the stripping. That was because Archie, on paper, had transferred all of his assets to Beulah. AHA was going after Archie's money wherever it was and charging Archie for his actions in the "hinder, delay and defraud" the AHA.[235] Nothing ever came of the suit and, presumably, Archie kept the money.

Rather than being concerned that people would discover his incredibly bad luck with regard to vessels and flying – and presumably his good luck at insurance payoffs – Archie actually advertised. When the Sweet-Wilson Expedition came to Kotzebue in 1946, Bruce A. Wilson reported that on the wall of the Kotzebue Grille he saw "a photo montage of ships turned over, ships smashed up, all done by Archie." Also framed on the wall of the Kotzebue Grille was a "touching testimony" from William B. Wilson who had once been a passenger of Archie's. "Archie Ferguson took me for my first ride," Wilson wrote, "and I have certainly made up my mind to stay on the ground."[236]

One of the unknown chapters in Archie Ferguson's life was that he was once considered as a Secret Agent for the United States government. According to Archie's FBI file, in 1950 and 1951, the OSI (Office of Special Investigation) for SAC (Strategic Air Command) was searching for Alaskans in the Arctic to be recruited into the SBA and E&E programs, the "Stay Behind Agent" and the "Escape and Evasion" programs. At that time the Pentagon firmly believed that the Soviets would invade Alaska. Anticipating this eventuality, the United States military establishment wanted agents who would stay "behind enemy lines" as the Reds advanced across the Arctic. Large caches of food, guns, medicine, radios and clothing – along with sabotage gear – were hidden in caches throughout the Arctic to supply these guerrilla bands once hostilities began.

However, after several interviews the OSI decided that although Archie was "loyal to this country and [was] crafty as well as capable," Archie "talk[ed] too much for this type of a program" and, under pressure and in the right conditions would "be for Archie" and would "deal with the enemy if it served his own ends."

Even these facts were not enough to eliminate Archie from the program. Apparently he was still under consideration for almost another year. Then, on October 15, 1951, SAC filed a memo to its files stating that Archie was no longer to be considered as a secret agent. Two days later, SAC in Anchorage sent a memo to "Director, FBI." While the memo clearly stated that Archie was not to be considered for any activity regarding the United States military, the next two paragraphs raised more questions than they answered:

> *The indices of the Anchorage Office have been searched on the above individual and all references connecting him with the Stage Program have been removed and destroyed. No record that the above-captioned individual is identified in any way with the Stage Program is contained in the files of the Anchorage Office.* [237]

While it would be easy to condemn Archie for his ongoing chicanery, it is also important to note that Archie was not the unfeeling pirate that many have painted him. While he did cheat the Inupiat unmercifully, there were quite a few families in Kotzebue that Archie was taking care of that no one knew about. No one starved if Archie knew they were in need. Archie's charity work was done quietly and with no publicity, but it was done frequently enough that even Archie's detractors recognized that the buccaneer did have a soft streak.

Archie also made it clear to Bob Erwin that he was *extremely* concerned about what would happen to his sons, Don, Ray and Frank when he died. "He wanted them to have enough money so that the Inupiat part of them did not drag them down." Archie recognized early that "economic means overcame color." If the three sons had enough money, there "wasn't anything anyone could do to them."

Also to his credit, Archie was a defender of the Inupiat against the rules and regulations of the federal government. When the game warden caught two Inupiat trapping for beaver too close to a beaver lodge, Archie was in a tizzy. How were the Inupiat supposed to know they were putting their traps too close to the beaver lodge? They couldn't read English. The game warden didn't particularly care. Inupiat were "railroaded a lot," Yost, a mechanic for Archie, remembered. So Archie rose to the defense and acted as a lawyer for the two Inupiat at the commissioner's hearing.

"I'm going to defend those guys," Archie snapped to Ed Yost frenetically. "This is their country. They were here before us. Look. You can't throw them in the slammer. You can't take money from them. They live here. They eat this meat. They're not hurtin' anything."

Archie won the case.

The 1950s had been a grand time for Archie. But by the middle of the decade, the ravages of age were catching up to him. Though he was in good health, those around him were not. Beulah died a particularly painful death in Seattle in 1956. In his inimitable script, Archie told Jack Bullock "beulh both kidneys aregone and theyare keeping by feeding he thu herveins it is terrible." When she died, little did Archie know that he had entered his last decade of life. Beulah's body was returned to Kotzebue and buried in the cemetery overlooking the town.

Though, as Alaskan legend would have it, that Archie cared "nawthin'" for the Lower 48 and "snarled-up mass of humanity" down there, he was spending more and more time in that "snarled-up mass of humanity." While the rest of Alaska was suffering from boom-to-bust woes, Archie was taking his family for vacations in Florida and spending winters in Mexico – while Hadley and the boys continued to live in Fairbanks. Archie maintained a home in Seattle where he had at least one royal blue Cadillac with "plaid upholstery on the seat covers."[238]

By this time Archie was spending more and more time in Mexico with his second wife, Linda. She was a real beauty, according to everyone who remembered her, and though she spoke little English with a terrible accent, she did understand quite a bit of America and its Customs and did not appear to mind being married to a man that was 40-years her senior. As late as 1958, Archie was still the King. Neil Bergt met him in his twilight years while Bergt was flying for Alaska Airlines. On his first morning in town, Bergt got the message that "Archie wants to see you."

Bergt went up to Archie's apartment and found him "sitting on the edge of his bed with no clothes on. He was a little, fat, old man with a big pot belly and scrawny little legs and his feet were in a pan of water and he had a young Mexican girl bathing his feet. I'll never forget that."

After a brief conversation, Archie said. "All right. You'll do." It was as if Archie had given his blessing to Bergt even though Bergt didn't even work for him.

"You'll do." That was all Archie had to say in 1958. That was all he had to say. Archie's word meant something in Kotzebue.

Archie and Marge Bogard in Seattle with a royal blue Cadillac.
courtesy of the Salinas Collection

THE END OF THE FRONTIER

"You might say he aroused my competitive spirit. Of the ten most difficult cases in my career, Archie would be in the top three."

...Max Pierce, IRS agent who collected from Archie Ferguson

By the mid-1950's the end of the Arctic as a frontier was coming fast. Wien and Alaska Airlines were landing in Kotzebue daily. For those with money, there was the unprecedented luxury of being able to choose between two airlines a day going to Nome, Fairbanks or Anchorage. During the summer, that number jumped to three flights a day.

There was another phenomenon as well: tourism dollars. As the income of Americans rose during the Eisenhower economic boom of the 1950s, Americans discovered the Arctic as a tourist destination. It was magical land where travelers could watch Inupiat do a blanket toss, eat whale blubber, pound a hammer on permafrost and read a newspaper outside at midnight. So powerful was the draw of the Inupiat on the imagination of tourists from the Lower 48 and around the world that Alaska Airlines eventually placed a grizzled, characteristic face of an Inupiat on the tail of its planes. Chester A. Seveck, the face on Alaska Airlines, added to the local charm by coming out and greeting people as they got off the plane in Kotzebue.

Many Kotzebue residents realized the value of tourism and went out of their way to encourage its growth. A chamber of commerce was started by Edith Bullock and Louis Rotman – who were very careful to make sure Archie was not extended an offer of membership – and though there was little for it to do to stimulate the visitor industry, it was apparent that tourism dollars could be as harmonic as the cycle of salmon returning to spawn. The rising of the midnight sun in June would draw tourists above the Arctic Circle like polar bears to a whale carcass. That meant MONEY into the local economy – HARD CASH rather than Ferguson bingles.

Other industries were moving in as well. Fishing was an up and coming way of making money for the one-man/one-boat entrepreneur and canneries sprang up along the coastline. As more and more fishermen moved into the Bering Sea, their conversations dominated the radio waves. That someone else would be monopolizing the air waves infuriated Archie. "We're [being] covered with fish," he said in disgust.[239]

Even during the winter, civilization was making its inroads. These were the days of the polar bear barons. Guides, some of whom had unsavory reputations, came north in January and stayed until June, each with a client list of well-heeled hunters who were coming to Kotzebue for an "Arctic vacation." Usually this meant lots of drinking and ongoing sexual encounters with Inupiat women, many of them under the age of consent. But these men were more than well-heeled, rich, white men. They were celebrities as well. This, however, did not stand in the way of their doing exactly what they wanted to do. When Roy Rogers came to Kotzebue, he was so drunk when he gave a performance for the hospital, he could not even remember the words to his television show's theme song "Tumbling Tumbleweeds."[240]

Venereal disease showed its face with a vengeance in this era as well and more than one suspicious death indicated that some of these white men felt that the expression "Free, White and 21" meant they owned the town. To a certain extent they were correct. As far as the white polar bear hunters were concerned, this was an open town and they made the most of it. Though Archie could not see it, Kotzebue was changing. This time, the change was not in Archie's interest. For years, Archie and Louis Rotman had been co-equal entrepreneurs. Both had stores with equivalent prices. Since Archie was unwilling to spend a dime on renovation, his establishment became ramshackle. Rotman, on the other hand, knew that it was necessary to "spend money to make money" and so he modernized.

When Rotman opened a new store, it was so stunning that it was given front page headlines in the *Nome Nugget*. The structure had a full cement basement, something uncommon in Kotzebue, and the first floor was "finished with chromium and plate glass." To make it easy for the customers to shop, "the store operat[ed] on a serve-yourself plan. Displays ranged from groceries, furniture and washing machines to a complete clothing department." Then came the extras. They included an air conditioner and an electric elevator, the latter causing a stir in the community because "everyone want[ed] to ride in the 'machine that goes up and down.'"[241]

After Rotman's death, Steve Salinas took over the reins of the Rotman empire and he maintained Louis's high standards for profitability. Archie, on the other hand, continued to be Archie and the gap between the two entrepreneurial empires widened until Archie's dismal little store became a decaying symbol of Archie's declining fortunes. Archie either could not or would not stay up with the times. While he had been clairvoyant in the mid-1940s, a decade later, he was blind. Eventually it ruined him. He kept doing the business the way he always had, burning bridges before and behind him until he had none left to set ablaze.

By the early 1950s, he had acquired such a reputation for knavery that anyone who actually did business with him was considered a bit daffy and many people would go to extreme lengths to avoid doing business with him at all. In September of 1953, for instance, Lyman Elsworth, an engineer for the Territory of Alaska, surveyed the routes for two additional roads in the community. One was two miles long along the beach and is today the main street in Kotzebue. The second one was to link the beach road to the expected dock.

But from the moment that there was word that a road was to be built, "everyone in Kotzebue connived to keep Archie from getting to do the work," Edith Bullock admitted. "If he got the contract, we knew what would happen. Archie would get all the money and [Kotzebue] wouldn't get a road." So the community leaders finagled a way to buy Archie's heavy equipment and do the road themselves. When Archie found out how he had been snookered, he was furious but there wasn't much he could do.[242]

Archie was also having other problems as well. He had "run out of insurance companies," Bill Stroecker, who worked for Key Bank Alaska in Fairbanks recalled. Now, when his barges really went down, there was no way to recoup the losses. He was also running out – or had run out – of wholesalers in the Seattle area from whom he could acquire groceries, lumber, film, equipment, supplies, spare parts, fuel oil, gasoline, etc. His credit rating was incredibly bad, at best, and all his business became "cash and carry" with the accent on the word *cash*. As bank and credit networks became more and more integrated, Archie could find fewer and fewer rubes. As his options pinched off, his fortunes continued to decline.

At some indeterminate moment in the mid-1950s, Archie's frontier days ended. Civilization finally caught up to Archie.

For years the IRS had been hopelessly outclassed by the Arctic entrepreneurs. Very few business people were making much of a living and those that were, like Archie, equated keeping records with drinking boiling cod liver oil. Kotzebue was basically a cash-based economy. Many, if not most, of the Inupiat were living on credit during the summer. Muskrat skins and other furs were just as good as cash throughout most of the winter. Actual dollars were not that easy to come by. Credit was the name of the game in Kotzebue and storekeepers had little, if any, paperwork to speak of.

Even if the IRS could have assessed an amount of tax owed, there was the problem of collecting. Kotzebue was 300 miles north of Fairbanks. Getting money out of a recalcitrant taxpayer north of the Arctic Circle was incredibly difficult. Even if there were assets to be seized, any property had to be put up for auction and, in those days, very few investors from out-of-town were interested in Arctic real estate.

Further, if the taxpayer converted his booty to cash and hid it, the IRS could spend the rest of eternity looking for assets. There was a lot of barren wilderness north of the Circle in which to hide assets, particularly if they were small enough to be carried and the taxpayer in question was a pilot.

The IRS was not unaware of these problems but had still been making its presence known for quite a few years, at least since the 1940s. In fact, ironically, one of the IRS agents even went down in a Ferguson Airways plane in the early-1940s.[243]

However, the IRS was an institution whose people Archie could not defeat. While he had danced around the Territorial law and federal regulations for years, little did he know that at last he had met his match.

Archie's tax problems were two-fold. First, he had spent the previous 25 years beating individuals, companies, and government agencies out of hundreds of thousands of dollars with a combination of guile, deceit and dubious business practices. He had become a master of dodge and weave. Whenever he was given a bill, he would deny he owed the money. When confronted with a demand to pay, he would allow the creditor to take him a court. Then he would dodge the court hearing and, if ordered to pay, he would force the creditor to find his cash. In the long run, creditors simply threw up their hands and took the loss. Archie was a master at d-r-a-g-g-i-n-g his legal feet and his wealth proved his staying power.

He was also become a master at moving his money so it could not be attached. Thanks to the genius of Fred Crane, Archie had a carton of incorporation papers. He would bleed his money from corporation to corporation, or to Beulah and later Linda, so it could not be found much less attached when Archie ran into legal problems. This made it all the more difficult for anyone to collect from Archie. Archie figured he had the IRS beaten. "I've got that Infernal Revenue Service beat!" Archie once told Fred Goodwin with pride. "It takes those sons-of-bitches five years to go through a company to find you ain't there no more. I'm five companies ahead of those sons-of-bitches and I'm not gonna live that long."

His second difficulty was that he had no records. Kotzebue was a community where everything was done on a cash basis. Archie used to keep his cash hidden in a milk can that was left over from the cow which had long since passed away. But when it came to actual records, he had none. While this shortcoming had been an asset when it came to dealing with the CAA, as Bess Cross had learned the hard way, with the IRS it was a curse.

Once the IRS focused on Archie, these two shortcomings were his undoing. Dodge as he might, he could only put off the inevitable. But he did try and did an admirable job – for a while. Vernon L. Snow, the Assistant Regional Counsel for the IRS out of San Francisco in the late 1950s remembered vividly that Archie was always one step ahead of the IRS. Every time the IRS was about to deliver papers to him, he'd disappear into thin air. When things got very hot, he went to Mexico.

When the IRS initially appeared at Archie's door, Archie treated them exactly as he did every other government official. He verbally danced about, told his stories and tried to talk his way out of paying any taxes at all. In fact, Archie claimed he owed no money. He had not, he claimed, made enough money to owe anyone anything, least of all the United States government. Further, he had not made enough in past years to be liable for taxes in those years either.

He didn't have that much paperwork because, of course, he hadn't made that much money.

This failed to impress the IRS.

Archie's attitude did not impress the IRS either.

But Archie didn't care.

As far as he was concerned, the IRS was simply another breed of government cat. A past master of dealing with the bureaucracy, experience had taught him he could "wait these boys out." All he had to do was be friendly and string them along until they, like their governmental predecessors, simply threw their collective hands in the air and left. So he played along. The IRS wanted records, fine. He gave them records. But not in the form they were expecting. When IRS agents arrived to examine what paperwork he had, Art Fields remembered, Archie handed over three barrels filled with paperwork and told the agents to look for themselves.

They did.

But it was not an easy task.

Interrogatories were difficult as well. First, they had to be conducted in Archie's Kotzebue Grille. As this was the only public place in town, *everyone* knew what was going on. Second, as Archie had a difficult time getting to the point, the process went on day after day, eight hours a day. Third, Archie was a past master at talking around in a circle and this he did well. Bob Erwin, who was the District Attorney of Nome, had gone after Archie for some civil claims for fuel tax, had learned the hard way that Archie's "no less than 20 interlocking corporations" whose legal interconnections were so nebulous that Erwin and his staff "could never unscramble to wit the corporations which appeared to owe always appeared to be defunct yet [Archie] always had assets and he went to Mexico regularly."

Linda was a bit easier. James R. Clouse, Jr. who was an Assistant United States Attorney at the time, recalled that Archie's new wife did not speak English very well. That made the questioning difficult. Linda had made "substantial sums" which she claimed had come from "babysitting." When Clouse pressed her further, she stated she had also occasionally won "at the tracks."

One of the reasons the IRS and United States Attorney did not get a lot of information from Linda was because she felt intimidated by the state trooper, Eugene Morris, who had come in from Nome with the IRS agents. Morris, the first State Trooper in Nome, was 6' 5", weighed 230 and appeared more as a hulking bear than a man to the petite Linda. Morris was yet another of the fascinating individuals of the Arctic. He had been sent to Nome, it was commonly believed, as "punishment." Prior to his career in law enforcement, Morris had hopes of being a big-league pitcher before he threw his arm out. The highlight of his baseball days was a 1 to 0 victory in a 14-inning pitching duel against legendary Hall of Famer Dizzy Dean who was barnstorming across the country after he retired. Morris also caused more than his fair share of laughter after he went down in an airplane and had to spend five days without food before being rescued. After that, whenever he traveled he always carried a "60 pound suitcase full of food."[244]

But Linda was easy to deal with compared to Archie. Erwin was in Kotzebue during the month that Archie was being interviewed by the IRS and recalled that Archie would talk and talk and talk until he had talked in a circle. "Archie was deposed for eight hours a day and by the time the IRS finished they could not make head or tail out of what he was saying."

The IRS also had a hard time tracking the money, as Clouse recalled. The "limited books and records available showed a rapid flow of assets from one corporation to the next, usually being transferred just prior to the IRS subpoenaing the same." Once, right after the agents demanded production of certain books and records they **knew** existed, the records were destroyed "as a result of a fire of unexplained and unknown origin."[245]

But unlike other government officials, the IRS agents were not of the humoring sort. They examined what records Archie had, listened patiently to his explanations and, after a brief period of time, stated that they felt that Archie had indeed made a profit on his enterprises in that year and previous ones and assessed Archie for what they thought he owed. The estimated bill was between $150,000 and $200,000 as well as penalties and interest, a whopping amount even today.

Then Archie made a critical mistake. Rather than continuing his pattern of bob-and-weave, he took the frontal approach.

"Ok, boys," he said in a challenge he was to regret, "now you've assessed it. Let's see you collect it."

This was not a problem for the two agents who made the original assessment. If the taxpayer refused to pay, it was up to another agent to do the actual collecting. In this case, it fell to Max B. Pierce, a veteran tax collector who was already handling several hundred cases in Fairbanks.

Looking over the paperwork, Pierce knew he had a tough job ahead of him. Archie had no easily traceable assets. Just to eyeball this legend of the north, Pierce flew into Kotzebue as though he was a tourist, walked into Archie's Kotzebue Grille, a camera over his shoulder, and asked Archie how business was.

"Things are just fine," said Archie.

Max smiled and when he got back to Fairbanks, he put together a summons for Archie to show cause he should not pay.

"My job was to find a way to collect the money," Pierce said flatly, and Archie was a "little upset" when he found that he had to talk with the IRS in person.

Was it difficult to collect from Archie? Absolutely, Pierce recalled. Archie was "past master at switching assets from one entity to another." He would form corporations as needed and drift money through them like water in a maze of sponges. He had no fewer than a half-dozen entities each with capital that appeared just as mysteriously as it disappeared.

It was an elaborate, clever ruse, as crafty a tax evasion scheme as Fred Crane could develop and Crane was no one's fool. But what neither Crane nor Archie had counted upon was the persistence of Max Pierce. Fred Crane tried to quash the summons. This was a highly unusual move as it was asking a federal court to order the IRS not to look at someone's records. It failed. Crane was doing what he should have been doing for his client, Pierce admitted, but the preponderance of evidence was on the side of the IRS. So was time. Not only did the IRS know that Archie *owed* the United States government money; they knew Archie had *assets*. It was just a matter of locating those assets and attaching them.

"It was like trying to unscramble scrambled eggs," Pierce remembered. After spending more than 600 hours on the Ferguson case and filling an entire drawer in a filing cabinet, Pierce realized the only way to collect from Archie would be to "pierce the corporate veil" and go after all the corporations at the same time. He summed this conclusion up in a memo to his superiors entitled "The Saga of Archie Ferguson, or, He Went That-a-Way." "You might say he aroused my competitive spirit," Pierce said in 1991. "Of the ten most difficult cases in my career, Archie would be in the top three."

Pierce's first step was to seize whatever loose assets could be found, in most cases automobiles, jewelry, cash in bank accounts, paintings, etc. While "the IRS code defines a levy as seizure by any means," Pierce recalled, "and I think, probably, our 'seizure by any means' went a little farther than the law should have allowed us because we actually searched" Archie's home. But search it the IRS did. One spring afternoon Max Pierce and another agent, Frank Doolin, known affectionately around the IRS as Frank "No Foolin'" Doolin, flew to Kotzebue looking for assets wherever they might be found. They even came with a large metal detector and a post hole digger because, according to one of their informants in Kotzebue, Archie had a 2-gallon freezer container full of gold buried in the sand underneath The Eskimo Building. (Other sources say it was a 5-pound coffee can with $750,000 worth of gold.

Archie later swore that he had the gold. If he did, the IRS never found it. But then, neither did Archie's nephews and adopted sons: Don, Frank or Ray.) Pierce and Doolin, quite literally, tore the place apart and found nothing of value but $1,000 in cash.[246] They even went so far as to search Linda's purse in case there was an undue amount of cash there. But they didn't catch Archie. "He beat us out of town to Mexico," Doolin recalled, three days before he and Pierce made it Kotzebue.[247]

Eugene Morris

The next step was to legally seize all of Archie's real estate and other tangible property. But it was hard to catch Archie. First, because of the convoluted nature of his ownership paperwork. Whatever the IRS seized, Archie continued to say that the property in question was actually not his property and therefore could not be served. Further, as he spent his winters in Mexico, it was hard to physically serve him with papers. While he was in Alaska, if he knew there was paperwork coming, he dodged it. If he got served, Fred Crane would quash it. Round and round the government and Archie went until the IRS finally decided it was time to put an end to the game.

"We were going to have a court hearing in Fairbanks in the middle of winter, of all times," Pierce recalled. "That's when Archie went to Mexico. The U.S. Marshal failed to serve him with a notice that there was going to be a court hearing so naturally Archie didn't show up." Everyone stood around in the court room waiting for an Archie that would never show up and the judge ruled in favor of the IRS.

But they didn't get that much. While the real estate went to the government, the only cash value the United States government ever got, in addition to the $1,000 in loose change from Archie's apartment in Kotzebue, was a house in Seattle the government sold for $25,000. (Max Pierce figured that he collected $28.89 per hour for the United States government on the Ferguson case. By comparison, his highest collectible dollars was on the North Slope when he collected a total of $250 million from various oil companies.)

When the IRS finally moved against Archie physically, they did it publicly. Agents other than Max Pierce and Frank Doolin showed up in Kotzebue and evicted him out of the theater right in the middle of the movie, "moved him right out of his apartment, right down the aisle" and out to door.

IRS ID of Max Pierce

One of the more unusual aspects of the case, Pierce recalled, was when they seized the movie theater they found that the attic was full of films Archie had rented but never returned. "There were *hundreds* of them," Pierce laughed, "and I don't know how the film companies got word that we had seized Archie's theaters but I got calls from all over the country. Those film distributors wanted their films back!"

In retrospect, Pierce felt that Archie was a "typical Alaskan of that era, just trying to make a living" and didn't give much of a thought to owing taxes. He just didn't "want the IRS or government interfering with the little empire he had in Kotzebue."

When the Notice of Sealed Bid was printed in the paper on June 1, 1962, the fingerprints of Fred Crane were clear. The IRS was seizing property from Archie Ferguson dba Kotzebue Mercantile, Kotzebue Grille, Midnight Sun Theater, Fergusons Pool Hall, Arctic Amusement Company, Inc., and Mutual Enterprises, Inc. Interestingly, N. G. Hanson bought Archie's store at the IRS auction, completing the cycle begun when Archie had won Hanson's store as part of a gambling bet a decade and a half earlier.[248]

That was the end of Archie's empire in Kotzebue.[249]

The actual IRS case against Archibald Robert Ferguson lasted until his death in 1967 and only ended when the agency was confident that the body in the coffin in El Paso was actually that of the Kotzebue bush pilot. "The last that I remember, there was that there was trouble getting his body

Frank Doolin searching for Archie's gold

across the border because they couldn't identify him. As it was the middle of winter in Fairbanks," Pierce recalled humorously, "I offered to go to El Paso to identify the remains."[250]

The last legal case filed against Archie was in November of 1964. Federal tax assessments against both Archie and Hadley – including interest and fees – totaled $117,659.29. Though the case was filed in 1964, the years for which Archie and Hadley were charged were 1943, 1944, 1945, 1946 and 1947. And in one year, 1947, the couple's "interest and lien fees" were almost three times higher than the initial unpaid balance. The court records revealed that the outstanding balance computed to November 6, 1964 to be

PERIOD	UNPAID BALANCE	INTEREST & LIEN FEES	TOTAL
1943	$ 8,085.11	$ 6,427.66	$14,512.77
1944	17,181.50	13,659.29	30,840.79
1945	24,313,63	19,369.84	43,683.47
1946	35,918.54	28,555.24	64,473.78
1947	5,258.55	18,889.93	24,148.48
Total:	$ 90,757.33	$ 86,901.96	$117,659.29[251]

As an ironic footnote to Archie's troubles, he was also hit with court costs: $142.32.[252]

In the end, even Fred Crane seemed to have turned against Archie. For legal bills owed, Archie had Don turn over the "Lrge NW dragline for Herring," Archie wrote Edith Bullock in July of 1962, "I hope [Crane and his partners] go Broke." He wrote similar sentiments to Alice Osborne,

Crane made Don give him our dragline te only thng that run he is adam rat for sure herei have give him over One thousand this past yr bes fifteen hundred of Grub few yrsago onthe Kivilan and his girls all stuck us he wouls not touch the case unless Don Signed t e drafline over him taylor an herning all together on Mud creek.[253]

That Archie had actually paid anything to Crane is surprising. But Archie might have been too harsh in his assessment of Crane. After all, Fred had fought the IRS for Archie and managed to keep The Eskimo Building from falling into their hands. The Eskimo was actually owned by Warren's children and they retained it and was the only financial legacy Archie left the three boys.[254] Further, Crane represented Hadley in her divorce from Archie and divorce proceedings rarely produce friends and often makes enemies of friends. Archie had other problems. He was broke, had no plane, no home, no store, no theater and no barge line. He also had no means of making a living in Kotzebue. Gathering what belongings they were allowed to keep, Archie and Linda moved to Candle.

Archie, ever the entrepreneur, went back to work at the profession he had learned long before he had become a pilot: mining. Working with John Belobraidich, they formed a mining venture called Avon Enterprises and proceeded to cull ground formerly owned by the Havenstrike Mining Company looking for the gold in the tailings which the original miners "forgot, didn't know about, or mined inefficiently."

But Archie's method of mining was frightening. To go after virgin ground, he had a crew operating a bulldozer under the permafrost with no bracing. Under normal conditions, a miner would extend a tunnel and add bracing to shore up the overburden. Otherwise there could be a collapse. Archie didn't bother with such niceties. He just dug. The deeper the bull dozers went, of course, the more stress there was on the permafrost. The crew excavated a cavern under the permafrost that was 30 feet deep and 200 feet wide. Even though the permafrost was 50 feet thick, there were more than a few men and women who looked at the permafrost ceiling with trepidation.

Archie wasn't using the newest equipment either, Ray Heinrichs remembered. In Candle he had an old cat with a seat made out of Blazo box with a plank that stuck out on both sides of the cab. "Show him how it works," Archie would yell and an Inupiat youth would then jam a crowbar into the gearbox to shift gears. "Ain't that nice?" Archie asked Heinrichs. "Just like new."

Even though he was down in his cups, Archie was still adept at the scam. Richard Foster, son of pioneer bush pilot Willy Foster, was stunned as he watched Archie borrow a piece of lead silver his father had found in Galena and then use it to hoodwink tourists into investing in a silver mine in Candle. Archie was the same old pilot too. When he flew in lumber, he strapped the longer pieces to his wings or the outside of the plane's fuselage.[255] He was the same old lighterage entrepreneur as well. But this time he was not using his own barges and his accidents weren't paper frauds. Dealing in herring oil, his barge really did break in half and go down.

Oddly, also on the barge when it went down was Al Capone's Cadillac, which had been owned by Johnny Herbert. Herbert had bought the car in California and brought it to Candle as an advertising gimmick for his bar. He had offered rides in the vehicle for a "dollar a ride up to [Mile] 19 and back." Archie got the use of the car when he got the mine but whether he owned the car is a matter lost in the sands of time. Whether Al Capone even owned the Cadillac is another matter lost in the sands of time. Capone never really owned anything. The IRS felt otherwise and, in 1931, the IRS won the debate.

Left to right, Gene Jack, Hadley, Archie and John Herbert.
Photograph courtesy of UAF.

(According to Ray Heinrichs, the car was a Packard and had been used to take miners to the local brothel. When the barge went down, it was barely loaded. In addition to the automobile, the cargo that was lost included some core drillings and about a dozen "barrels of bones" which had been unearthed by a Swiss anthropologist. When the barge was righted, the only cargo that was saved was an old caterpillar generator, "that you could find abandoned just about anywhere in Alaska," Heinrichs said laughing.)

Archie's biggest killing in Candle days might have been ivory. In those days, when miners came upon mastodon tusks, they generally pulled them out of the gravel pit and stacked them in a pile. As far as the miners were concerned, the ivory was trash. Archie, however, saw a possible product and bought up the tusks for pennies. Richard Foster vividly remembered Archie standing in front of a tusk pile "ten feet high and 15 feet in diameter" that he was sawing into smaller pieces so he could get them into his plane. When Foster asked what Archie intended to do with them, he replied that he was going to "sell them for $3 a pound in Mexico."

Once again, there was the question of the amount of Archie's money. While some assert that Archie made money hand-over-fist at Candle, others say he barely made enough on which to live. Art Fields remembered that Archie had bought the Candle mine for $6,000 and had the "biggest clean-up they ever had." At least one other person firmly believed that Archie pulled "a third of a million" out of Candle.

More than one person interviewed also felt that Archie was spending so much time in Mexico because he was smuggling gold out of the United States. It was also insinuated that Archie knew which gold claims to mine after the war because, as a pilot, he knew which claims were the richest and which men did not return from the hostilities. As far as the richness of his claim was, Tom Packer, who actually did some gold panning with Archie on his claim in Candle remembered that he and the state trooper then in Kotzebue, Jim Hemphill, spent a day gold panning and came away with "3/4 an ounce of gold." That would be about $300 today. For a one-man, pan-and-water operation, $300 a day was not a paltry wage.

But he was still the same old Archie. One time he was crossing the Mexican-United States border and he had his cat Hercules. He didn't have any record of vaccinations for Hercules but, in Archie's words, "You know if you take [the Customs people's] minds off what they're supposed to be don' sometimes they forget to ask all them questions." So Archie convinced the customs agents that Hercules was really half-rabbit and half-cat. The beast would only eat cabbage, Archie claimed, and he was being badgered by people who wanted to put the specimen on exhibit.

The Customs Agents got so excited, or so Archie claimed, that they didn't ask to see any vaccination records. While this may be a stretch of the truth, apparently some of the tourists who saw Hercules at the border and witnessed the exchange between Archie and the Customs agents believed him. Several weeks later the Fairbanks *Daily News Miner* ran a letter from Clay Childress of Lawrenceville, Illinois, stated he "would like to buy, or information, leading to offspring resulting from mating of rabbit and cat."[256]

But the luster of the Arctic seems have gone out of Archie's life. In [257]a letter to Jack Bullock, Archie wrote "I just dread going back up there jack."[258] Actually, Archie didn't have to worry about living in Candle much longer. It burned to the ground in 1966. With the last of his Arctic ties extinguished, Archie and Linda headed south. They lived in Artesia, California for a few months and in 1967 crossed the border into Mexico. Archie never returned. On February 4, 1967, he suffered a fatal heart attack and died in La Barca, Jalisco, Mexico.

But even in death Archie generated myths. More than one person was suspicious of Archie's death and there were insinuations of a strange demise quickly covered by the Mexican Police and the United States State Department. But this may be a bit more high drama than actual fact. Archie's death certificate indicates that he died of a heart ailment, not unusual for a man of his age, 71.

As far as the quick burial is concerned, Archie's son, Don, remembered with agonizing clarity that such was not the case. After Archie's death, Linda kept the body in the van she and Archie had been using in Mexico. She apparently did not have enough cash to have the body buried so she called Don for assistance.

"She didn't speak English that well," Don recalled, "and I kept telling her to find a *Padre* to have the body buried. The next thing I knew, Archie's body was in El Paso." Ray Heinrichs' wife, Marie, remembered that Linda had tried to cross the border with Archie's corpse sitting upright in the van as if he were a passenger.[259] That did not fool the United States Customs agents. They would not allow the body into the country. Even if they would have granted it entrance, neither Linda nor the rest of the Ferguson clan had the money to ship it to Kotzebue.

If Archie died rich, no one knew where the money was. In fact, had it not been for two friends of Archie, the body of the gnarly bush pilot might have ended up in a pauper's grave on the Mexican side of the border. Then-State Senator Bob Blodgett of Teller called the United States State Department to get the body across the border. At that time the mortal remains were "lying on a bunk in a Mexican jail." Edith Bullock provided the $800 necessary to ship the body to Seattle by rail and then to Kotzebue by air.

Two weeks later, on February 19, Archie was laid to rest in the Kotzebue cemetery, south of the old airstrip, near his son, Glenn, his brother, Warren, and his parents. The airstrip was still there but the new airport had moved all the traffic to the edge of town. If Archie had his way, though, he probably would have wanted to be buried by the old landing strip where he could hear the ghostly throb of the Wacos, Travelaires, Cessnas, Stinsons and Norsemans as they leaped into the sky on their way to Point Hope, Shungnak and Selawik. He might not have liked the new airport with the 727s and 737s landing twice a day.

But then again, with the new airport there were more sheep to fleece and that would have thrilled Archie as much as rattle and shake of a gull wing Stinson, gassed and ready to fly, headed into the wind on a Marsden matting runway with a load of mail for Kiana, Kobuk and Shungnak.

Thus passed Archie Ferguson, the wild-eyed, crazy, unforgettable pilot, lighterage con man and living legend of the north. He was a colorful, often comic character but he was a man who loved living and lived on his own terms, one of the most redeeming characteristics of being in the Alaskan Arctic.

EPILOG

There are many more Eskimos in the North than can now be supported by diminishing wildlife food resources. There are nowhere near enough jobs to go around for conventional financial support. But the new Eskimos are moving. They're building hotels, buying jade mines for jewelry crafts, extending skin sewing ventures, investing in mining exploration, in office buildings and in apartments. And they are hiring whites to teach them, which will take a little understanding on everybody's part: taking care of hotel rooms and waiting tables isn't exactly the kind of work Eskimo women folk are cut out for (33 showed up for training one day, 6 the next), while on another front a harried white hotel clerk on the evening of the grand opening [of the Nullugvik Hotel in Kotzebue owned by NANA Corporation] went lunging up the stairs after a gang of Eskimo youngsters who were having a ball charging up and down the halls, in and out of neatly furnished new rooms, feeling the slick hallway rails and smooth finish of the walls.

"Hey, you kids!" he shouted (in vain). "Time to go home! Everybody go home now!"

"Take it easy, Mac," somebody laughed. "Those kids are the stockholders. They're your bosses!"

. . . Robert Henning
Alaska Magazine
July, 1975[260]

I t has been more than half a century since the passing of Archie Ferguson. But it has been a monumental 50 years for the Arctic. Not all of the change has been for the better.

Ironically, for a man of Archie's ilk, he died a shade early. In 1972, as a result of the Arab Oil Embargo and the skyrocketing prices of gasoline at the pumps across the United States, the American oil companies were able to convince the United States Congress of the wisdom of a TransAlaska Pipeline. What they wanted was an 800-mile, 48-inch, insulated conduit which could carry about 2 million barrels of oil a day from Prudhoe Bay to Valdez on Prince William Sound. This would be a domestic supply of petroleum, under American air cover from well head to market, that could supply 15% of the nation's daily thirst for diesel and gasoline.

However, there was a major problem. When Alaska became the 49th state, the compact between the newly-formed state and the United States government contained a proviso for Native lands which, paraphrased, amounted to the bland statement that the Statehood Act was "subject to aboriginal rights to be determined later." However, "later" was one of those terms in the English language which had no meaning. As the TransAlaska Pipeline legislation was winding its way through the United States Congress, the Alaska Natives, collectively, saw a political wedge to resolve their guaranteed but delayed aboriginal rights. After all, if no one knew for sure which lands were aboriginal, there was a good chance that some of the lands to be crossed by the TransAlaska Pipeline would be Native lands.

Holding the pipeline as a political hostage, the Natives were able to negotiate what was known as the Alaska Native Claims Settlement Act, ANCSA. Under ANCSA, passed in December of 1971, the Federal government recognized that the Natives were entitled to 44 million acres of land. For this consideration, the Natives guaranteed that there would be no blocking of the construction of the pipeline and certain "aboriginal rights" were "extinguished." It was believed then that the "aboriginal rights" being "extinguished" meant that there would not be a reservation system in Alaska similar to that which existed in the Lower 48. To date, no one is exactly legally sure what those "aboriginal rights" are.

As a sweetener, the Natives, collectively, were also given a one-time cash payment of $900 million. But the Federal government would not give the money directly to individual Natives. Part of the agreement was that the

Natives would form regional corporations and, beneath them, village corporations. The $900 million would then be dispensed to these corporations and each would decide how their portion of the money would be allocated. One of the 13 regional corporations was in the Kotzebue Area: NANA.

NANA sought to consolidate its local hold on tourism. It built the largest hotel in the Arctic, the Nullagvik – at a cost of $2.6 million just to fly in the building materials.[261] Over the years it also bought out Gene Joiner's jade mountain properties. NANA's single largest investment was the Red Dog Mine, a $450 million joint venture with Cominco, a Canadian multi-national mineral extraction firm.

But even with legislative and financial clout, the transition period from aboriginal to computer ages has not been easy for the Inupiat. It has been a matter of moving forward and, at the same time, maintaining their heritage. This has not been easy for the whites brought cultural changes that did not sit well with the Inupiat. As an example, when the Quakers came to Kotzebue, they outlawed dancing, and the Inupiat adhered to this rule for decades. But not forever. In the 1940s, two Inupiat, Paul Green and Abraham Lincoln, decided that they wanted to dance. But they had a problem other than the prohibition: they had no drum. As dancing had been forbidden for so long, there had not been a reason to own a dance drum.

There was a dancing drum in Kotzebue, an antique, but it was in the possession of a white man, Paul Davidovics, who owned a roadhouse. Davidovics agreed to let the two Inupiat use the drum as long as they danced at his roadhouse as entertainment. Dancing at the Davidovics Roadhouse was a mainstay for years.

Humorously, when the Bureau of Indian Affairs finally gave the Inupiat written permission to dance in BIA schools, the Inupiat again faced the problem of finding a drum. It was too late in the year to find a walrus stomach to use in the construction of the instrument, so they made their instrument with the vulcanized rubber from weather balloons provided courtesy of the CAA station in Kotzebue. When Mrs. Berryman, Tom Berryman's wife, a "real Christian woman," tried to stop the dancing, the Inupiat just waved the written permission from BIA and smiled. Only thus did Inupiat dancing return to Kotzebue.[262]

Health-wise, the state of the Native has improved substantially over the last several decades. Infant mortality among Natives since 1950 has been cut by more than 75% and the overall death rate by half. Tuberculosis, which accounted for 43% of Native deaths in 1946, only claimed 13 lives between 1980 and 1989. During that same decade, no Native deaths resulted from measles, whooping cough, rheumatic fever, syphilis, typhoid or polio and life expectancy among Natives jumped from 47 years in 1950 to 67 by the turn of the century.[263]

But the health gap between Native and non-Native is still great. Infant mortality rates for Natives are twice that of non-Natives and death by accidents are three times higher for Natives than non-Natives. Natives are twice as likely to drop out of school and unemployment rates for Native men are twice that of Non-native men.[264] Though Natives only represent 16% of Alaska's population, they account for 40 percent of the enrollment for public assistance programs.[265] The suicide rate for Native men is three times that of whites – and higher in the high risk age group of 20 to 24. Overall, Native suicide rates are **14 times higher** than the national average.[266]

Alcoholism, one of the severest problems, continues to affect the Native population deeply. In the Arctic, the alcoholism rate is 50 percent higher than among any other Native groups in the state. Almost half of the admissions to alcohol rehabilitation programs in Alaska are Natives. Natives also account for 30% of all alcohol-related arrests and 55% of all liquor law violations. Morbidly, they account for 49% of the alcohol-related deaths and 28 percent of cirrhosis deaths. 79% of all Native suicides had detectable levels of blood alcohol. Alaska Natives also have one of the highest Fetal Alcohol Syndrome birth rates **in the world** (4.2/1000 live births).[267]

There have been other changes in the Arctic as well. With the advent of money, as in cash, the entire economic structure of the Arctic community has changed. Gordon Osborne's branch of the Nome Miner's and Merchant's bank was bought out by Bank of the North whose business was taken over in 1986 by National Bank of Alaska that, in 2001, was bought by Wells Fargo. Loans were extended, a surprise to many Arctic residents who had previously been forced to fly to Nome, Fairbanks, Anchorage, Seattle or elsewhere for money in the past.

Money has brought quite a change in day-to-day living as well. In the late 1960s, Dave Johnson of the ACS ran telephone cable throughout the community and many homes installed a phone. Edith Bullock remembered when she got a Princess phone and everyone came by to look out at. A telephone in your own home! What a wonder of civilization! Why, with a phone in your own house you didn't have to go to the ACS and wait two or three hours for your call to go through to faraway places like Fairbanks and Anchorage! And the person on the other end wouldn't be all garbled![268]

The first coin-operated laundry, "Bonnie's Bubble Room," appeared in 1965, the same year as the filtrated water system.[269] Residents could then drink water right out of the tap, a luxury that many people in Los Angeles cannot claim today. [Prior to that, interestingly, water was provided by Archie during the summer through a two-barge operation. He would have one barge slowly filling with water from lagoons in the Teller area while he was selling water from a second barge in Kotzebue. Every few weeks he would switch the barges.[270]

By 1975 there were flush toilets in most buildings. Cable television followed in the late 1970s along with pizza parlors, pull-tab businesses and video stores. Today it is not unusual to wait for a pizza being made by an Inupiat wearing a "Guns & Roses" T shirt while you watch a live baseball game in Florida on ESPN. But, in 1992, Kotzebue did not have a movie theater.

The diet of the Arctic has changed quite a bit as well. With four flights a day, getting food into Kotzebue is much easier than when Archie was alive. Many of the Inupiat still subsistence hunt but more and more are doing their "hunting" at the supermarket. One of the standing jokes among some Natives is how they went "subsistence hunting" at Safeway and, 'POW! shot a beefsteak.'

The greatest impact on the Arctic has been made by the people who shaped it. No book on Kotzebue would be complete without crediting Edith and Jack Bullock for their telling influence on the course of Arctic history.

While Archie was the archetype Frontier exploiter, Jack and Edith Bullock could be called the gold standard for ethics in the Arctic. After watching how Archie unscrupulously cheated white and Native alike, Edith and Jack formed a corporation with Louis Rotman to compete head-on with Archie's lighterage business. Started in 1951 under the name B & R for "Bullock and Rotman," their barge line offered fuel oil and gasoline to the same customers Archie had been serving for years.

Bert Belz and Louie Rotman

It did not take long for Archie to be driven out of business. Actually this was not that difficult. Archie could not or would not sell an honest product or service. Then he wouldn't pay for the product or service he received. He often sold gasoline that had been contaminated with diesel oil because he didn't clean out his tanks properly. Other times, the fuel he sold froze because there was water in it.[271] With B & R, there was no question that the product the consumer received was top of the line. In the end, B & R took all of Archie's customers.

B & R itself was an instrument of change in the Arctic. When the Bullocks started the lighterage service, the Inupiat crew ate fish, caribou and pilot bread and coffee. By the time the Bullocks sold out to Pacific Inland Navigation in 1969 – who later sold out to Crowley Maritime – they were ordering supplies just as if the crews were white. The diet of the Inupiat on the barges was like that of their white crew: vegetables, meat, eggs and, particularly, mayonnaise.

Louis Rotman sold out to the Bullocks because he "had a heart attack every time one of the barges was at sea," Edith remembered with a laugh. In addition to the oil and gasoline concession, the Bullocks also provided lighterage to the United States government in the building of DEW Line sites. Jack Bullock, operating out of Seattle, stunned military transport personnel in 1958 by transporting more cargo north in a shorter time than they had calculated under their best case scenario.

Edith Bullock also deserves credit for her steadfast support of the Inupiat in the face of exploitation by unscrupulous whites. As a small example, in the 1960s, with the polar bear hunters coming to town, there was so much money to be made that the Inupiat did whatever they could to absorb a trickle of it. One way for the Natives to make money was to sell artifacts they owned or found along the beach. When Edith discovered that there was a market for the ancient workings, she passed the word among the Inupiat that they should not be selling the artifacts because these items were part of their heritage. This did little to stem the sale of the artifacts, so she bought a book on Alaskan artwork and began buying the best pieces. These were eventually donated to the City of Kotzebue. Other pieces were donated to the Anchorage Museum of History and Art where they remain to this day. Jack and Edith were separated in 1960 and divorced in 1966. Edith moved to Anchorage in 1969 where she served on many boards including the University of Alaska. She was named Alaskan of the Year in 1979 by the Anchorage Chamber of Commerce. She died in 1994.

Jack Bullock went to Seattle where he started Alaska Barge Transport. During the Vietnam War he off loaded hundreds of tons of supplies in Vietnam – along with enough private sector washing machines which he smuggled into the country – to open a laundry in Saigon "a block square," Ray Heinrichs remembered. Caught in a corruption investigation, Jack took the blame for the shenanigan and returned to the United States broke. He went through two more marriages, one of them which left such bitterness that as this book was being written the ex-wife was insinuating legal action as to the contents of the two or three paragraphs on Jack.[272] Jack eventually died of cancer of the voice box in 1989. Throughout his life he was a man who was always willing to reach into his pocket to financially help others, but he died broke. After Edith's death in 1994, it was revealed that she had been her ex-husband's anonymous financial benefactor. In the final years of Jack's life, she had given money to Gene Joiner which was then given to Jack for his medical and living expenses. Jack died without ever knowing it was Edith who had been paying his bills for years.[273]

In 1991, when this book was written, Warren's three sons were still alive. But Ray and Don have suffered heart attacks and Frank has survived two strokes. Don ran a small business in Fairbanks and Ray was still flying out of Kotzebue. Frank retired from the State Senate in 1988 for health reasons. He had done so much for his constituents that October 18 is officially Frank Ferguson Day in Kotzebue. Archie is remembered with Ferguson Airfield in Selawik and an annual dog sled race.

With regard to progeny, if Archie had been alive in 1991, he would have had 22 grandchildren. Included in the growing family are names from the past including Ray's daughters Hadley, named after Archie's first wife, and Juanita, named after Archie's sister. Don's family includes a Warren, after Archie's brother, Don, Jr., and an Archie, Jr. who works for Ward Air, owned by Marge Ward, daughter of Clara Rotman Salinas.

In the 1990s, Max Pierce, the IRS agent who collected from Archie, was still alive in Anchorage as were Sam Shafsky, Judge von der Heydt, Bob Erwin, Rose Marie Lauser, C. R. Kennelly, Tommy Richards, Sr., Ray and Marie Heinrichs, Vincent Doran and Neil Bergt, now the owner of Mark Air. Bill Boucher, Sig Wien and Robert Jacobs live in Fairbanks. Frank and Ray Ferguson still lived in Kotzebue as does Art Fields, Sr., and Clara Rotman Salinas. Charles Cole was the Attorney General of Alaska for three years in the early 1990s.

Father Segundo Llorente, the priest who had gone to battle against the Ferguson bull, later served as a missionary in Bethel, Akulurak, Kwiguk, Sheldon Point and Alakanuk. In 1960, while in Alakanuk, he was elected to the Alaska State House by a write-in campaign pushed by a Seattle group who signed their literature "Committee for Good Government." This made Llorente one of the first Roman Catholic priests in American history to be elected to a legislative office.[274]

Father Segundo Llorente

His election raised eyebrows among his superiors as the 51-year old priest was already well-known for his unconventional ways. He had been appointed by the Territorial Court as an official marriage counselor and had "performed ceremonies (though not Catholic ones) for both Protestants and divorced couples."[275]

Llorente was quickly asked by his Bishop, Gleeson, to resign because, with the election of John F. Kennedy to the Presidency, there was a fear that "priests would be running and perhaps stampeding for elected office." The shrewd man that he was, Llorente submitted the letter of resignation to his Bishop asking the Bishop to forward it to Governor Egan.

According to the *Nome Nugget,* in the letter of resignation, Llorente cited "several reasons" which he would "rather not have discussed in the press." Reporters speculated that Llorente's actions had something to do with "fish-buying activities in the Yukon Delta area where Father Llorente live[d]."

The Bishop was a shrewd man himself. By design or accident, he kept the letter of resignation long enough that it became "too late to resign." [276] Only after he was seated did Llorente decide to become a Democrat because, Llorente noted, if he sided with the Republicans, the State House would be evenly split and "it would paralyze all meaningful legislation."[277] Llorente later wrote of his experiences in Alaska MEMORIES OF A YUKON PRIEST which was published in 1988. He died in 1989.[278]

Gene Jack died of cancer in California in 1988 and Hadley Ferguson, Archie's first wife, died the year after Archie in Kotzebue, on October 28th. Jimmy Donovan, Archie's first passenger, went on to become a gold miner in Shungnak. He was unsuccessful and finally killed himself with a shotgun. When his body was found, it was discovered that "mice had eaten his eyes." Paul Davidovics, with the 99 children, died in 1943. Don Emmons, Archie's pilot who had to "drop" his common law wife, was killed in Ketchikan in October of 1954. He was in a pulp mill when he fell into a debarking or "chipping" machine. Emmons had a reputation around Ketchikan as being cantankerous and constantly saying that he was going to be worth a million dollars when he died. Shortly after his death, the talk around Ketchikan was that "Don Emmons was finally in the chips."

Archie's friend Jim Robbins died in a plane wreck in Idaho in 1958. He took off from Denver in a Twin Apache and disappeared. Eight months later a sheepherder found the plane and what were presumed to be Robbins' bones.[279]

In retrospect, Robbins is an interesting character for both Alaska and American history. Robbins was a mechanical genius and, in 1951, invented a machine capable of boring the full diameter of a tunnel. This sped up the mining process significantly as it eliminated conventional drilling and blasting. Since 1952, the Robbins Company, now run by Richard Robbins, Jim's son, has custom-designed 168 TBM, Tunnel Boring Machines. The 'grandson' of the TBM design invented by Jim Robbins was used in the building of the Chunnel, the subway under the English Channel between Dover and Calais. Interesting from an aviation point of view, Jim Robbins' daughter, Barbara, married John Lindbergh, son of the famed aviator Charles and author Ann Morrow.[280]

Chet Brown, the man Archie hired by wire to come north to teach him to fly, remained in Alaska for a number of years but his flying took him all over the world. In the early 1960s, he was in Thailand where he served the government as their aviation counselor. He married a princess and started Thai Air, the national airlines of Thailand. In 1962, he was flying supplies to guerrillas in Laos when his plane, a Lockheed Hudson, smashed into a mountain in the fog. Brown was co-pilot that day and not at the controls when the plane crashed. The cause of the wreck was determined to be pilot error. Brown is buried in Bangkok. Maurice King, the second pilot to teach Archie to fly, disappeared after taking off from the Malaspina Glacier on July 27, 1951.

"Queen" Bess Cross served one term in Juneau, in the 17th Territorial Legislature, 1945-46. She introduced a few bills, two of which merit mention. House Bill 103 called for an "absolute prohibition of the importation, manufacture, barter and sale of drugs and alcoholic beverages," ironic because of her bootlegging conviction. The other bill was HB 77, which would have required "persons operating commercial planes carrying passengers to obtain instrument rating from the Civil Aeronautics Administration." HB 77 did not go over well. It came out of the six-person Committee on Roads and Highways with six votes against it and made it the floor where it went down to defeat 19 to 5. She paid O. D. Cochran, the senator from Nome, to sponsor a bill to incorporate the village of Deering. [Author's note: This tidbit came from a transcription of a recording. The person doing the transcription was not an Alaskan and misspelled many village and geographic names. The actual village in the transcript was "Darien," which the author assumes is "Deering."] When the bill was introduced on the floor, Senator Grenold Collins of Anchorage "smelled a rat," and said he didn't think the legislature should pass this legislation "without finding out a little more about it. The village of Deering is an Inupiat village and I [don't] see any need to have it incorporated and I [haven't]seen any word from the people of the village that they want to incorporate."

Cochran asked for a recess and cornered Collins in the hallway. "Now, Gren," Collins reported Cochran as saying. "You know damn well what this is about. Bess wants to sell booze to the Inupiat. You can't have a liquor place there unless the town in incorporated." Collins said he didn't believe this was a good idea to which Cochran replied, "I don't believe in it either [but] I'm [Bess Cross'] attorney and I have to play along to some extent. We'll go back in there and you get up and tell 'em what it's all about and I'll give you hell on the floor and then we'll have a vote." So Collins did, and Cochran did, and the bill failed.[281]

After her single legislative term, Bess Cross returned to Kotzebue. She divorced John Cross by the end of the decade and opened a restaurant, The

Arctic Adventurers Club right across the street from and in direct competition with Archie's Kotzebue Grille. (Her silent partner was Boris Magids, a fact that came out after the death of Magids and the United States government wanted to acquire the property for a jail[282].) She also raised eyebrows around Kotzebue by taking an "Eskimo Lover." She left Kotzebue in the early 1960s and ended up in the Sitka Pioneer Home at the end of the decade. Later she was "transferred" to the Fairbanks Pioneer Home. She left Alaska for the last time and died in Seattle on April 14, 1971. John Cross subsequently married Bessie and had three children. After putting in more than 21,000 hours of flying and logging more than 2 million miles over Alaska, John Cross died in Kotzebue in 1981. The International Airport at Fairbanks is named in his honor.

Robert K. Baker, the game warden who had "both friends" in attendance, married Clara Rotman's daughter, Marge. Together they formed Baker Air Service. Robert was killed landing on a proverbial dark and stormy night on St. Lawrence Island during an emergency flight. Robert Baker is memorialized in an airfield in Kiana.

Gene Morris, the State Trooper in Nome who intimidated Linda Ferguson by being so large, was transferred to Anchorage where he was promoted to patrol sergeant. That proved to be his undoing. In the big city, he was completely out of place. "He could not only care less [but] he didn't give a damn if the cop cars ran out of fuel or not," Erwin remembered. Morris was quickly transferred to Wrangell and then to the Pribilof Islands where he spent his last six years as a trooper doing a phenomenal job. He was a man who genuinely liked the Inupiat and went way out of his way to help. He was covered with awards when he retired. He moved to Arizona where he was killed in a hunting accident.

Trooper Hemphill divorced, re-married and was eventually stationed in Nome. Tom Packer left the Post Office and worked for both the Miner's and Merchants Bank and Bank of the North before working for Wedbush Morgan Securities, Inc. Dave Johnson, much liked in Kotzebue and a close friend of Gene Joiner, died in Anchorage in 1988.

The "Master of the Lie Box," Ed Dankworth, the State Trooper who gave Steve Salinas the polygraph twice went on to become the head of the Alaska State Troopers, an Alaska State Senator and, in 1992, is a powerful lobbyist in the Alaska capitol. Tommy Richards, Sr., calls "Bish"

Donald Gallahorn, the "Little Louis Rotman," after his grandfather. Bish inherited management roles in the Rotman-Salinas Empire and went into business with his half-aunt, Yvonne Salinas, daughter of Steve Salinas. The company, R & S, for "Rotman & Salinas" has city and corporation gravel contracts, rental units, and real estate holdings and, when it was legal, a liquor store and bar. Linda Ferguson has had very few contacts with her former in-laws. She lived in Anchorage for a number of years and eventually re-married. Numerous attempts to contact her by the author proved fruitless.

Fred Crane did not outlive Archie by very long. As Archie began his long battle with the "Infernal" Revenue Service, Crane was convinced to apply for reinstatement to the bar. Statehood was coming fast and Fred was advised to resolve his legal difficulties before Alaska became a state and a new layer of bureaucracy was added. Thus, in 1958, after practicing without a license for more than 20 years, Crane applied to United States District Court Judge Walter Hodge of Nome to be reinstated. Hodge did so under the specific condition that Fred practice in Nome.[283] There was only one lawyer there, James von der Heydt, but he was about to be named to the Federal bench and was going to leave the area. Crane agreed to the condition and the moment he was reinstated, he "promptly moved to Fairbanks." Why didn't Hodge object? He had other things on his mind. In August, 1959, he was appointed to the Alaska Supreme Court.[284]

Back in Fairbanks, Crane went back into private practice with another frontier character, Warren Taylor I. Taylor was the epitome of cantankerous curmudgeon who held the dubious distinction of having the "longest successful string of DWI defenses in the Alaska in the 1950s – if not today."[285]

Throughout the legal circle of Fairbanks, Taylor was known as a "cantankerous, obstructionist criminal defense lawyer" who was "preposterous to deal with, extremely unpleasant, devious, willfully misleading" and was always calling the prosecutors "names under his breath." A legislator as well, it was said that every member of the Fairbanks Bar voted for Taylor to get him out of Fairbanks for at least four months each year. Doug Baily, former Attorney General for the State of Alaska, remembered Warren Taylor as a lawyer who would "pull every trick in the book and then some" in the courtroom but was an absolute teddy bear on a personal level. One weekend Baily went to Warren's mine as Warren's guest and spent an enjoyable day but the second the two were back in the courtroom Taylor was back to the "insulting, insinuating, scowling defense lawyer."[286]

Charles Cole, former Attorney General for the State of Alaska, remembered that Crane and Taylor were ideal legal partners. It was common knowledge that the two paid themselves in a very odd fashion. "The first one there in the morning would [open the mail and] take the checks." Cole, however, felt that Crane's legal abilities by then were "somewhat over-rated. He knew nothing about discovery" and did little preparation. Once, Cole remembered Crane, acting as a defense attorney, walked into the court room and said, "'Will the Defendant please stand up and identify himself.'"

Even in Fairbanks, Crane maintained his reputation as a drinker and womanizer. He always had "at least four or five Eskimo women anywhere from 18 to 25" living with him and while everyone assumed that he was having wild sexual affairs, the truth was probably a bit different. Fred was diabetic by this point in life and was having severe prostrate problems. He was still a heavy smoker and "carried nitroglycerine with him all the time."[287] The strain of his rough life told on his face as it "looked like a road map" and his body, once forgiving of his alcoholism, was now rebelling against him.[288] More than once, Bob Erwin had to go over to Crane's apartment and pick him up off the floor because of his deteriorating metabolic condition.

But he maintained his rock-solid reputation as a defender of the Inupiat, both in and out of the court room. It was well known in the Arctic that if a Native came to town, Fred would cover the cost of meals at the Model Cafe. John Bonich, who ran the Model Cafe, kept a running tabulation on the Inupiat and then Fred exchanged the bill for legal services. Fred also took an active role in opposing "religious groups which had taken advantage of the Inupiat," Erwin remembered "and he was always fighting with them for their over-paternalism."

Returning to public service, Crane served as the DA in both Nome and Fairbanks. But he was hardly the conventional prosecutor. His techniques were Territorial and many were clearly extra-legal. For instance, attorney Robert H. Wagstaff remembered a homicide where a woman had shot her husband in Fairbanks and the Grand Jury refused to indict. When the police chief asked Crane why the case had been dropped, Fred replied,

"If ever there was a son-of-a-bitch who needed killing, that was him."

"Fred," said the Chief. "You're making us look like fools!"

"Did you ever think about that?" returned Fred.

One of the shenanigans for which Crane is most remembered was revealed by Fred, publicly, at an Alaska Bar Association gathering in the late 1960s. Speaking as the District Attorney of Nome, Fred was explaining how he had handled the problem of LSD coming into Nome. He knew the drug was coming into town and he also knew who was transporting the illegal substance. Rather than following the guidelines of search and seizure, which he believed to be "silly,"[289] Fred took the law into his own hands. He got a hold of a "young, attractive woman" and offered her a number of dollars to be available that night to befriend the construction worker in question. Then he called his friend "Reggie the Rat" and "made an arrangement" for "$20 presently and another $20 to be paid after com-

Fred Crane in his last year

pletion of the task" to stand by at the Board of Trade Bar (BOT) where an out-of-towner would reasonably appear.

The construction worker showed up in the BOT as anticipated and Fred immediately pointed him out to the woman he had hired. As soon as the woman and the construction worker "appeared to be progressing toward a very friendly relationship in the back of the bar," Fred and "Reggie the Rat" went up the street to the Nugget Inn. There Reggie broke into the construction worker's room, located and removed the LSD. Fred paid "Reggie the Rat" and took the LSD out to the breakwater and tossed it into Norton Sound.[290]

Crane was also accused of generating false testimony in the arson case of Salinas. In signed affidavits, two then-Kotzebue residents stated they had been paid to give false testimony. Later the two thought their predicament through and went to the U.S. Marshal, R. W. Oliver, and admitted their transgressions. Apparently nothing ever came of the matter.[291]

It is thus not surprising that Crane's FBI file is interesting. Requested through a Freedom of Information Act request, there were 27 pages of references to Crane but only seven were released and of these, one was completely blacked out. The bulk of the pages withheld were from the same file, "44-17239." One of the two reasons given for not releasing documents 30-years old was that it would reveal the name of a "confidential source." Of the memos that were released, one, dated August 10, 1961, requested an investigation into the possibility that Fred Crane may have violated an individual's civil rights because he and his "associates" wanted Nome to be "an open town for bootlegging and vice." Supposedly Crane forced more than one person to sign false statements to "get" another person. The matter was sent to the District Attorney for the Second Judicial District for consideration and that was the end of the file. Nothing came of the investigation.[292]

In late 1968, Crane invited the Alaska Bar Association to have its annual convention in Nome. But a few months before the meeting was to be held, Crane died. However, since all the arrangements had been made well ahead of time, the convention was held on schedule and Fred was honored posthumously for his "dual reputation of being a tough old codger and the champion of the underdog."[293] The Saturday night before the banquet, many old friends of Crane's were drinking heavily and playing poker when someone remarked that in Nome no one was buried in the winter. The bodies were kept in storage until the thaw made it possible to dig graves. Someone then suggested that they prop up Fred Crane for one last night of merriment. According to Erwin and three other sources, Crane's body was taken out of the locker at the Nome Hospital and transported to the BOT where it was put in the ice locker behind the bar. Crane was finally buried in Nome on Memorial Day, 1969.

While Fred and Archie were in their seventies when they died, Salinas died young, at 57, of a cerebral hemorrhage in February of 1980. He had gone outside to remove some snow from around the Rotman Store entrance, turned on a small snow plow and collapsed on the ground. He was flown to Providence Hospital in Anchorage where he died.

One of the many ironies of the Arctic is that Gene Joiner outlived both Archie and Fred Crane by more than two decades. As those two men passed into history, Joiner continued to build his reputation as an eccentric. He had the first Cadillac in Kotzebue which he parked beside his two-room home and occasionally drove it out to the airport, a grand total of about a mile. He also started the now-traditional Fourth of July Miss Arctic Circle Pageant.

In November of 1969, Joiner's PA 12, Piper Supercruiser, finally gave out on him about 60 miles from Kiana. He survived the crash but rather than walk the 16 miles to a shelter cabin owned by a man he didn't like, Joiner decided to walk the 60 miles into Kiana. He did spend at least one night in an abandoned cabin on his way to the village but slept without heat to prevent his already-frozen feet and fingers from thawing which would have caused him additional, intense pain.

After spending 12 days in 50-below-zero weather he stumbled into Kiana more dead than alive. More than once he wanted to die, he later told friends, but he kept walking because he "didn't want to be a question mark, someone who went out and never came back."[294] (What kept him going, he later told Dr. Neilson, was "tremendous craving" for a "big can of tomato juice" he knew he could get at Blankenship's store in Kiana.)

Joiner was transported to the Alaska Native Hospital in Anchorage where he was eligible for treatment because he had been in the Merchant Marines. The prognosis was not good. The frostbite was so severe that all of his toes and the top digits of his fingers had to be removed. A substantial section of his right heel had to be cut away as well.

But the pain and his own closeness of death did not seem to affect him at all. "Touch me," he said to Baptist Minister, Reverend Richard Miller who came to visit him. "I'm a living miracle."

That was as humble as Joiner got. As soon as he could dial a phone, he was on it. He rang Ray Heinrichs and told him to bring over steak and lobster from the Anchorage Westward Hotel. Heinrichs and his wife were living on a "tight budget and eating beans" at the time but complied though Joiner never offered to pay them back for the food Ray brought to the hospital. Then Joiner phoned Martin to bring him fruit. Martin went down and watched Joiner treat the hospital room just like his home in Kotzebue. "He'd take grape seed and spit them out on the floor to get the nurses goin' and he wanted rotten bananas and throw the skins on the floor."

Gene Joiner in Rancho Mirage. Note his missing fingers.
Photograph courtesy of the Riverside Press Enterprise.

But the survival trek had taken a physical toll on Joiner. He could not take the cold as well after the wreck and his metabolic condition deteriorated. Already having problems with diabetes and cancer of the prostate, he now suffered from heart trouble, high blood pressure and arthritis. He would occasionally have blackouts and forget where he was. Once, as he told Richard Foster, he was in his plane coming to Nome when he had a blackout. He awoke to find himself with full right rudder, the plane flying in an uncoordinated manner, with his head sticking out of the window of the aircraft and screaming at the top of his lungs. As Joiner became older, he spent more and more time in Mexico going to health clinics. The heat did wonders for his outlook but there was little that could be done for his internal difficulties. Believing that the drugs prescribed for him were doing him more damage than good, he eventually swore off of them altogether, fearing addiction more than pain.

Being off the drugs made him more susceptible to mood changes which sometimes led to comedy. His daughter remembered one time when he got off the plane from Alaska, groggy from the flight and in a bad mood from the lack of medication. When he discovered that his flight to Palm Springs was leaving without him – and was still visible moving into takeoff position on the tarmac, he "bounded through the gate and began running after the plane." He made it as far as the landing strip but was escorted back to the terminal by "about 40 people" and held momentarily under suspicion of attempted hijacking of an airliner.

Joiner finally got his "Big Lick," as Ozrow Martin referred to it, in 1974. After NANA Corporation was formed, one of their first acquisitions were Joiner's claims on Jade Mountain. Joiner had built the jade market up to the point where it was a reasonable investment for the regional corporation, particularly since there were Inupiat in Kotzebue trained to work the jade into commercial products. They also had contracts with Chinese factories. (Today, Jade is the State Gem.)

A deal was negotiated and Joiner signed a bill for sale for "several hundred thousand dollars," which Joiner demanded in cash. NANA did not have cash but gave him a check on the Wells Fargo Bank in San Francisco. The check was given on a Friday under the assumption that Joiner would take a few days to tie up his affairs before he went south.

This was not the case.

On the proceeding Monday morning, Joiner was first in line at the Wells Fargo Bank in San Francisco demanding his "several hundred thousand dollars" in cash. Since he was dressed *a la Joiner*, the bank had a hard time believing that this ragged man was indeed worth several hundred thousand dollars.

Joiner, who called himself "impatient" and "loud," put up, in his words, "quite a fuss" over his "sale of the century."[295] Erwin's recollection was a bit different. He recalled stories of Joiner sitting in the bank "screaming and hollering for two hours," as the bank verified that he was entitled to receive the money. Then they packed the "several hundred thousand dollars" into his empty suitcase and out the door Joiner went. His next stop was Boaz, Alabama, a city in which he had not lived in 50 years and with relatives of his with whom he had not corresponded during the same time period. He made the rounds and was greatly amused at the shock he created by being a "ragtag old man in a fairly dirty suit carrying several hundred thousand dollars in cash in a suitcase."[296]

With a fortune in his hands, Joiner could now do anything he wanted. He bought a small house on the outskirts of Rancho Mirage. The home had originally been built by a construction firm owned by Hollywood sex-symbol Hedy LaMarr and was far from the center of town. Over the years, however, the exclusive community moved in on Joiner and he eventually became part of the suburbs. As Joiner's little house was zoned residential, he created unending headaches for the city fathers. In addition to the piles of junk in his yard, he had an ever-increasing collection of 1956 Fords. The one on which he was working was usually in the garage but the rest stretched around his house, bumper to bumper, regardless of the zoning restrictions. At one time, Jim West from Nome, remembered that Joiner had ten of them in his front yard. "They call me 'Mr. 56' down here," Joiner told him proudly.

Inside, Joiner's home in Rancho Mirage was treated exactly the same as his home in Kotzebue. The only difference was that instead of an airplane engine in the living room it was that of a 1956 Ford. He was still smoking too. The last time Jim West say him, Joiner said that he was "smoking four packs of Camels a day and had to cut back to three packs."

Perhaps for the first time in his life, Joiner had the money to be extravagant. But he was extravagant in a manner that was pure Joiner. Being a well-informed history buff, he discovered that English law had changed in the 1970s such that anyone could buy a Title of Nobility as long as there was no property involved. At the first auction, he went to England and offered a bid that was accepted. Thereafter, Gene Joiner was officially Lord Crepping from Colchester. (Colchester is in Essex, the county immediately adjacent to London on the northeast.) Oddly, of all the achievements in his life, the Title of Nobility thrilled him the most. His daughter remembered that Joiner was "absolutely thrilled to death that his name would go down with the likes of Eleanor of Aquitaine."

But just sitting at his home in Palm Springs was difficult so Joiner began a new career. He decided to become a violin maker. In spite of the fact that he had no digits on the tops of his fingers, he was nevertheless quite adept at using the tools necessary to make the musical instrument. Swearing that he was going to make violins *better* than Stradivarius, he went all over the world looking for the right kind of wood. He did manage to build a couple of violins but none of them approached the quality of the finely-made instrument by the Italian Master.

When Joiner died in May of 1988, his daughter handled his affairs and had the body shipped to Boaz, Alabama. Only later did she discover that

Joiner had wanted to be buried next to Emily Boucher in Seattle where a small, flat jade headstone had already been installed for him.

As an interesting twist to the life of Gene Joiner, he got one last laugh from beyond the grave. Cheap throughout his entire life, he had stored a number of jade boulders in Seattle at Mayflower. One at a time he had sold the boulders, most of them to Ray Heinrichs who ran Kobuk Valley Jade in Girdwood, Alaska until his death in 2004. Several years after Joiner's death, Ray Heinrichs received a letter from Mayflower in Seattle informing him that he owed several years rental on a warehouse in which sat three gargantuan jade boulders. Heinrichs wrote to Mayflower and stated that he had only bought three boulders from Joiner and they had already received shipment. The boulders in question were Joiner's, not his. The next letter from Mayflower was a shock. Enclosed was correspondence to Mayflower in which Joiner, the skinflint, stated that all boulders remaining at Mayflower belonged to Heinrichs.

But the "legacy of Archie" still lived. In 1969, Don Ferguson flew into the Anchorage International Airport and landed at George Grant's air salvage shop. Don was flying a 207 and walked into Grant's office, looked around and *a la Archie Ferguson* asked if there were any FAA around. When Grant told him no, Don walked back to the door and gave a hand wave to the people in the plane. As Grant watched, "18 people got out of this airplane, a plane that normally held six people and the pilot. Kids and some babies, they just kept coming."

They had all come in from Kotzebue. Had Archie been alive, he would have thought that Don was truly following in his footsteps.

BIBLIOGRAPHY

Secondary Sources

BASEBALL ENCYCLOPEDIA. Macmillan Publishing Company, 1990.

BITS AND PIECES OF ALASKAN HISTORY. (Two Volumes), Alaska Northwest Publishing Company, 1981 and 1982.

Brink, Frank. SOUNDS OF ALASKA. Anchorage, 1964. (record)

Clifton, Robert Bruce. MURDER BY MAIL AND OTHER POSTAL INVESTIGATIONS. Dorrance & Company, 1979.

Day, Beth. GLACIER PILOT. Comstock, 1981.

Franck, Harry A. THE LURE OF ALASKA. Blue Ribbon Books, 1939.

Harkey, Ira. PIONEER BUSH PILOT. University of Washington, 1974.

Helmericks, Harmon. THE LAST OF THE BUSH PILOTS. Bantam Books, 1969.

Janson, Lone E. MUDHOLE SMITH. Alaska Northwest Publishing Company, 1981.

Jasper, Patricia B. and Beverly M. Blasongame. A GATHERING OF SAINTS IN ALASKA. Salt Lake City, Hiller Industries, 1983.

Jones, H. Wendy. WOMEN WHO BRAVED THE FAR NORTH. Grossmont Press, Inc., San Diego, 1976.

Karst, Gene and Martin J. Jones, Jr. WHO'S WHO IN PROFESSIONAL BASEBAL, Arlington House, 1973.

MANIILAQ. Compiled by Ruth Ramoth-Sampson and Angeline Newlin and published in book form by Federal Grant G008006779 in 1978. This copy was at the Z. J. Loussac Library in Anchorage.

Naske, Claus-M. and Herman E. Slotnick. ALASKA, A HISTORY OF THE 49TH STATE. William B. Eerdsmans Publishing Company, 1979.

Orth, Donald J. DICTIONARY OF ALASKA PLACE NAMES. United States Printing Office, 1967.

Potter, Jean. FLYING FRONTIERSMEN. New York, Macmillan, 1956.

Potter, Jean. THE FLYING NORTH. New York, Bantam, 1983.

Ricks, Melvin. ALASKA BIBLIOGRAPHY: AN INTRODUCTORY GUIDE TO ALASKAN HISTORICAL LITERATURE. (Edited by Stephen W. and Betty J. Haycox.) Alaska Historical Commission, 1977.

Roberts, Arthur O. TOMORROW IS GROWING OLD. Newberg, Oregon. The Barclay Press, 1978.

Rychetnik, Joe. BUSH COP. Boxwood Press, 1991.

SAN FRANCISCO, THE BAY AND ITS CITIES. Compiled by Workers of the Writer's Program of the Work Projects Administration in Northern California, 1947.

Skehan, Everett M. ROCKY MARCIANO, Biography of a First Son. Houghton Mifflin Company, 1977.

Satterfield, Archie. THE ALASKA AIRLINES STORY. Alaska Northwest Publishing Company, 1981.

Stefansson, Vihjalmur. THE ADVENTURE OF WRANGEL ISLAND. Macmillan, 1925.

Warbelow, Willy Lou. EMPIRE ON ICE. Great Northwest Publishing and Distributing Company, Inc., 1990.

Waring Associates, Kevin. FINAL TECHNICAL REPORT, KOTZEBUE SOCIOCULTURAL MONITORING STUDY, submitted to Minerals Management Service, United States Department of the Interior, December, 1988.

Primary Sources

Alaska Magazine

Anchorage Daily News

Anchorage Times

Arctic Sounder

Collins, Grenold and Dorothy. Papers in the possession of the University of Alaska Anchorage Archives.

Fairbanks Daily News Miner

Hadley, Martha E. THE ALASKAN DIARY OF A PIONEER QUAKER MISSIONARY. Xeroxed, spiral-bound, typed manuscript of the diary of Martha E. Hadley, 1899-1903, in the possession of the Z. J. Loussac Library, Anchorage, Alaska. 1969. These papers have been published in book form.

Harris, Gladys Knight. Collection of photographs in the possession of the Southwest Museum in Los Angeles.

Heller, Margaret. Papers in the possession of the University of Alaska Anchorage Archives.

"In the Matter of Fred Crane, Petitioner, Appearing for the Purpose of Quashing a Subpeona," Alaska Archives, Juneau, Record Group 507, Series 429, Box 2, File #4214.

Ketchikan Alaska Chronicle.

Lester, Jean. FACES OF ALASKA FROM BARROW TO WRANGELL. (Self-published in 1992): Box 33, Ester, Alaska, 99725.

Llorente, Segundo. MEMOIRES OF A YUKON PRIEST. Georgetown University Press, 1988.

McKotzebugle.

Mukluk Telegraph. (Mukluk Telegraph is also the name of the internal newsletter for the Alaska Native Services.)

Nome Nugget.

Poor, Henry Varum. THE CRUISE OF THE **ADA**. (Self-published, 1945.)

Simpson, Jimmy. "Homin' Home to My Home in Kotzebue." Sourdough Records.

Squire, Cark. "Alaska Jade is Tough Stuff," *Seattle Sunday Times Magazine,* June 5, 1955.

TEWKESBURY'S WHO'S WHO IN ALASKA AND BUSINESS INDEX, 1947.

Transcript of an Interview of Jim Hutchison by Cliff Cernick on July 15, 1990 in the possession of the Ferguson Collection of the Levi Papers, UAA. *Tundra Times.*

Wilson, Bruce A. and Marylee. Diary of the Sweet-Wilson Expedition, 1946, in the possession of the Alaska State Library, Juneau.

World War I Selective Service System Registration Cards, 1917-1918, microfilm in the possession of NARA.

Interviewees

Doug Baily

Leroy Barker

Neil Bergt

Bill Boucher

Edith Bullock

Fred Chambers

Frank Doolin

Vincent Doran

K Doyle

Linda Drohman

Ida Evern

Cliff Everts

Bob Erwin

Art Fields, Sr.

Dr. Robert I. Fraser

Fred Goodwin – (no relation to the Kotzebue Goodwins)

George Grant

Jay Hammond

Raymond Hawk

Harold Herning

Jim Hutchison

Robert Jacobs

Mabel Johnson

C. R. Kennelly

Rose Marie Lauser

Leo Mark-Anthony

Ozrow Martin

Helen McConnell

Roger McShea

Reverend Richard Miller

Graham Mower

Jan Morrow

Dr. Charles Neilson

Patricia Neilson

Mary Oldham

Alice Osborne

Drue Pearce

Ray Petersen

Max Pierce

Burleigh Putnam

Tommy Richards, Sr.

Pat Rodey

Ransom "Tony" Schultz

Sam Shafsky

Warren Tilman

Orville Tosch

Robert Wagstaff

Jim West

Sig Wien

Roscoe J. Wilke

Paul Wilson

Frank Whaley

Ed Yost

Letters and Quips

Randy Acord

Robert "Bob" Blodgett

Cliff Cernick

Gary Chandelar

Jean Potter Chelnov

James R. Clouse, Jr.

Charles Cole

Ed Dankworth

Helen Denton

Josh Eagle

Mrs. Don Emmons

Archie Ferguson, Jr.

Don Ferguson, Sr.

Minnie Ferguson

Ray Ferguson

Jerry Finke

Neil Fried

Perry Green

Marie Heinrichs

Willie Hensley

Hadley Hess

Mrs. Jack "Bobbi" Herman

Caroline Hudnall

Frank Irick

Harold Little

Marvin Magnus

Fr. Neill R. Meany, S. J.

Doug Millard

Ken Oldham

Jean Oldham

Georganne Phillips

Roberta Ravenscroft

Joan Ray

Louis Renner, S.J.

Dorothy Richards

Marilyn Richards

Richard Robbins

Jim Ruotsala

Joe Rychetnik

Clara Salinas

Yvonne Salinas

Pasquale M. Spoletini

Bill Stroecker

Glenda Tabor

Alaine Tate

Flip Todd

Willy Lou Warbelow Young

Endnotes

1   Helmricks, BUSH PILOTS, page 75.

2   Potter, FRONTIERSMEN, page 154.

3   Hammond.

4   Shafsky. Archie was not averse to renaming things to suit his unique view of the world. After Archie flew in Randy Acord's Beachcraft Bonanza, he kept referring to it as the "banana with a tailwheel in front." Comments to Levi by Randy Acord, February, 1998.

5   Archie's Death Certificate indicates he was born in Fallmont, Ohio. The Ohio Historical Society was contacted and stated that no such town exists. A search of the 1900 Census also indicated that the Fergusons were no longer in Ohio.

6   Handout from the Fremont, Ohio, phone book. Fremont, incidentally, was the hometown of President Rutherford B. Hayes. He died there in 1893. Know by a variety of epithets including "His Fraudulency" and "Old 8 to 7," his was the third and last-to-date electoral tie in a Presidential election. He was known by these names because his electoral victory was secured by a vote of a special committee of the House of Representatives. The special committee of 8 Republicans and 7 Democrats voted "8 to 7" on all disputes thus electing the Republican Rutherford B. Hayes to the Presidency.

7   Beaverton Schools to Levi, Ferguson Collection in the Steven C. Levi Papers, UAA Archives.

8   Kay Kennedy interview with John Cross housed at the UAF Archives.

9   World War I Selective Service System Registration Cards, 1917-1918, in the possession of NARA.

10 "Alaskan Bush Pilots Recapture Flights of Fancy," *Senior Voice*, March, 1992, and Goodwin.

11 Roberts, *Tomorrow,* page 248.

12 Fields.

13   Putnam.

14   "Edith Bullock" from Lester, FACES OF ALASKA FROM BARROW TO WRANGELL.

15   Dr. Rabeau, now deceased, told Dr. Neilson that in the late 1940s there were only two motor vehicles in Kotzebue that were functional and they had a collision.

16   The date is in dispute, some say 1926 others 1927.

17   Harkey, PIONEER, page 178-9.

18   Harkey, PIONEER, pages 157-8.

19   This tidbit came from Don Ferguson.

20   Conversation with Ransom "Tony" Schultz, August 20, 1991 and Shafsky.

21   Conversation with Ransom "Tony" Schultz, August 20, 1991 and Shafsky..

22   Richards, Sr.

23   "Ferguson's Cow Weathering 1st Winter All Right," *Nome Nugget*, January 10, 1938.

24   Potter, FLYING NORTH, page 219.

25   Llorente, pages 64-65.

26   Yost.

27   Putnam.

28   Comments by Harold Herning. Mrs. Don Emmons gave the name of Dr. Anthony.

29   Shafsky comments.

30   "Munz Makes Daring Rescue," *Nome Nugget*, December 17, 1945.

31   Comment by Jim Ruotsala.

32   Heinrichs stated that Archie had some Kobuk Jade claims.

33   Conversation with Jerry Finke at Hanson's in Nome, 1990 and Hadley Hess, Ray Ferguson's daughter.

34   Edna Ferber described Clara in her book ICE PALACE gracious, elegant and "the Nefertiti of the North" according to Marilyn Richards.

35   Goodwin.

36   Llorente, 62.

37   Yost. One of Davidovics alleged 99 children was Ira Ferguson, son of Minnie, Warren's widow. A photo of Frank Davidovics and his wife can be found in Harry A. Francks' THE LURE OF ALASKA, Blue Ribbon Books, 1943, page 210.

38   "News About Town," *Mukluk Telegraph*, June 1, 1950.

39   Warren had a liquor license in 1935, 1936, 1937 and 1938. On a list of signatures in favor of his liquor license in June of 1936, Warren wrote "This is all the residents that are in Kotzebue at the present time, please wire me

collect soon as my license is in the <u>mail</u>." Below that Warren wrote, "I am out of business till I hear from you." (Nome Civil Files #3318, 2403, and 3356, in the possession of NARA.)

40   Art Fields comment.

41   "Warren Ferguson Tells of Mining in North," *Nome Nugget*, April 22, 1936.

42   Comments by Helen Denton, daughter of Logan Varnell.

43   Art Fields, interview and comments. When Warren's death was first noted in the *Nome Nugget*, the headlines actually read "Archie Ferguson Breaks Thru Ice and Drowns," October 23, 1939. "Body of Warren Ferguson is Recovered at Kotzebue," *Alaska Weekly,* June 14, 1940.

44   Fields and Marilyn Richards.

45   Little.

46   Don and Ray were adopted with papers; Frank was adopted "Eskimo style," IE., with no paperwork.

Robert Ravenscroft. This is what Ray said but there are guardianship 'papers' in the Commissioners logbook for Noatak-Kotzebue. That logbook is in the possession of the State of Alaska Archives and the probate record numbers are 11986, 11987, 11988, 11989. The paperwork is somewhat convoluted. Warren's will, written in 1933 and filed in 1939 <u>after</u> he died, gives Minnie $100 a year in groceries and supplies for five years from the Ferguson store and leaves the rest to Archie. Archie is also made guardian of Warren's children. But there appears to be some kind of twist in the application of the will. Someone tried to claim Warren's property and Archie had to fight off this unnamed adversary. Archie raised the issue that Warren's signature might have been forged and also claimed that Warren's property might be awarded to a nonfamily member. That non family member is not mentioned and was not Minnie as she was specifically mentioned in another section of the will. In the end Archie prevailed. For the historical record, the Commissioner was Delbart Cary.

47   From an interview with John Cross by Mike Dalton, undated, at the University of Alaska, Fairbanks Archives.

48   Archie also dodged debts owed by Warren and was taken to court at least once for bills Warren had signed for but for which Archie refused to pay. (Nome Civil Court File #3604 in the possession of NARA.)

49   Letter from Alice Royce, F.R.'s sister, to Juanita Ferguson, November 18, 1937, a copy of which is in the Ferguson Collection of the Levi Papers, UAA. The copy was supplied by Glenda Tabor.

50   Potter, FLYING NORTH, page 192.

51   Conversation with Potter, July 22, 1989.

52   Phone conversation with Jean Potter and Steven C. Levi.

53   Pilot Certificate of Archie Ferguson, a copy of the file is in the Ferguson Papers of the Levi Collection, Archives, UAA.

54   Grant.

55   Goodwin.

56   "Bombs Open Up Ice-Jam in Kobuk River," *Nome Nugget*, June 7, 1948.

57   "Bush Pilot William Munz Dies at 82," *Anchorage Times*, March 2, 1992.

58   BITS AND PIECES OF ALASKAN HISTORY, Alaska Northwest Publishing Company, Volume I, page 58.

59   "Alaska Lives On Air," *Nome Nugget*, November 10, 1944.

60   Phone conversation of Doug Millard to Steven C. Levi.

61   Clifton, MURDER, page 31.

62   Osborne, Alice, "Archie Ferguson," *Alaska Flying*, No. 17.

63   Potter, FLYING NORTH, p. 206.

64   Wednesday, July 17, 1946 diary entry for Sweet-Wilson Expedition.

65   Kennelly.

66   BITS AND PIECES OF ALASKAN HISTORY, Alaska Northwest Publishing Company, 1981, Volume I, page 76.

67   July 27, 1946, Diary of the Sweet-Wilson Expedition.

68   Fields.

69   Wien and Herman.

70   Letter from Mrs. Jack "Bobbi" Herman to Steven C. Levi, in the Ferguson Papers of the Levi Collection, UAA.

71   Comments by Mrs. Don Emmons.

72   Letter from Bud Miller, January 14, 1990.

73   Hutchison.

74   Goodwin.

75   Goodwin.

76   Whaley and Goodwin but different version. This is primarily Goodwin's.

77   Goodwin.

78   Wilke.

79   Goodwin.

80   Worthy of humorous footnote in aviation history, Wien used to charge its pilots $1 each time they lost a lead weight. After Fred Goodwin lost a few, he discovered that he could use the bung on a 55-gallon oil drum as a substitute. It was just as heavy as the lead weight and had an eye through which the antenna could be attached. Goodwin later stated that he "put Wien out of [the] business of selling lead weights . . . but there were a lot of empty oil drums laying around with no bungs in them."

81   Shafsky.

82   Potter, FLYING NORTH, page 164.

83   Potter, FRONTIERSMEN page 154.

84   Letter from Don Ferguson, October 20, 1989.

85   Goodwin.

86   Potter, FLYING NORTH, 227-229.

87   Potter, FLYING NORTH. Quite a few bush pilots remember this story, though many different locations were given for where this actually occurred. Ray Petersen confirmed that Archie refused to use the 'code of the day' on this – and many other – occasions.

88   Wilke.

89   also called *aktuhaak*

90   Also called *ivalu*,

91   "Main Trails & Bypaths," *Alaska Magazine*, May, 1983.

92   "Veteran Alaska Flyer Turns from Planes to Boats," *Nome Nugget*, February 11, 1946. Harold Little remembers two sets of cubs, a second pair bought for $50 apiece in 1951.

93   Conversation with Don Ferguson and Whaley.

94   Mower interview, Levi papers, UAA.

95   Goodwin.

96   While there are turkeys that can fly, as Arkansas hunters can attest, even these wild birds would have trouble flying inside a Cessna Airmaster.

97   "Hunt Wolves By Airplane," *Nome Nugget*, April 7, 1937.

98   Potter, FLYING NORTH, page 207.

99   Goodwin.

100   Goodwin.

101   Dorothy Collins in Collins Papers, undated letter, University of Alaska Anchorage archives.

102   Bess Cross Appeals Conviction to District Court," *Mukluk Telegraph*, June 9, 1951.

103   Interview with Fred Goodwin.

104   Second Division Returns and historical profiles from the Alaska Legislative Affairs Agency.

105   "Mr. Cross Wins Election," *Nome Nugget*, December 6, 1944.

106   Conversation with Ruth Jefford, June 8, 1990.

107   Helmricks, page 79. The letter, says Ray Petersen, was actually written to Burleigh Putnam.

108   Communications, United States Post Office, Anchorage, February, 1992.

109   July 17, 1946, Diary of the Sweet-Wilson Expedition.

110 George Grant.

111 Ida Evern.

112 von der Heydt.

113 von der Heydt.

114 Heinrichs.

115 Letter from Bud Miller, January 14, 1990.

116 Helmricks, page 87.

117 Grant.

118 *Mukluk Telegraph,* August 31, 1950.

119 Boucher.

120 Alaine Tate and Bill Boucher comments.

121 Neilson and "**North Star** Cruises Alaska's Wild West, " *National Geographic*, July, 1952, page 69.

122 Lauser and Fields.

123 Conversation with Heinrichs, April, 1990.

124 Martin.

125 Martin.

126 Boucher. The author cannot verify many of these claims.

127 Drohman.

128 Boucher letter.

129 Heinrichs comments.

130 Acord comments to Steve Levi in February of 1898.

131 Hutchison.

132 Boucher comments.

133 Conversation with Edith Bullock.

134 Conversation with Don Ferguson, February 25, 1990.

135 Squire, Clark, "Alaskan Jade is Tough Stuff," *Seattle Sunday Times,* June 5, 1955.

136 Conversation with Ray Heinrichs. There is also an article on Archie and the jade in the *Seattle Sunday_Times,* June 5, 1955. The article also includes a photograph of Archie and a jade boulder, Beulah Levy with a jade bracelet and "a cloverleaf of jade" owned by Jim Robbins.

137 Boucher.

138 Bullock.

139 Comment by Mary Oldham.

140 Erwin.

141 Boucher letter.

142 Neilson.

143 "$100,000 Boulder," *Alaska Sportsman*, July, 1963. Eventually the boulder

was sold to John Haley of Fairbanks.

144 Martin Interview. Martin said that Debbie Reynolds was approached by Joiner to plate her swimming pool. A letter to Ms. Reynolds produced no response.

145 Of absolutely no interest except to an historian with a sense of irony and humor, the Soviets were considering colonizing Wrangell Island in 1927. They intended to send Inupiat with families and wireless radios to live on the island. The article, "Wrangell Island to be Colonized," appeared in the January 7, 1926, *Fairbanks Daily News-Miner*. In the same edition on the same page, humorously, is an article on a professor of psychology who claimed that "petting may lead to insanity" and, next to that clip, the story of a Russian professor who claimed that rocks had gender and therefore, by logical extension, sex lives.

146 Loman to Command and General Staff School, December 27, 1939, War Department File, 272-57, NARA, Washington D. C.; Stefansson, ADVENTURE.

147 Neilson.

148 Foster.

149 *Mukluk Telegraph*, January 31, 1951.

150 Boucher.

151 Neilson.

152 Joiner supposedly had an "affair of some sort" with a naturalist from Unalakleet named Sally Carrigher but this cannot be confirmed, Warbelow.

153 "C.A.B. Interfering with Schools" and "Hunting Season Closed for Game Warden," *Mukluk Telegraph*, January 31, 1951 and September 16, 1950.

154 "CAB Officials Accepting Bribes," *Mukluk Telegraph*, April 28, 1951.

155 Shafsky.

156 "C.A.B. Working for Moscow," *Mukluk Telegraph*, June 15, 1950.

157 "C.A.A. Inspector Lands Safely," *Mukluk Telegraph*, November 25, 1950.

158 "Democracy In America Example to the World," *Mukluk Telegraph*, June 9, 1951.

159 "News About Town," *Mukluk Telegraph*, July 29, 1950.

160 Erwin.

161 Gene Jack interview with Kay Kennedy, UAF Archives. However, one interview, Marvin Magnus, noted that Archie sold out to Wien a number of times.

162 "Long-Range Alaskan Radar Sites Will Give President 20-Minute Attack Lead," *Nome Nugget*, March 13, 1959.

163 Oldham comments.

164 Al Adams in conversation with author, September 19, 1997. Al Adams later became one of the most powerful state senators in Alaska's history. He served from 1980 to 2000.

165 Johnson.

166 Ferguson vs. Ferguson, divorce papers in the Ferguson Collection of the Levi Papers, UAA.

167 United States vs. Hadley Ferguson, U. S. Attorney's Papers, Nome, Territorial Case File "F," RG 118, NARA.

168 Bullock.

169 von der Heydt and Everts.

170 Putnam.

171 Mower.

172 Erwin.

173 Miller.

174 Erwin.

175 Conversation with Don Ferguson, February 25, 1990.

176 Mower.

177 Goodwin.

178 Kennelly.

179 United States of America vs. Fred Crane, Criminal Docket 4472, August 13, 1941, Third District Criminal Records in the possession of NARA.

180 Wilke.

181 Conversation with Don Ferguson and in a letter, September 10, 1991.

182 Miller.

183 Hawk.

184 Conversation with "K" Doyle, August 28, 1991.

185 Kennelly.

186 von der Heydt.

187 "Game Warden," *Mukluk Telegraph*, June 9, 1951, translated by Tommy Richards.

188 Evern.

189 Pierce.

190 Edith Bullock, July 21, 1989.

191 von der Heydt.

192 Heinrichs.

193 Yost.

194 Yost.

195 Johnson.

196 Pierce.

197   Putnam.

198   Herning.

199   Yost.

200   Satterfield, ALASKA AIRLINES, page 157.

201   Erwin.

202   Mower interview, Levi papers, UAA.

203   BITS AND PIECES OF ALASKAN HISTORY, Alaska Northwest Publishing Company, 1981, Volume I, page 56.

204   Fields and comments by Hadley Hess, Ray's daughter.

205   "Dave Bronaugh Finds A. Ferguson," *Nome Nugget,* March 19, 1947.

206   Conversation with Sam Shafsky, January 10, 1990.

207   Heinrichs.

208   Archie refused to pay the back wages of his dead pilot, Leo Malloy, to the pilot's father. Malloy filed
papers against Archie in Nome in January of 1945. There is no indication if the case was resolved. (Nome Civil File #3562 in the possession of NARA.)

209   Mower interview, Levi Papers, UAA.

210   Warbelow, page 240.

211   Jones, WOMEN WHO BRAVED THE FAR NORTH, page 147.

212   Leo Mark-Anthony to the author, April 5, 2002.

213   "Alaskan Flyer, Visiting Seattle, Dislikes Boats," *Ketchikan Alaska Chronicle,* February 9, 1946. The article appeared in the *Anchorage Daily Times* on the same day.

214   Heinrichs.

215   Conversation with Bill Sheffield and "Fairbanks Group Hears Sheffield Promote Arctic Coal Mining," *Anchorage Daily News,* January 20, 1992.

216   John Miller of the Alaska Oil and Gas Association and BP STATISTICAL REVIEW OF WORLD ENERGY, June, 1991.

217   Shafsky.

218   Shafsky.

219   "Kotzebue Will Be Townsite Soon," *Nome Nugget*, March 30, 1956.

220   Comment by Willie Hensley.

221   Miller.

222   "Knife Death Ruled Suicide," *Anchorage Times,* November 5, 1955.

223   Natividad Salinas' FBI file in the Levi Papers, UAA Archives. Both the arson charges and the involuntary servitude charges are included on the same forms and thus there is reason to believe they are inter-related.

224   "Two Believed Dead in Fire at Kotzebue Office of Alaska Air," *Nome Nugget,* December 19, 1955. Author is not sure this is the fire for which Salinas

was convicted of arson. Other documents indicate that Salinas was indicted for arson of the Kotzebue Grille which Salinas had purchased from Archie. This article did not mention the Kotzebue Grille.

225 This comment was from Willie Hensley. It is probably true as the Alaska and U.S. Archives could not find any records for Salinas with regard to his prison record. Further, Caroline Hudnall, Legal Technician of the Alaska Supreme Court, stated that in her 26 years with the Alaska Court System, she had "never heard of a single case of expungement."

226 "Steve Salinas is Indicted for Arson," *Nome Nugget*, March 5, 1958.

227 Neilson.

228 Neilson.

229 Comments by Willie Hensley.

230 Marilyn Richards.

231 "Muktuk Enterprise Starts at Kotzebue; Chicago is Market," *Tundra Times*, May 3, 1965.

232 Erwin.

233 Ferguson, Archie R., File 8859, United States District Court, Nome, RG 21, NARA.

234 "Strike Oil at Kotzebue," *Nome Nugget*, November 1, 1950. The news story says that the oil was discovered on "school reserve lands for the hospital" but Edith Bullock remembered it being on Archie's land. Archie had a lot of land he claimed as his so this author tends to believe Bullock because he finds it hard to see Archie getting excited about oil on someone else's property. According to some Kotzebue residents, there are still oil leaks in the same area today.

235 "$40,000 Suit Filed Against Kotzebue Trio," *Nome Nugget*, September 18, 1953.

236 July 17, 1946, Sweet-Wilson Expedition Diary.

237 FOIA memos in the Ferguson Collection of the Levi Papers, UAA.

238 Conversation with Frank Irick, September 18, 1991.

239 Satterfield, ALASKA AIRLINES, page 9.

240 Oldham.

241 "Modern Rotman Store Opens at Kotzebue," *Nome Nugget*, December 3, 1951. (When Ray Heinrichs got to Kotzebue in 1960, there was no elevator in Rotman's.)

242 "Plans for New Kotzebue Roads," *Nome Nugget*, September 14, 1953 and Bullock reminiscence.

243 Undated news article from the *Nome Nugget* for September 4th. Author believes the year to be 1941 or 1942.

244 Erwin.

245 Letter from James R. Clouse, Jr., September 7, 1990, Levi Papers, UAA.

246 In a conversation with the author in October of 1995, Doolin stated that he was still convinced that Archie had buried "several coffee cans full of gold nuggets on and around his property."

247 Written on the back of the photograph of Doolin and his metal detector in the possession of Max Pierce.

248 The case against Archie's properties which were left to his sons can be found in the NARA Fairbanks Civil cases, Record Group 21, Box 9 as cases 15-62 and 16-62, United States vs. Arctic Amusements, Inc., and United States vs. Mutual Enterprises.

249 "Archie Ferguson Property Seized," *Anchorage Times,* May 8, 1962.

250 Pierce.

251 About $1 million in 2016 dollars.

252 United States versus Archie Ferguson, Fairbanks Civil Case F28-63, Box 20, Record Group 21, NARA.

253 Letter from Archie to Bullock, July 16, 1962, and an undated letter from Archie to "Gordon and Family" Osborne, in the Ferguson Collection of the Levi Papers, UAA.

254 Little.

255 Rhodes, Herb, "People of the Great Land," *Greatlander,* July 28, 1971.

256 Rhodes, Herb, "People of the Great Land," *Greatlander,* July 28, 1971.

257

258 Letter to Jack Bullock, June 8, no year.

259 Marie Heinrichs.

260 "Main Trails and Bypaths," *Alaska Magazine,* July, 1975.

261 "Main Trails and Bypaths," Alaska Magazine, July, 1975.

262 Conversation with Willie Hensley.

263 "Alaska Health Facts," State of Alaska, Department of Health and Social Services, July 1, 1991.

264 "Changes in the Well-Being of Alaska Natives Since ANCSA," University of Alaska, Institute of Social and Economic Research, November, 1984.

265 "Poverty Among Alaska Natives," University of Alaska, Institute of Social and Economic Research, May, 1986.

266 Hlady, M.D., W. Gary and John P. Middaugh, M.D. "The Epidemiology of Suicide in Alaska, 1983-1984," Alaska Medicine, November/December, 1987.

267 State of Alaska Alcoholism and Drug Abuse Plan, 1990-1992, Department of Health and Social Services.

268 Bullock.

269 "Ketchikan to Barrow," *Alaska Magazine,* January, 1965.

270 Randy Acord to Steven Levi, February, 1998.

271 Johnson.

272 Graham M. Hicks of Miller, Nash, Wiener, Hager & Carlsen to Steven C. Levi, April 30, 1993.

273 Told to the Author by Ray Heinrichs.

274 "Maverick Among Eskimos," Time, January 13, 1961, pages 66-7. The first Roman Catholic to be elected to national office was Gabriel Richard, 1767-1832, who was elected to the United States House of Representatives in 1823.

275 "Maverick Among Eskimos," *Time,* January 13, 1961, pages 66-7.

276 "Father Llorente Sends Resignation From State House," Nome Nugget, December 31, 1969.

277 Llorente, MEMOIRS, Chapter 21.

278 While Llorente was in Alaska, he was reluctant to use the word or concept of Hell because the Inupiat, in Llorente's words, "said that if it is hot in Hell they would have to haul no wood and do no work and that they wanted to go there," Anchorage Weekly Times, July 15, 1937.

279 When Emmons' death was announced in *Alaska Magazine*, it was stated he had been pulled beneath a log carriage, "Ketchikan to Barrow," Alaska Magazine, January, 1955. The details on the finding of Robbins' bones comes from Sam Shafsky. The news announcement that Robbins plane had been found was from "Missing Pilot Found Dead Atop Idaho Peak," Nome Nugget, August 14, 1959.

280 Comments by Harold Herning and Richard Robbins, son of Jim, now CEO of Robbins Company in Kent, Washington.

281 Collins papers, page 82 of the tape transcriptions.

282 Kotzebue Jail File, United States Attorney's Records, Nome, RG 118, NARA.

283 Erwin and von der Heydt disagree as to where Crane was supposed to practice. As he practiced in neither Nome nor Kotzebue after being re-instated; it makes little difference.

284 Erwin and "Judge Hodge Resigns to Accept High Court Post," *Nome Nugget,* August 14, 1959.

285 Told by Warren A. Taylor II, grandson of Warren A. Taylor I, October 12, 1991.

286 Baily Interview.

287 Conversation with C. R. Kennelly, July 5, 1990.

288   Erwin.

289   Erwin.

290   Baily.

291   "In the Matter of Fred Crane, Petitioner, Appearing for the Purpose of Quashing a Subpeona," Alaska Archives, Juneau, Record Group 507, Series 429, Box 2, File #4214.

292   Crane's FBI file in the Levi Papers, UAA. It is also interesting to note that in 1960, Crane attempted to raise $250,000 for a bowling alley in Kotzebue in which he was one of the incorporators. This is a surprising amount of money – $2.7 million in 1990 dollars – for a bowling alley. That it was in Kotzebue, one might wonder how the incorporators expected to receive a reasonable rate of return on their money – much less any return. "New Corporation Listed in Kotzebue," *Nome Nugget,* December 28, 1960.

293   "Pioneer Attorneys Honored By Alaska Bar Convention," *Fairbanks Daily News Miner,* July, ?, 1969.

294   Miller.

295   The quotes are from Joiner through Boucher.

296   Erwin originally noted that the city was Philadelphia. It was most likely Boaz, Alabama, where Joiner's family lived.

Made in the USA
Middletown, DE
31 May 2022

66466284R00116